THE SIGNIFICANCE OF DREAMS

Developments in Psychoanalysis Series

Series Editors: Peter Fonagy, Mary Target, and Liz Allison

Other titles in the series:

Developmental Science and Psychoanalysis: Integration and Innovation
    Edited by Linda Mayes, Peter Fonagy and Mary Target

Mentalizing in Child Therapy: Guidelines for Clinical Practitioners
    Edited by Annelies J. E. Verheugt-Pleiter, Jolien Zevalkink
    and Marcel G. J. Schmeets

*Taboo or not Taboo? Forbidden Thoughts, Forbidden Acts in Psychoanalysis
and Psychotherapy*
    Edited by Brent Willock, Rebecca C. Curtis and Lori C. Bohm

*Destructiveness, Intersubjectivity, and Trauma: The Identity Crisis of Modern
Psychoanalysis*
    Werner Bohleber

*Early Development and its Disturbances: Clinical, Conceptual, and Empirical
Research on ADHD and other Psychopathologies and its Epistemological
Reflections*
    Edited by Marianne Leuzinger-Bohleber, Jorge Canestri and Mary Target

THE SIGNIFICANCE OF DREAMS
Bridging Clinical and Extraclinical Research in Psychoanalysis

Edited by
Peter Fonagy, Horst Kächele,
Marianne Leuzinger-Bohleber,
and David Taylor

Routledge
Taylor & Francis Group

LONDON AND NEW YORK

First published 2012 by Karnac Books Ltd.

Published 2018 by Routledge
2 Park Square, Milton Park, Abingdon, Oxon OX14 4RN
711 Third Avenue, New York, NY 10017, USA

Routledge is an imprint of the Taylor & Francis Group, an informa business

British Library Cataloguing in Publication Data

A C.I.P. for this book is available from the British Library

ISBN-13: 9781780490502 (pbk)

Typeset by Vikatan Publishing Solutions (P) Ltd., Chennai, India

CONTENTS

v

ABOUT THE EDITORS AND CONTRIBUTORS

Peter-André Alt studied German language and literature, political science, history, and philosophy at the Freie Universität Berlin. He earned his doctorate in 1984 and completed the habilitation process in 1993. Since 1995, Alt has been a full professor of German language and literature, first at Ruhr-Universität Bochum (1995–2002), then at the University of Würzburg (2002–2005), and since 2005 at Freie Universität Berlin. Alt has published sixteen books on German literature of the seventeenth to the twentieth centuries, including works on literary allegory and hermeticism in the early modern period, the literary and cultural history of dreams, the Enlightenment, the aesthetics of evil, psychoanalysis and literature, Friedrich Schiller, and Franz Kafka. His publication record also comprises ninety articles in international journals and numerous essays for German newspapers (among them *Frankfurter Allgemeine Zeitung* and *Süddeutsche Zeitung*). From 2007 to 2009, Alt served as the dean of the Department of Philosophy and Humanities, and from 2007 to 2010 he was a member of the Academic Senate, of Freie Universität. He was the spokesperson of the Friedrich Schlegel Graduate School of Literary Studies from 2007 until 2010, and has been the director of the Dahlem Research School since 2008. On May 12, 2010, Alt was elected the seventh president of Freie Universität.

Tobias Baehr is a clinical psychologist at Fachklinik Hofheim, Germany, a clinic for psychiatry and the treatment of psychosomatic disorders. He is a former scientific researcher at the Sigmund-Freud-Institut, Frankfurt am Main. He has contributed to publications on interdisciplinary research in questionnaire validation, sleep and dream research, as well as imaging technique studies in neurosciences.

Emil Branik, M.D. is a consultant in the psychiatry and psychotherapy of children, adolescents, and adults; a psychoanalyst (DGPT); and director of the department for child and adolescent psychiatry and psychotherapy, Asklepios Klinik Harburg, Hamburg, Germany. He is the author of numerous publications on various topics within the fields of clinical psychiatry and psychotherapy of children, adolescents, and adults as well as psychosomatics, especially issues of inpatient psychotherapy and psychic consequences of migration and the Holocaust.

Steven Ellman was professor in the Graduate School of City University of New York (CUNY) where he was director of the PhD program in clinical psychology. He is now, after thirty years as a professor at CUNY, professor emeritus. He has published more than seventy papers in psychoanalysis, sleep and dreams, and the neurophysiology of motivation. He has published several books including *Freud's Technique Papers: A Contemporary Perspective* (Karnac, 2002) and *When Theories Touch: A Historical and Theoretical Integration of Psychoanalytic Thought* (Karnac, 2010). He has been president of IPTAR twice, program chair, and he is a training and supervising analyst at IPTAR. He is also clinical professor at New York University's post-doctoral program in psychoanalysis and psychotherapy. He was the first president of the Confederation of Independent Psychoanalytic Societies (CIPS). CIPS is the national professional organisation of the independent International Psychoanalytic Association (IPA) societies of the United States. He is a member of the IPA and was previously on its executive council.

Tamara Fischmann, Priv.-Doz. Dr. rer. med., and psychoanalyst (DPV/IPA), is a staff member and scientific researcher at the Sigmund-Freud-Institut Frankfurt am Main, where she is chief methodologist in psychoanalytic empirical research, specialising in dream research. Her publications include those on interdisciplinary research in bioethics, dream research, attachment and ADHD, as well as imaging technique studies in neurosciences.

Peter Fonagy, Ph.D., FBA, is Freud Memorial Professor of Psychoanalysis and Head of the Research Department of Clinical, Educational, and Health Psychology at University College London. He is Chief Executive of the Anna Freud Centre, London. He is director of UCL Partners Mental Health Programme and is National Clinical Lead on the Improving Access to Psychological Therapies for Children and Young People. He is consultant to the Child and Family Program at the Menninger Department of Psychiatry and Behavioral Sciences at the Baylor College of Medicine, Houston, Texas. He holds visiting professorships at the Child Study Center, Yale University and at McLean Hospital, Harvard University. He is on the editorial board of twenty-five journals and currently chairs the research board of the International Psychoanalytical Association. He is a clinical psychologist and a training and supervising analyst in the British Psychoanalytical Society in child and adult analysis.

Birgit Gaertner, Ph.D., is a psychologist and psychoanalyst (DPV/IPA). She is professor of psychoanalytical psychology at the University for Applied Sciences, Frankfurt am Main, Germany. Her research activities are in the field of early prevention, psychodynamics of pregnancy and early mother–child interaction, and clinical typology of children with ADHD symptoms.

Lorena Katharina Hartmann, DipPsych, is a staff member at the Sigmund-Freud-Institut, Frankfurt am Main, Germany and Ph.D. student with the research interests of attachment and mentalisation.

Stephan Hau is professor in clinical psychology, Department of Psychology, Stockholm University. He is a psychoanalyst in private practice. From 1990 to 2004 he was a member of the research staff of the Sigmund-Freud-Institut, Frankfurt am Main, Germany. His special areas of research interest include experimental dream research, psychotherapy research, social psychology, and mass group behaviour.

Juan Pablo Jiménez is professor of psychiatry and director of the Department of Psychiatry and Mental Health East at University of Chile (Santiago), and visiting professor at University College London. He is a training and supervising analyst in the Chilean Psychoanalytical Association. He has held a number of important positions, including president of the Chilean Psychoanalytical Association (1994–1998), member of the House of Delegates of the International Psychoanalytic

Association (IPA) and representative at the Council (1994–1996), and president of the Latin-American Psychoanalytic Federation, FEPAL (2007–2008). He is a member of the International Research Board and of the Conceptual Integration Committee of the IPA. His research interests centre on issues of clinical epistemology and integration between clinical psychoanalysis and empirical research.

Vladimir Jović, MD, Ph.D., is a psychiatrist and psychoanalyst in private practice in Belgrade, assistant professor at the School of Psychology, Faculty of Philosophy of the University of Pristina in Kosovska Mitrovica, and a consultant at the Centre for Rehabilitation of Torture Victims of International Aid Network in Belgrade, Serbia.

Horst Kächele is the former director of the University Clinic for Psychosomatic Medicine and Psychotherapy at Ulm University, Germany (1990–2000), also former director of the Research Centre for Psychotherapy, Stuttgart (1988–2004); he teaches now at the International Psychoanalytic University in Berlin. He is a training analyst of the German Psychoanalytic Association and a member of the Society for Psychotherapy Research. For more details see his homepage: www.horstkaechele.de

Katrin Luise Laezer, Ph.D., is currently completing her post-doctorate thesis in psychoanalytical psychology at the University of Kassel, Germany. She works as a lecturer and research assistant at the Sigmund-Freud-Institut, Frankfurt am Main. Her research interests focus on early development and maltreatment of children, prevention, attachment, ADHD, and ODD. She is in psychoanalytic training at the Frankfurt Psychoanalytical Institute.

Marianne Leuzinger-Bohleber is professor of psychoanalytical psychology at the University of Kassel, Germany, and director of the Sigmund-Freud Institut, Frankfurt am Main. She is a training analyst of the Germany Psychoanalytical Association and a member of the Swiss Psychoanalytical Society. She is Vice-Chair of the Research Board of the International Psychoanalytical Association (IPA), chair of the research committee of the German Psychoanalytical Association (DPV), visiting professor at University College London, and member of the "Action Group" of the Society for Neuropsychoanalysis. Her research topics include clinical and extraclinical research in psychoanalysis, developmental psychoanalysis, and early prevention, dialogue between psychoanalysis and the neurosciences, and contemporary German literature.

Hanspeter Mathys, D.Phil., studied clinical psychology, psychopathology, and theology at the University of Zurich. He is a clinical psychologist at several psychiatric hospitals in Switzerland and a senior researcher at the Department of Clinical Psychology, Psychotherapy and Psychoanalysis, University of Zurich with a research focus on dream communication. He is in private psychoanalytic practice in Zurich.

Nicole Pfenning-Meerkoetter is a clinical psychologist, working as a researcher at the Sigmund-Freud-Institut, Frankfurt am Main, Germany. She is completing her PhD thesis on the conditions of knowledge production in current psychoanalytic research. Since 2005 she has been in psychoanalytic training (German Psychoanalytical Association). Her research interests focus on attachment, therapy effectiveness studies, and depression.

Bent Rosenbaum is a specialist in psychiatry, M.D. sci., associate clinical research professor, University of Copenhagen Faculty of Health Sciences, and professor, Institute of Psychology, University of Copenhagen. He is a psychoanalyst in private practice and training analyst in the Danish Psychoanalytic Society. He was president of the Danish Psychoanalytic Society (2004–2011) and is currently chair of the programme committee and the research committee. He is European chair of the IPA New Group Committee and was president of the Danish Psychiatric Society from 1998 to 2000. His special areas of research interest include psychoanalytic psychotherapy for people with psychosis and psychoanalysis of personality disorders; general and developmental psychopathology; trauma; suicidology; group analysis; and semiotics.

Michael Russ Dr. rer. med., is a clinical neuropsychologist. His fields of professional experience and research are cognitive neurology, neuropsychology, and fMRI. He is affiliated to the Sigmund-Freud-Institut, Frankfurt am Main, Germany as a scientist conducting the fMRI investigations of the LAC depression study.

Margaret Rustin is a consultant child and adolescent psychotherapist at the Tavistock and Portman NHS Foundation Trust, and was head of child psychotherapy 1985–2007. She is an honorary associate of the Institute of Psychoanalysis, London. She has lectured and written widely on child psychotherapy theory and practice and on teaching psychoanalysis. She has jointly edited *Closely Observed Infants* (Duckworth, 1989), *Psychotic States in Children* (Karnac, 1997), *Assessment* *in Child Psychotherapy* (Karnac, 1999), and *Work Discussion: Learning from Reflective Practice in Work with Children and Families* (Karnac, 2008); and is joint author with Michael Rustin of *Narratives of Love and Loss* (Verso, 1987) and *Mirror to Nature: Drama Psychoanalysis and Society* (Karnac, 2003). She has a private practice in London.

Brigitte Schiller is a child and adolescent psychotherapist, member of the training board, and head of the outpatient department of the Institute for Analytic Child and Adolescent Psychotherapy in Frankfurt am Main, Germany.

Aglaja Stirn, Priv. Doz. Dr. med., is head physician of the clinic for psychosomatic medicine and psychotherapy in Hamburg-West, in Germany. She is a staff member at the Frankfurt am Main university hospital's clinic for psychiatry, psychosomatics and psychotherapy. She is a specialist in psychotherapeutic medicine, psychotherapist, psychoanalyst, group analyst, and sexual therapist. Her publications include those about eating disorders, body modification, Buddhist art, and north-east India, as well as imaging technique studies in neurosciences.

David Taylor is a training and supervising analyst of the British Psychoanalytical Society. He is chair of the International Psychoanalytical Association's Clinical Research Sub-Committee. Currently he is the clinical director of the Tavistock's long-term research study evaluating the benefits of psychoanalytic psychotherapy in the treatment of chronic and refractory depression (TADS). Previously, he was a consultant psychotherapist and head of unit in the Adult Department of the Tavistock & Portman NHS Foundation Trust where he was also the medical director from 2000–2005. Publications include the book *Talking Cure* which he edited to accompany a BBC TV series about the Tavistock, along with papers on topics such as depression, dreams, psychotic parts of the personality, and the nature of psychic conflict. He has been an invited lecturer and supervisor in Australia, Brazil, India, USA, and Taiwan, as well as regularly supervising and teaching in Heidelberg and Vienna as well as in other European centres.

Sverre Varvin, M.D., Dr Philos, is a training and supervising analyst and Norwegian Psychoanalytic Society senior researcher at the Norwegian centre for studies on violence and traumatic stress, affiliated to the University of Oslo. His main research areas are traumatisation and treatment of traumatised patients, treatment process, traumatic dreams, and psychoanalytic training. He has held several positions in the IPA, including vice-president and board representative. Presently, he is chair of the programme committee for the next IPAC in Prague and member of the China Committee.

Rudi Vermote is a practising psychoanalyst and full member of the IPA. He is professor of psychiatry at the Departments of Psychiatry, Psychology, and Sexual and Familial Sciences at the Catholic University Leuven (KUL), Belgium. He is the director of postgraduate training of psychoanalytic psychotherapy and of the unit for hospitalisation-based psychotherapy, in-patient and day treatment, at the University Psychiatric Centre of the KUL, Campus Kortenberg. His empirical research is about process outcome in the treatment of personality disorders. He has lectured and published on the concepts of Bion on psychic change. He is currently the president of the Belgian Society of Psychoanalysis. He is a member of the editorial board of *Tijdschrift voor Psychiatrie* (the Belgian-Dutch Journal of Psychiatry) and of the *International Journal of Psychoanalysis*. He has been an active member of the European Psychoanalytical Federation (EPF) Working Party on Initiating Psychoanalysis for ten years.

Lissa Weinstein is an associate professor in the Doctoral Program in Clinical Psychology at the City University of New York and a graduate of the New York Psychoanalytic Institute. Her interests include the interrelationship of neurobiology and psychoanalysis, sleep and dreams, as well as film and literature studies. She is the winner of several awards, among them the Heinz Hartmann Jr. Award along with Dr Arnold Wilson for outstanding publication in the theory or practice of psychoanalysis, for their papers on the relevance of the work of Lev Vygotsky to psychoanalysis, and the Margaret Marek award from the International Dyslexia Association for her book *Reading David: A Mother and Son's Journey through the Labyrinth of Dyslexia*. Her current research centres on the role of repetition in the psychoanalytic process and in the overcoming of traumatic states. Her film papers have appeared in *Projections, Projected Shadows*, and *Psychoanalytic Inquiry*. A story entitled "A Dimension of More than Sight and Sound" recently appeared in *Fiction*.

SERIES EDITORS' PREFACE

After the first hundred years of its history, psychoanalysis has matured into a serious, independent intellectual tradition, which has notably retained its capacity to challenge established truths in most areas of our culture. Above all, psychoanalytic ideas have given rise to an approach to the treatment of mental disorders and character problems, psychodynamic psychotherapy, which has become a thriving tradition in most countries, at least in the Western world. With an ever-expanding evidence base, founded on randomised controlled trials as well as investigations of brain function, psychodynamic psychotherapy can aspire to legitimacy in the world of science, yet retains a unique perspective on human subjectivity which continues to justify its place in the world of humanities and all spheres where human culture is systematically studied.

The biological psychiatrist of today is called to task by psychoanalysis, as much as was the specialist in nervous diseases of Freud's time, in turn of the century Vienna. Today's cultural commentators, whether for or against psychoanalytic ideas, are obliged to pay attention to considerations of unconscious motivation, defences, the formative impact of early childhood experience, and the myriad other discoveries which psychoanalysts brought to twentieth century culture. Twenty-first century thought implicitly incorporates much of what was discovered by psychoanalysis in the last century. Critics who try to pick holes in or even demolish the psychoanalytic edifice are often doing this from ramparts constructed on psychoanalytic foundations. A good example of this would be the recent attacks by some cognitive behaviour therapists upon psychodynamic approaches. Vehement as these are, the critics have to give credit to psychoanalysis for its contribution to cognitive therapeutic theory and technique. These authors point to the advances they have made in relation to classical ideas, but rarely acknowledge that the psychodynamic approach has also advanced. An unfortunate feature of such debates is that often attacks on psychoanalysis are addressed to where the discipline was fifty or even seventy-five years ago.

Both the epistemology and the conceptual and clinical claims of psychoanalysis are often passionately disputed. We see this as a sign that psychoanalysis may be unique in its capacity to challenge and provoke. Why should this be? Psychoanalysis is unrivalled in the depth of its questioning of human motivation, and whether its answers are right or wrong, the epistemology of psychoanalysis allows it to confront the most difficult problems of human experience. When else is the motivation of both victim and perpetrator of sexual abuse going to be simultaneously considered? What other discipline will take the subjectivity of a newborn, or in fact, an in-utero infant as a serious topic for study? The discipline, which has found meaning in dreams, continues to search for understanding in relation to acts of the greatest humanity and inhumanity. It remains committed to attempting to understand the most subtle aspects of the intersubjective interplay that can occur between two individuals, one struggling to overcome the barriers that another has elected to create in the path of their own progress through the world. Paradoxically, our new understanding of the physical basis of our existence—our genes, nervous systems, and endocrine functioning—rather than finally displacing psychoanalysis, has created a pressing need for a complementary discipline which considers the memories, desires, and meanings which are beginning to be recognised as influencing human adaptation even at the biological level. How else, other than through the study of subjective experience, will we understand the expression of the individual's biological destiny, within the social environment?

It is not surprising, then, that psychoanalysis continues to attract some of the liveliest intellects in our culture. These individuals are by no means all psychoanalytic clinicians, or psychotherapists. They are distinguished scholars in an almost bewildering range of disciplines, from the study of mental disorders with their biological determinants to the disciplines of literature, art, philosophy, and history. There will always be a need to explicate the meaning of experience. Psychoanalysis, with its commitment to understanding subjectivity, is in a leading position to fulfil this intellectual destiny. We are not surprised at the upsurge of interest in psychoanalytic studies in universities in many countries, which is driven by the limitations of understanding that modern science, including modern social science, all too often provides. The books in this series will aim to address the same intellectual curiosity that has made these educational projects so successful. The courageous accounts of psychoanalysts meet a fundamental human need for discovering the meaning behind actions, and meet this need head on. While some may consider psychoanalytic accounts speculative, we must not forget that in relation to many descriptions of action, feeling, and cognition, the explorations of psychoanalysis based in the consulting room have proved to be profound and readily generalisable. No one now doubts the reality of childhood sexuality, no one believes the conscious mind, in any sense, to represent the boundaries of subjectivity. Non-conscious conflict, defence, the mental structures that encode the quality of early relationships into later interpersonal functioning, and the motivation to become attached and to look after others, represent early psychoanalytic discoveries that have become an inalienable part of twenty-first century culture.

The theme of our series is a focus on advances in psychoanalysis—hence our series title "Developments in Psychoanalysis". In our view, while psychoanalysis has a glorious and rich history, it also has an exciting future, with dramatic changes and shifts as our understanding of the mind is informed by scientific, philosophical, and literary enquiry. Our commitment is to no specific orientation, to no particular professional group, but to the intellectual challenge to explore questions of meaning and interpretation systematically, and in a scholarly way. Nevertheless, we would be glad if this series particularly spoke to the psychotherapeutic community, to those individuals who use their own minds and humanity to help others in distress.

In this series we are aiming to communicate some of the intellectual excitement which we feel about the past, present, and future of psychoanalytic ideas, and which we enjoy seeing in our students each year. We hope that our work with the authors and editors in the series will help to make these ideas accessible to an even larger group of students, scholars, and practitioners worldwide.

Peter Fonagy, Mary Target, and Liz Allison
University College London

FOREWORD

It is with great pleasure that I have accepted to write a few words to introduce this rich and stimulating book. The core of this volume is based on the presentations and discussions of papers given during the 12th Joseph Sandler Research Conference which was dedicated to the topic of "The Significance of Dreams: Bridging Clinical and Extraclinical Research in Psychoanalysis".

The Joseph Sandler Research Conference has taken place in London for a number of years, but has since 2008, thanks to the support of the Sigmund Freud Institute and the dedication of Professor Marianne Leuzinger-Bohleber, most successfully been organised in Frankfurt. When Joseph Sandler became Freud Memorial Professor in 1984 at University College London, he wanted to counteract what he felt was a tendency among psychoanalysts to be inward looking. He had observed that psychoanalysts who dedicated most of their working time to clinical work and had thus amassed a great deal of clinical knowledge felt naturally tempted to share and discuss clinical and conceptual ideas with like-minded colleagues. This certainly was the source of a great deal of rich development of ideas within psychoanalysis but tended to ignore the work of certain psychoanalytic colleagues who were doing research in institutions, and of experimental psychologists, and neurobiologists who researched and questioned certain facets of psychoanalytic theory. In an attempt to correct this tendency, Joseph Sandler organised regular international meetings on various central psychoanalytic topics, inviting psychoanalytic practitioners and clinicians as well as more academic researchers to share and discuss some of their new ideas. He tried to have research papers discussed by psychoanalysts and psychoanalytic presentations, both conceptual and clinical, discussed by researchers. This new approach was not always easy to organise but was met with enthusiasm, opening the door to psychoanalysis to a wider audience. A year after his untimely death, Peter Fonagy, with the support of the International Psychoanalytical Association, founded the Joseph Sandler Research Conference, which has been taking place every year on the first weekend in March.

In the last decade, some of the particularly successful conferences became the basis for a publication. This last book on the significance of dreams is particularly timely as it discusses and illustrates some of the important new understandings and changes in the conceptualisation, use, and interpretations of dreams. I would like here to express my gratitude to Peter Fonagy, David Taylor, Marianne Leuzinger-Bohleber, and Horst Kächele for agreeing to be the editors of this volume, and extend also my warm thanks to the Sigmund Freud Institute and the IPA who, each in their own ways, have importantly supported the publication of this book.

Anne-Marie Sandler

INTRODUCTION

Marianne Leuzinger-Bohleber and Peter Fonagy

Long before Sigmund Freud wrote *The Interpretation of Dreams*, people listened to and tried to understand their dreams, taking them as prophetic signs from the gods, or as expressions of severe inner conflicts. In the Bible, the prisoner Joseph, a dreamer and oneiromancer, was asked to interpret the pharaoh's strange dream of the seven lean and the seven fat cows. Through the dream, said Joseph, "God hath shewed Pharaoh what he is about to do" (*Genesis* 41:25). In *Hamlet*, the young prince suggests that dreams have the power to disrupt complacence: "I could be bounded in a nutshell and count myself a king of infinite space, were it not that I have bad dreams" (*Hamlet* 2.2.234).

Dreams are also a recurrent subject of paintings as the cover of this book with a reproduction of "Nightmare" by the Swiss painter Johann Heinrich Füssli illustrates. "Nightmare" is the most famous of his paintings and exists in different versions, all painted around 1781.

Do current psychoanalytical treatments still consider dream interpretation to be a *via regia* to knowledge of the unconscious?

Some remarks on clinical research on dreams in psychoanalysis

Artists seem to have known for centuries that the capacity to dream and to remember dreams is part of human creativity and problem solving, and thus of psychic health. Someone who cannot remember his own dreams misses a major possibility to be in dialogue with his unconscious and thus with his mind's attempts to find symbolic and creative solutions for unsolved problems of the present and past. In this context, Bohleber (2011) talks about the "creative unconscious".

Excessive restriction of psychic or physical freedom can cause individuals to lose their ability to dream. In turn, the institutions or societies to which these people belong lose their capacities for innovation and creative problem solving. This has serious consequences, particularly in the realm of education, but also for psychic and physical health more generally. This volume will therefore be of interest not only to psychoanalysts and psychotherapists, but also to educators, educational and social scientists, as well as people interested in individual and cultural creativity.

Such insights have been mainly developed through psychoanalytic clinical research. As one very successful manager reported during an interview from the large follow-up study of the German Psychoanalytical Association in the 1990s:

> The most important result of my long psychoanalysis is that I am in a constant dialogue with my unconscious mind which gives me an inner orientation, a feeling of "being on earth", to be myself. If I am not able to remember my dreams for a longer period of time, e.g., then I realize that I have to step back in order not to lose myself. It will have severe consequences for me if I deny that my psyche and my mind need some inner space in order to express themselves in my dreams and my fantasies. If I neglect this I am losing my creativity and the basic feeling that I am living my own life in spite of all the challenges, which I have to deal with in my everyday job. If I don't take care of this I finally get sick—then something has been simply too much …. (Patient ZA, see Leuzinger-Bohleber, Rüger, Stuhr & Beutel, 2002, p. 92).

This is just one among myriad examples. In the space of this introduction, we cannot give an overview of the huge clinical psychoanalytical literature on dreams. Over 19,000 articles in the Psychoanalytic Electronic Publishing archive make reference to dreams, a citation pattern that intriguingly has remained more or less unchanged over the history of psychoanalysis.

In order to give readers an insight into current clinical discourse on dreams, we take four papers that were presented on 5 August 2011 during the keynote panel on dreams at the 47th Congress of the International Psychoanalytical Association, held in Mexico City. The papers are by Elias Mallet da Rocha Barros (São Paulo), Luis J. Martín Cabré (Madrid), Harold P. Blum (New York), and Fred Pine (New York). (Versions of these papers were also published before the conference in the *International Journal of Psychoanalysis*, 2011, volume 92.) These papers are illustrations of a number of threads running through current clinical theory about dreams: (1) dreams are a pre-symbolic transitional stage in thought fulfilling a key function in the patient's processing of emotional material, particularly of an overwhelming or traumatic kind; (2) dreams are key to a comprehensive understanding of the patient's unconscious attitudes and preconscious thoughts, particularly in relation to the clinical situation; (3) dreams on the couch are part of a complex pattern of communication established between patient and analyst over a considerable period charged with the burden of carrying content concerning all aspects of transference and countertransference communication. These points have been part of clinical analytic discourse for decades, and these recent examples show that they remain topical issues. After reviewing these central concerns we then outline some other focuses of the current psychoanalytic discourse on dreams.

Clinically, all the speakers, perhaps representing modern psychoanalysis, seemed to agree that dream interpretation was still one important "via regia", as Freud had seen it, to knowledge of the unconscious. At the same time, they all emphasised that psychoanalysts use dreams in their treatments to gain insights not only into unconscious wishes (which were the focus of Freud's interpretations), but also into the characteristics of primary object relations, into traumas, and into other features of mental life.

Dreams give clinical access to the primary process, i.e., to psychic processes that are not yet mentalised, and have not yet started to be experienced as mental rather than physical or perceptual phenomena. For most contemporary psychoanalysts, dreams therefore provide a rare opportunity to access unconscious and preconscious fantasies and thinking. Da Rocha Barros compared dreams with a "private theatre" in which "meaning is generated and transformed":

> The dreams of our patients can be viewed as playing the part of a playwright who brings to light a very private theatre of the patient's psychic reality and shows the way in which it has come into being and has been transformed since early childhood .... [The] psychical working out function performed by dreams is a form of unconscious thinking which transforms affects into memories and mental structures. It also comprehends a process through which meaning is apprehended, built and transformed. (Da Rocha Barros, 2011, p. 270).

In other words, underscoring the first clinical function we listed above, dreams may serve to metabolise emotional life and are connected to the capacity to mentalise, to create an internal world, a subjectivity (Fonagy, 2007).

For Martín Cabré (2011), beyond the construction of subjectivity, dreams had a twofold importance in clinical work. First, they are an incomparable source of information on the affects prevailing in the analytic space. They can therefore serve as an indispensible aid to the work of construction. Second, they reactivate and can symbolise emotions stemming from sometimes traumatic experiences which are stored in implicit memory and date back to the earliest periods of relational life and to a phase of presymbolic, preverbal mental functioning. They therefore open avenues for reconstructive work in psychoanalyses.

From a clinical point of view, said Martín Cabré, it is very important to discriminate between traumatic and non-traumatic dreams. Ferenczi (1931) pointed out that traumatic dreams can hardly be understood as fulfilments of unconscious wishes. But they do have the potential to enervate traumatic experiences. Ferenczi called this "traumatolysis"— a process, according to Martín Cabré, "whereby traumatic experiences were dissolved and undone" (2011, p. 273).

Blum (2011) elaborated on the clinical communicative functions of dreams, showing that dreams have a communicative function in general, but particularly in clinical contexts. They can be seen as an analysand's gifts to the analyst or as magical messages. Dreams may open insights into early object relationships that have never been symbolised. By talking about a dream and trying to understand its meaning, analyst and analysand alter its sensory (mostly visual) and affective contents. Therefore, the manifest dream should not only be considered as an envelope for its latent content. The content of the latent dream may also contain important unconscious meanings concerning early object relationships, conflicts, anxieties, etc. Thus, in psychoanalytic sessions, the meanings of dreams are usually explored from the surface downwards.

Pine (2011) denied that dreams have a special role in clinical work. Referring to an *IJP* controversy (Pine, 1998), he suggested that other information (such as transference–countertransference observations, reports of an analysand's "moments of meeting" (Stern & the Process Study Group, 1998) in both the analytic situation and in the outside world, slips, etc.) could be as productive as dreams for gaining insights into unconscious fantasies and processes.

Recently, other clinical discussions of dreams have focused on nightmares and post-traumatic dreams. Surprisingly, these have not until now been major subjects in the psychoanalytic literature. Their neglect was prevalent even during the last decades, when trauma became one of the central topics in international psychoanalysis. Since they could not reasonably be considered wish-fulfilling, Freud placed post-traumatic nightmares in a special category of dreams (1933a). Even today, many psychoanalysts believe that post-traumatic dreams have no latent meaning. Lansky (1995, p. 8) characterised such a view thus:

> Freud's assumptions about the nature of posttraumatic nightmares are tantamount to an implicit model of posttraumatic nightmare. Those assumptions, shared for the most part by psychoanalytic and non-psychoanalytic thinkers alike, are (1) that the nightmare portrays the essence of what is traumatic about the trauma; (2) that the nightmare has no latent content of any importance, that is to say, that the nightmare is more like an affectively charged memory than a true dream; (3) accordingly, that the manifest content is not a product of transformation of the dreams work's service defensive functions or portraying wishes as fulfilled; (4) therefore, the conflict represented in the nightmare scenario, usually one involving fear of external danger (occasionally with conscious remorse), is the central or only conflict to be addressed in the therapy; and (5) the nightmare is itself part of the stress response reaction, as inflammation is to physical tissue, and is (somehow) driven into existence by the trauma that is represented in the manifest content of the nightmare.

Lansky questions these assumptions based on a critical review of psychoanalytical papers by Adams-Sylvan and Sylvan (1990), Blitz and Greenberg (1984), Jones (1910), Kohut (1977), Lidz (1946), Mack (1965, 1970), Moses (1978), and Wisdom (1949), as well as on contributions from sleep researchers like Fischer, Byrne, Edwards & Kahn (1970), Hartmann (1984), and Kramer (1991).

Lansky himself carried out a large clinical study in an inpatient psychiatric unit at the West Los Angeles VA Medical Center. Between 1987 and 1993, all the patients—many of them were Vietnam War combat veterans—were asked about their nightmares via questionnaire. Their nightmares were also investigated in clinical interviews and psychoanalytic therapy sessions. This offered Lansky's research group "the opportunity to appreciate the complexity of the posttraumatic nightmare" (Lansky, 1995, p. 5). Lansky summarised his conclusions thus:

> The central line of thinking ... does indeed support a revised concept of wish fulfillment, one that draws heavily on an understanding of shame, narcissistic injury and narcissistic rage and their relation to disruptive mental states in the light of which even the possession of an intact sense of self within the scenario of a terrifying anxiety dream can be seen as a wish. (p. 6).

Working with traumatic dreams might thus have an important therapeutic effect, as the case reports in this volume by Juan Pablo Jimenez, Margaret Rustin, and Marianne Leuzinger-Bohleber also illustrate.

Another interesting clinical phenomenon that has recently been the focus of attention is the so-called countertransference dream. This is a dream of the analyst which features or includes a patient. For some writers, such as Zwiebel (1985), analysing such dreams allows for an understanding of current unconscious communications between patient and psychoanalyst.

Interdisciplinary research and theoretical pluralism in contemporary psychoanalysis

Another field of contemporary psychoanalytical dream research is *conceptual research* (see, e.g., Leuzinger-Bohleber & Fischmann, 2006), which was the focus of the 47th IPA Congress. Three central concepts in psychoanalysis—the unconscious, sexuality, and dreams—were taken up in keynote papers aiming to develop or even integrate existing psychoanalytic theories. Clearly, dreams are still considered to be among the core phenomena of contemporary psychoanalysis.

All our illustrative Mexico City keynote speakers seemed to agree that data gained in clinical work with patients constitutes the unique field of discovery in psychoanalysis. Freud (1927a) described this idea in his famous formulation of the "Junktim Forschung", the inseparable bond between therapy and research. This bond is also evident in contemporary struggles to develop psychoanalytic concepts and theories.

However, the speakers also had clear differences in their understandings of conceptual research in contemporary psychoanalysis. In particular, their different ways of developing the central psychoanalytical concept of the dream seemed to be closely connected to their varying positions on the status of psychoanalysis as a scientific discipline (see also Ahumada & Doria-Medina, 2010; Leuzinger-Bohleber, Dreher & Canestri, 2003). Some of the authors held that theoretical clarifications or even theoretical integrations—central aims of the conference—could be achieved by psychoanalysts themselves, through discourses taking place exclusively within the psychoanalytic community. Others argued that new, innovative developments in psychoanalysis would depend on an exchange with the outside scientific and societal world. This includes an interdisciplinary and international dialogue with other scientists, as well as with politicians, the media, and the arts.

A radical formulation of the latter position came from Steven Ellman (e.g., Ellman, 2010), whose work generated controversy during the final panel of the 2011 IPA Congress and is included in this volume. Ellman discussed his extensive experimental research into sleep and dreams, illustrating the ways in which he used interdisciplinary knowledge to make new theoretical integrations. The result is a new drive theory that brings together Freud and Fairbairn. It takes a developmental view of unconscious mental life and puts forward a new understanding of the function of dreams. Ellman sees the baby as both pleasure- and object-seeking, and dreams as strongly connected to early developmental processes. Furthermore, says Ellman, dreams remain a form of self-regulation and problem solving throughout life (see his contribution in this volume).

The speakers also took different positions concerning *theoretical pluralism in contemporary psychoanalysis*. Some of the speakers implicitly shared the opinion of many psychoanalysts who think that the diversity of psychoanalytic theories allows us to perceive ever-new patterns in complex clinical material. These patterns can then be made use of in the joint process of acquiring knowledge with our patients. Some of the speakers argued persuasively that looking at clinical material from a Freudian, post-Kleinian, French, American object-relational, or South American perspective leads to specific insights. These insights can be deepened, supported, or sometimes even contradicted by shifting to another theoretical stance. Other speakers thought that theoretical integration is absolutely necessary. Still others warned that attempting such integration risks losing the conceptual and clinical richness developed in the different psychoanalytic cultures and regions (see, e.g., Ferro, 2011).

Some colleagues seemed to share the epistemological and methodological concerns of Charles Hanly (2010), who argued that further pluralism in psychoanalysis could lead to a fragmentation of psychoanalytic theorising. This, in turn, could lead to the proliferation of institutions fostering eclectic, *anything goes* approaches. Hanly warned that such approaches might promote fuzzy thinking, thinking that could indicate a neglect of psychoanalysis' continuous struggle to understand the "not understandable"—i.e., the complex, mainly unconscious psychic realities of our patients.

A healthy multiplicity of clinical perspectives and theory-informed observations does not relieve us of the need to recognise irreconcilable contradictions between various theoretical explanations of clinical phenomena. These contradictions need to be the subject of intra-psychoanalytic dialogue. Through such dialogue, we will be able to recognise both commonalities and divergences in our conceptual approaches. This is a prerequisite for further developing psychoanalytic theories, for finding innovative integrations, and for developing a culture of respectful, fruitful scientific debate within the IPA.

A historical perspective on the relationship between psychoanalysis, science, and society

Underlying the differences that emerged during the 2011 IPA Congress may be fundamental tensions between different conceptualisations of the nature of psychoanalysis and of its relationship to other areas of scientific enquiry. Freud himself grappled with such tensions. As a young man, he was very interested in philosophy and the humanities. Only later did he turn with remarkable passion to the natural sciences. In the laboratory of Ernst Brücke's Institute of Physiology, he became acquainted with a strict positivistic understanding of science that attracted him throughout his whole life. Eventually, however, he turned away from the neurology of his time because he recognised its methodological limitations: the discipline was not appropriate for conducting research into the nature of the psyche.

With *The Interpretation of Dreams*, the founding work of psychoanalysis, Freud initiated his new method of "pure psychology" (1900a). Nevertheless, he kept thinking of himself as a physician making exact observations, just as a natural scientist would. His wish for a precise, empirical examination of hypotheses and theories protected him, as Joel Whitebook (2011) argues, from his own predilection for wild speculation. Thus, Freud, as a "philosophical physician", could establish a new *science of the unconscious*. In developing psychoanalysis, he initiated a complex discourse between the natural sciences and the humanities.

This discourse has been fraught with difficulties. Makari (2008) characterises these well when he describes an inevitable tension in psychoanalysis between a wish to assert again and again one's own identity as a psychoanalyst (e.g., by promoting the basic feeling of belonging to the psychoanalytic community and by continuing its specific tradition of thought), and an openness to challenges and discoveries from the non-psychoanalytic world (e.g., academic research or developments in globalised society).

Psychoanalysis as a discipline—not just individual analysts—has had to face such problems of identity. Two opposing dangers have threatened it throughout its history. On the one hand, there was the possibility that psychoanalysis would be swallowed by another academic discipline and stripped of its unique methodology. On the other hand, there was a possibility that it would keep its identity but be marginalised as a non-scientific cult or a secret religiously structured society.

One of Freud's great, lasting achievements was to preserve both psychoanalysis' disciplinary independence and the integrity of psychoanalytic research. He secured these ends in large part by founding the IPA in 1910. By creating this institution, he resisted subsuming psychoanalysis under the disciplines of medicine, the humanities, or the cultural sciences. At the same time, he created an organisation that could foster psychoanalysis' identity and its methodological rigour.

Makari (2008) sees the decision to found a loyal psychoanalytic organisation outside the universities as an ambivalent step that alienated important scientific colleagues such as Eugen Bleuler. It also led to well known splits in the psychoanalytic movement—for example, the split between Freud and Jung. Makari shows in great detail that Freud brooded heavily over the danger connected with his decision to get rid of his "rebellious sons" (p. 290f.). Expelling certain members from the IPA could make it seem like a cult that was under Freud's autocratic control. To avoid this, Freud tried very hard to define psychoanalysis as a science.

As we know, the struggle for an adequate understanding of the *Wissenschaft* (science) of psychoanalysis goes on. As noted above, this was a latent topic in the 2011 IPA Congress discussions on dreams.

Related concerns about the role of psychoanalysis in modern societies also emerged during the congress. More than ever before, psychoanalysis is shaped by constant, global competition for political, financial, and medical acceptance. Many of us believe that psychoanalysis is both an efficient method for treating patients and a theoretical framework in which deeper understandings of societal problems (such as violence, anti-Semitism, right-wing radical adolescence, religious fanaticism, and terrorism) can be achieved. It is generally felt that if psychoanalysts can convincingly demonstrate and disseminate the unique and indispensible results of their research in clinical and cultural fields, they will not be marginalised.

At the same time, however, there is a danger that by attempting to play a more significant role in society, psychoanalysis will end up conforming to a conventional understanding of science, one that is inappropriate for a *Wissenschaft des Unbewussten* (a "scientific discipline of the unconscious"). Striving for public credibility, particularly through the expert-obsessed media, could cause psychoanalysis to lose its inconvenient but unique status as a method for true self-investigation and self-exploration. Thus, in its very attempt to preserve its relevance, psychoanalysis might efface itself.

It is only by remaining psychoanalytic that our discipline can have real value for society. Psychoanalysis is still convinced that individuals will only find their sense of self and identity if they explore their unique unconscious worlds of fantasies and conflicts—if they examine how their specific life experiences and biographies determine their individual ways of feeling, thinking, and acting. The sceptical *Weltanschauung* of psychoanalysis is still in opposition to the *Zeitgeist* of anything goes and to the endless commercialisation of human resources and capacities.

It is partly because of this opposition that psychoanalysis can continue to offer necessary criticisms of contemporary culture. It is therefore essential that the psychoanalytic community communicates the richness of its clinical and extraclinical research—including research on dreams—to the scientific community, the public, and the media in an authentic way (see, e.g., Pfenning-Meerkötter, in press).

In this volume, we take up these controversial discussions in the hopes of contributing to an understanding of one of contemporary psychoanalysis's central clinical phenomena and concepts: the dream.

Short overview of the contributions in this volume and their scientific context

The majority of the papers collected in this volume were originally presented at the 12th annual Joseph Sandler Research Conference, which took place in Frankfurt in March 2011. The conference title was "The Significance of Dreams: Bridging clinical and extraclinical research in psychoanalysis". This topic was very much in keeping with the work of Joseph Sandler and his wife, Anne-Marie. The Sandlers always showed a unique and innovative openness to all forms of research in psychoanalysis, and were dedicated to building bridges between psychoanalysts working in their private offices, psychoanalytic researchers in institutions and at the universities, and non-psychoanalytic researchers and intellectuals (see the foreword by Anne-Marie Sandler).

The Sandlers' noble stance cannot be taken for granted: the discourse between psychoanalysts with different methodological and epistemological convictions has not always been open, friendly, and productive. The same is true for the relations between psychoanalysis and other disciplines. Nevertheless, many analysts, including the authors whose works appear in this book, carry on in the Sandlers' tradition. We are proud to present some of their important contributions here.

David Taylor (London) is an internationally known psychoanalytic clinician. Currently, the Clinical Director of the Tavistock Adult Depression Study, he has formerly held the posts of clinical director of the Tavistock's Adult Section and of the Tavistock's Medical Section. Recently, he has collaborated with the Sigmund Freud Institute on its LAC Depression Study, in which his *Manual for Psychoanalytical Treatments of Chronic Depressed Patients* is used. In several papers, he has built bridges between clinical research in psychoanalysis and extraclinical research, considering scientific, conceptual, empirical, and interdisciplinary issues. In his chapter, "The re-awakening of the psychoanalytic theories of dreams and dreaming", Taylor looks at the part to be played by clinical research in further advancing our understanding of dreams and dreaming.

Margret Rustin (London) is one of the most internationally famous child psychoanalysts working today. In her chapter, "Dream and play in child analysis today", she elaborates on her clinical observation that not many of her child analytic colleagues seem to work with dreams in their treatments. She compares this with the central place that dreams had in the work of both Melanie Klein and Anna Freud. Rustin's interesting thesis is that this could indicate the contraction of intermediate space in children due to "changes in childhood", which include increasing overexposure to media and frequent overstimulation. A second hypothesis is that contemporary child psychoanalysts more frequently treat children who have suffered severe early trauma. These children have severe deficits in symbolisation, mentalisation, and dreaming. Rustin illustrates her arguments with impressive case examples that show the parallels between dreaming and playing in children (2011).

In his chapter, "The manifest dream *is* the real dream: the changing relationship between theory and practice in the interpretation of dreams", the Chilean psychoanalyst and researcher Juan Pablo Jimenez (Santiago de Chile) discusses how contemporary clinicians have an understanding of the manifest dream that is different from that of former generations. Dream interpretations are not built on "static interpretations of dream symbols" or exclusively on the associations of the patient. Rather, they are created by both the analyst and the analysand in a "co-construction". Jimenez illustrates these ideas—and his artful technique—through detailed accounts of psychoanalytic sessions with a chronically depressed and severely traumatised patient.

Another extensive case study of a severely depressed, traumatised patient is presented by Marianne Leuzinger-Bohleber (Frankfurt) in her chapter, "Changes in dreams. From a psychoanalysis with a traumatised, chronic depressed patient". She argues that changes in the quality of the manifest content of dreams, as well as changes in working with dreams, may be seen as genuine psychoanalytic indicators of structural changes in psychoanalyses. This is a topic which Leuzinger-Bohleber has studied both clinically and extraclinically for years (1987, 1989). In the ongoing large LAC Depression Study, changes in dreams are one of the domains for investigating therapeutic transformations, as will be shown in several case studies by experienced psychoanalysts (see www.sigmund-freud-institut.de).

In addition to the authors above, who focus on clinical research in psychoanalysis, several contributors to this volume present work on empirical, experimental, and interdisciplinary dream research.

Horst Kächele (Ulm, Germany), the head of the famous annual Ulmer research workshops, and the *Sonderforschungsbereich 129: Psychotherapeutische Prozesse* (Psychotherapeutic Processes) of the DFG (German Research Foundation), has inspired generations of empirical psychotherapy researchers. In his chapter, "Dreams as subject of psychoanalytical treatment research", Kächele presents examples of the empirical dream research he began in the 1970s. In one of his earliest studies, he and a doctoral student found that analysands in Jungian psychoanalyses dream in Jungian dream symbols, while those in Freudian psychoanalyses more frequently dream in Freudian dream metaphors. In a second study, his research group analysed dreams applying the CCRT method developed by Luborsky and Crits-Christoph (1990). Finally, Kächele summarises studies of the changes in manifest dream content and dream work in psychoanalytic sessions, work which Leuzinger-Bohleber (1987, 1989) carried out in the 1980s in the frame of the *Sonderforschungsbereich 129*. In the widely read third volume of *Psychoanalytic Practice*, Kächele has published a new summary of these analyses, carried out new analyses of some of the data, and has revisited the dreams of the specimen case "Amalie" (see Kächele et al., 2006).

In "The work at the gate. Discussion of the papers of Juan Pablo Jimenez and Horst Kächele", Rudi Vermote (Brussels) compares clinical and empirical research. He underlines similarities in the contributions of Jimenez and Kächele. In particular, says Vermote, they combine the openness and curiosity of the clinical and the empirical researcher. Using three clinical examples, and drawing on the work of theoreticians such as Bion and Matte Blanco, Vermote illustrates how difficult it is to find adequate models for explaining complex clinical phenomena. Ultimately, he formulates a kind of paradoxical solution: on the one hand, he pleads for an attitude of radical openness in each new clinical situation; on the other hand, he demands ambitious and elaborated theoretical models for explaining clinical observations. Thus, he offers a highly ambitious vision of conceptual research in psychoanalysis.

Two excellent examples of such ambitious conceptual research are included in this volume. The first comes from Steven Ellman (New York), and is presented in his chapter, "When theories touch: an attempted integration and reformulation of dream theory". For many years, Ellman was the head of a large laboratory for experimental dream and sleep research at the City University of New York (CUNY). His neurobiological and experimental research focused on the function of REM sleep, on endogenous stimulation, and on early mother–child interaction. He has published several seminal papers and books in this field. In the chapter included here, he integrates clinical psychoanalytical insights concerning dreams, the results of experimental dream research, and newer developmental studies. The result is a conceptual framework that sheds new light not only on dreams and coping with dreams in psychotherapies, but also on the very nature of unconscious mental life.

The second ambitious conceptual chapter, "'It's only a dream.' Physiological and developmental contributions to the feeling of reality", is by Lissa Weinstein (New York). She worked in Ellman's laboratory for years and has developed conceptual integrations similar to his. Based on her studies of REM dreams and REM deprivations, she explores the reflective mentations of the dreamer. Among individuals, she says, there is a great diversity in the quality and quantity of this mentation. In the second part of her chapter, she connects findings from these laboratory studies with insights from attachment research. She postulates time windows that are crucial for early self-development and in which sleep and dream patterns play an important role: the ways in which a primary object reacts and adapts to the idiosyncratic physiological sleep/dream rhythms of the infant have dramatic consequences for the infant's development.

In his discussion of these two papers Peter Fonagy (London) underscores the success of both authors in arriving at an integration of an object relations (or attachment) model with the classical Freudian model of the drives. He illustrates how the authors modify both approaches to a certain degree emphasising pleasure, and uses the metaphor of brain stimulation to describe their approach to drive theory and the role of self-reflective function in their exploration of object relations theory. Fonagy stresses that by presenting a parsimonious view of both these constructs, by stripping away the non-essentials, they are able to arrive at a relatively smooth integration that has the potential to advance our collective theoretical constructions.

The chapters by Ellman and Weinstein are closely connected to another exciting field of research, where controversial discussions have been taking place since the 1950s. This field examines the neurological and physiological correlates of dreaming. As mentioned above, Freud created a purely psychological scientific discipline because he realised the methodological limitations of the neurosciences at that time. Nevertheless, he never gave up hope that progress in the natural sciences and neurosciences would one day allow us to "objectively" test some of the basic assumptions of psychoanalysis. Habermas (1968) characterised this hope as the "*szientistisches Selbstmissverständnis der Psychoanalyse*" (the "scientific self-misunderstanding of psychoanalysis"). Now, however, remarkable progress in our understanding of the brain has led many contemporary psychoanalysts to engage in the productive dialogue with the natural sciences for which Freud hoped, even in a core field of psychoanalysis, the dreams.

Of particular note is the new scientific discipline of neuropsychoanalysis, which has been developed and championed by Mark Solms and colleagues. Initially, the discovery of REM sleep by Aserinsky and Kleitman (1955) separated the psychological and physiological worlds of dream research. Working in this vein, Hobson and McCarley (1977) formulated the well known thesis that dreams are nothing more than a coincidental neocortical interpretation of *Neuronenrauschen* ("neuronal stimulation") during sleep. This has been called the "paper-basket theory" of dreaming. For Hobson and McCarley, the psychoanalytic search for the unconscious meanings of dreams was absurd. Through careful studies of patients with brain lesions, however, Solms and Karen Kaplan-Solms have been able to refute the thesis of Hobson and McCarley (Kaplan-Solms & Solms, 2000). In a recently held debate between Solms and Hobson, Solms's findings and arguments won over the audience of eminent scientists. This was seen as a great triumph for psychoanalysis (Domhoff, 2005). The controversy continues, however, as newer publications by Hobson (2009) indicate. In these works, he accepts that dreams have meanings and are aimed at problem solving, but he denies that there is an unconscious dimension to such mental processes.

Many psychoanalytical researchers, also working experimentally, have contributed to the contemporary development of Freud's dream theory. Of particular note is Wolfgang Leuschner, Stephan Hau, and Tamara Fischmann's research group. In the sleep laboratory of the Sigmund Freud Institute in the 1980s, they collaborated with Howard Shevrin to perform innovative experiments on the unconscious and preconscious reactions of dreams to subliminal stimuli. More recently, in cooperation with Wolf Singer at the Max Planck Institute and the team of the Hanse Neuropsychoanalysis Study (Anna Buchheim, Horst Kächele, Gerhard Roth, Manfred Cierpka, Georg Bruns, et al.), a research team at the Sigmund Freud Institute has been following this tradition in a new way. Tamara Fischmann, Michael Russ, Tobias Baehr, and Marianne Leuzinger-Bohleber (Frankfurt) summarise their ongoing study on "Changes in dreams of chronic depressed patients. The Frankfurt FmRI/EEG Study (FRED)". They present a single case study discussing the problems and opportunities associated with comparing changes in dreams in clinical and extraclinical psychoanalytic research. The patient, presented in the extensive case study in Chapter Five, also reported his dreams in the sleep laboratory, which enabled the research team to investigate the changes in the manifest dream contents from a theory-driven, systematic analysis applying the coding system of Moser and v. Zeppelin (1996) (for more details see www-sigmund-freud-institut.de).

The same method is used in another study of post-traumatic dreams and symbolisation by Sverre Varvin (Oslo), Tamara Fischmann (Frankfurt), Vladimir Jovic (Belgrade), Bent Rosenbaum (Copenhagen), and Stephan Hau (Stockholm). In their chapter, "Traumatic dreams: symbolisation gone astray", the authors summarise a large ongoing study in Belgrade with patients who have been traumatised by war. The authors give an impressive short overview of the historical context and outline some of the unbearable difficulties faced by psychoanalysts as they try to help severely traumatised patients. Some of these patients were also investigated in the sleep laboratory. Different methods for approaching the post-traumatic dreams, e.g., by the Enunciation Method, the "Moser method", and a clinical psychoanalytical approach are discussed. At the end of the chapter, there is a summary of the conceptual and clinical specifics of psychoanalysis with this group of patients.

Hanspeter Mathys (Zurich) in his chapter, "Communicative functions of dream telling", discusses an additional aspect of dreams in psychoanalytic treatment. From his perspective, the main focus is not what the dream means but how the analysand tells it and talks about it. Introducing a dream to the conversation establishes a triadic mode of communication out of a dyadic one. Reference to an intrapsychic product that is one's own but at the same time also seems foreign makes relational regulation possible and creates an atmosphere where the analysand feels comfortable presenting topics they cannot otherwise bring up. On the basis of the findings presented, a differentiated attitude of reception is proposed for clinical work with dreams.

Katrin Luise Laezer (Frankfurt), Birgit Gaertner (Frankfurt), and Emil Branik (Hamburg) in their chapter, "ADHD—illness or symptomatic indicator for trauma?" take up the thesis of Margaret Rustin in this volume. They discuss their observation that often children diagnosed with ADHD (attention deficit hyperactivity disorder) do not primarily suffer from a genetic or neurobiological impairment but—due to severe traumatisations in their first years of life—did not have a chance to develop the capability to dream ("rêverie"), symbolise, or mentalise. They lack an intermediate space, a trustful inner world of objects, and adequate self regulation. This is illustrated by a case study, which was carefully discussed by "expert validation". The case study is part of qualitative-clinical psychoanalytical research, which is combined with extraclinical research, in an ongoing study, comparing the effects of psychoanalytical and behavioural treatments of children with ADHD (see www.sigmund-freud-institut.de).

Nicole Pfenning-Meerkötter, Katrin Luise Läzer, Brigitte Schiller, Lorena Hartmann, and Marianne Leuzinger-Bohleber (Frankfurt) report in their chapter "No intermediate space for dreaming? Findings of the EVA Study with Children at Risk" on child analytic treatments offered in kindergartens for at-risk children. In close cooperation with the Institute for Psychoanalytic Child and Adolescent Psychotherapy, the research team of the Sigmund Freud Institute tried out a new form of "outreaching psychoanalysis" that takes place in locations other than private offices. The case study is part of the ongoing early prevention studies at the Institute. In all studies, clinical and extraclinical psychoanalytical research are combined (see EVA project, www. sigmund-freud-institut.de).

In the projects presented in this volume, psychoanalytic researchers have had to resolve a specific tension. On the one hand, they have had to argue that the proper research phenomena of psychoanalysis—unconscious fantasies and conflicts—are not directly observable. These phenomena therefore require the particular research methodology of psychoanalysis, which uses the precise observation of free associations, dreams, slips of the tongue, etc., as well as of transference and countertransference reactions in psychoanalytic sessions. To validate these observations, psychoanalysis has developed specific truth criteria that allow analysts to confirm some hypotheses and falsify others. The validity of these criteria relies on the close cooperation of analysts and analysands in the psychoanalytic setting. This genuinely psychoanalytic form of research has no substitute. On the other hand, however, the results of this research can often only be reported anecdotally and not measured. This creates a tension between psychoanalytic research and the standards of empirical science, which require potentially falsifiable hypotheses, transparent reporting of data, deductive justifications for conclusions, replicable experiments, conclusions that can be evaluated by fellow researchers, systematic controls for subjective factors, etc.

The editors of this volume believe that this tension should not be denied; it should be reflected upon through a dialectic between clinical and extraclinical research. This requires the building of bridges between psychoanalysis and other disciplines. In our view, such bridges are essential to preserving the future of psychoanalysis as a profession and as a scientific discipline.

Often, psychoanalysis' dialogue with literature and the arts has been much less conflicted. The last chapter of this volume, "Orders of the imaginary. Freud's *The Interpretation of Dreams* and the literature of classical modernity", reminds us of this other tradition. Peter-André Alt (Berlin), Professor of Literature and Cultural Sciences at the University of Berlin, shows how three of Freud's contemporaries—the writers Hugo von Hofmannsthal, Arthur Schnitzler, and Franz Kafka—were inspired by *The Interpretation of Dreams*. In spite of or in response to Freud's scientific clarity, each of these writers created his own works of ambiguity, and thus "gave back the mystery to the dream".

We would like to thank all the authors of this volume for helping us to build bridges between the psychoanalytic and the non-analytic scientific community. We also would like to thank David Taylor and Horst Kächele, who, in cooperation with the Research Board of the International Psychoanalytical Association (IPA), helped conceive of the conference and write an application for financial support from the

DFG. We are grateful for the support of this organisation, the IPA, and the Sigmund Freud Institute.

Great thanks must also go to Eva Karduck, Lisa Kallenbach, Yadigar Imamoglu, Johann Wirth, and Tamara Fischmann, who helped with the translations. We would also like to thank Renate Stebahne, Magdaléna Bankovi ová, and Marie-Sophie Loehlein, the many young scientists of the Sigmund Freud Institute and, last but not least, Axel Scharfenberg, Herbert Bareuther, and Klaus-Dieter Albrecht. Without this team we would have never been able to organise such a conference. Finally, many thanks to Anne Annau who helped to prepare this volume.

References

Adams-Sylvan, A. & Sylvan, M. (1990). A dream is the fulfilment of a wish: Traumatic dream, repetion compulsion, and the pleasure principle. *International Journal of Psychoanalysis*, 71: 513–522.

Ahumada, J. L. & Doria-Medina, R. (2010). New Orleans congress panel: What does conceptual research have to offer? In: M. Leuzinger-Bohleber, J. Canestri & M. Target (Eds.), *Early Development and Its Disturbances: Clinical, Conceptual and Empirical Research on ADHD and Other Psychopathologies and Its Epistemological Reflections* (pp. 267–279). London: Karnac.

Aserinsky, E. & Kleitman, N. (1955). Two types of ocular motility during sleep. *Journal of Applied Physiology*, 8: 1–10.

Blitz, R. & Greenberg, R. (1984). Nightmares of the traumatic neurosis: Implications for theory and treatment, In: H. Schwartz (Ed.), *Psychotherapy of the Combat Veteran* (pp. 103–123). New York: Spectrum.

Blum, H. P. (2011). Response. *International Journal of Psychoanalysis*, 92: 275–277.

Bohleber, W. (2011). Response. *International Journal of Psychoanalysis*, 92: 285–288.

Cabré, M. (2011). Response. *International Journal of Psychoanalysis*, 92: 272–274.

Da Rocha Barros, E. (2011). Response. *International Journal of Psychoanalysis*, 92: 270–272.

Domhoff, G. W. (2005). The content of dreams: Methodologic and theoretical implications. In: M. H. Kryger, T. Roth & W. C. Dement (Eds.), *Principles and Practice of Sleep Medicine (4th ed.)* (pp. 522–534). Philadelphia: Saunders.

Ellman, S. (2010). *When Theories Touch: a Historical and Theoretical Integration of Psychoanalytic Thought*. London: Karnac.

Ferenczi, S. (1931). On the revision of the interpretation of dreams. In: *Notes and Fragments: Final Contributions to the Problems and Methods of Psychoanalysis* (pp. 238–243). London: Hogarth, 1955.

Ferro, A. (2011). *Avoiding Emotions. Living Emotions.* London: Routledge.

Fisher, C., Byrne, J. V., Edwards, A. & Kahn, E. (1970). A psychophysiological study of nightmares. *Journal of the American Psychoanalytic Association,* 18: 747–782.

Fonagy, P. (2007). *Violent Attachment.* Unpublished paper given at the conference, "In Gewalt verstrickt. Interdisziplinäre Erkundungen". Kassel University, Germany, March.

Freud, S. (1900a). *The Interpretation of Dreams. S. E., 4.* London: Hogarth.

Freud, S. (1927a). Postscript to a discussion on lay analysis. *S. E., 20*: 251–258. London: Hogarth.

Freud, S. (1933a). New introductory lectures on psycho-analysis. *S. E., 22*: 5–182.

Habermas, J. (1968). *Technik und "Wissenschaft" als Ideologie.* Frankfurt am Main, Germany: Suhrkamp.

Hanly, C. (2010). Logic, meaning, and truth in psychoanalytic research. In: M. Leuzinger-Bohleber, J. Canestri & M. Target (Eds.), *Early Development and Its Disturbances: Clinical, Conceptual and Empirical Research on ADHD and Other Psychopathologies and Its Epistemological Reflections* (pp. 209–218). London: Karnac.

Hartmann, E. (1984). *The Nightmare.* New York: Basic.

Hobson, J. A. (2009). REM sleep and dreaming: Towards a theory of proto-consciousness. *Nature Reviews Neuroscience, 10*: 803–813.

Hobson, J. & McCarley, R. (1977). The brain as a dream-state generator. *American Journal of Psychiatry, 134*: 1335–1348.

Jones, E. (1910). *On the Nightmare.* London: Hogarth, 1951.

Kächele, H., Albani, C., Buchheim, A., Grünzig, H.-J., Hölzer, M., Hohage, R., Jimenez, J. P., Leuzinger-Bohleber, M., Mergenthaler, E., Neudert-Dreyer, L., Pokorny, D. & Thomä, H. (2006). The German specimen case, Amalia X: Empirical studies. *International Journal of Psychoanalysis, 87*: 809–826.

Kaplan-Solms, K. & Solms, M. (2000). *Clinical Studies in Neuro-psychoanalysis.* New York: Karnac.

Kohut, H. (1977). *The Restoration of the Self.* New York: International Universities Press.

Kramer, M. (1991). The nightmare: A failure in dream function. *Dreaming,* 1: 277–285.

Lansky, M. R. (1995). *Posttraumatic Nightmares: Psychodynamic Explorations.* Hillsdale, NJ: The Analytic Press.

Leuzinger-Bohleber, M. (1987, 1989). *Veränderung kognitiver Prozesse in Psychoanalysen. Band 1 und 2.* Berlin: Springer (PSZ).

Leuzinger-Bohleber, M. (2007). Forschende Grundhaltung als abgewehrter "common ground" von psychoanalytischen Praktikern und Forschern? *Psyche—Z Psychoanal, 61*: 966–994.

Leuzinger-Bohleber, M., Dreher, A. U. & Canestri, J. (Eds.) (2003). *Pluralism and Unity? Methods of Research in Psychoanalysis*. London: International Psychoanalytical Association.

Leuzinger-Bohleber, M. & Fischmann, T., in cooperation with the Research Subcommittee for Conceptual Research of the IPA (2006). What is conceptual research in psychoanalysis? *International Journal of Psychoanalysis, 87*: 1355–1386.

Leuzinger-Bohleber, M., Rüger, B., Stuhr, U. & Beutel, M. (2002). *"Forschen und Heilen" in der Psychoanalyse. Ergebnisse und Berichte aus Forschung und Praxis*. Stuttgart, Germany: Kohlhammer.

Lidz, T. (1946). Nightmares and combat neuroses. *Psychiatry, 19*: 37–39.

Luborsky, L. & Crits-Christoph, P. (1990). *Understanding Transference: The Core Conflictual Relationship Theme Method*. New York: Basic.

Mack, J. (1965). Nightmares, conflict and ego development in childhood. *International Journal of Psychoanalysis, 46*: 403–428.

Mack, J. (1970). *Nightmares and Human Conflict*. Boston: Houghzon Mifflin.

Makari, G. (2008). *Revolution in Mind: the Creation of Psychoanalysis*. London: Duckworth.

Moser, U. & Zeppelin, I. v. (1996). *Der geträumte Traum. Wie Träume entstehen und sich verändern*. Stuttgart, Germany: Kohlhammer.

Moses, R. (1978). Adult psychic trauma: The question of early predisposition. *International Journal of Psychoanalysis, 59*: 353–363.

Pfenning-Meerkötter, N. (in press). *Wissensmanagement in psychoanalytischen Forschungsprojekten* [dissertation]. Kassel University.

Pine, F. (1998). Sexuality in clinical psychoanalytical treatment. *International Journal of Psychoanalysis, 79*: 160–161.

Pine, F. (2011). Panel at 47th IPA Congress, Mexico City, unpublished.

Rustin, M. (2011). Dream and play in child psychoanalysis. (See chapter in this book.)

Stern, D. & the Process Study Group (1998). Non-interpretative mechanisms in psychoanalytic therapy. *International Journal of Psychoanalysis, 79*: 903–921.

Whitebook, J. (2011). Sigmund Freud—A philosophical physician. (See chapter in this book.)

Wisdom, J. O. (1949). A hypothesis to explain trauma-re-enactment dreams. *International Journal of Psychoanalysis, 31*: 13–20.

Zwiebel, R. (1985). The dynamics of the countertransference dream. *International Review of Psycho-Analysis, 12*: 87–99.

PART I

CLINICAL RESEARCH ON DREAMS

CHAPTER ONE

The re-awakening of psychoanalytic theories of dreams and dreaming

David Taylor

In 1908, Henri Poincaré (1854–1912), the French mathematician and philosopher of science, gave a celebrated series of lectures at the Société de Psychologie in Paris. One of his lectures had as its principal subject the psychology of mathematical discovery. The interest of his observations endures. They were published later that same year as chapter three of his widely read *Science et Méthode*. It was immediately translated into English and has been reprinted as recently as 2001. Poincaré's observations are based upon his own experiences. They carry weight because Poincaré, a mathematical genius, was responsible for some of the most important mathematical discoveries of his age. They made possible many significant recent advances in modern science. The importance of his theory about what are now known as automorphic functions is equal to that of the calculus (Ayoub, 2004; Weisstein, 1999; Birkhoff, 1920).[1]

In his lecture, Poincaré took his discovery of these automorphic functions as a case study of the process of mathematical discovery. To him, it appeared to have three components. In the first, he would work at a theoretically important aspect of his problem for some days, but typically would fail to find the solution which he had sensed to be there. This work involved hard and detailed mental reasoning of a mathematical and logical kind. In the second stage, increasingly frustrated, he would give up on his work and abandon it for an entirely different pursuit—perhaps a holiday. Then suddenly after a few hours—or it might be days, weeks, or sometimes even months—*the* solution would come to him.

Thus he recalled, "I ... began to study arithmetical questions without any great apparent result, and without suspecting that they could have the least connection with my previous researches. Disgusted at my want of success, I went away to spend a few days at the seaside and thought of entirely different things. One day, as I was walking on the cliff, the idea came to me, again with the same characteristics of conciseness, suddenness and immediate certainty, that arithmetical transformations of indefinite ternary quadratic forms are identical with those of non-Euclidian geometry."

Although he usually experienced a sense of certainty about the correctness of his intuition, Poincaré found that there was always a third stage. In this he felt a compulsion to check that his solution was correct. Sometimes this might take just a few hours .... "I had all the elements, and had only to assemble and arrange them. Accordingly I composed my definitive treatise at a sitting and without any difficulty." But equally it might take days or weeks of the same hard kind of mathematical deduction and analysis as had been necessary at the beginning.

Poincaré's immediate sense of what was happening in his mind was that all three stages were necessary. He reasoned that unconscious or subliminal mental processes were as important as those that were conscious and more familiar. In the first stage, he considered that the creative mathematician was trying out all possible connections between the mathematical objects which might be involved. Although characteristically he fails to find *the* solution, he succeeds in loosening all the connections previously thought to exist. Graphically, Poincaré compared this to the way that the atoms which go to make up the molecules of a gas may under certain conditions become unhooked. He imagined the stage when he seemed not to be thinking about the problem at all as actually involving unconscious processes consisting of repeated attempts to recombine these free atoms. Only the combination which joins the mathematical objects together in a way that brings about order, coherence, and wholeness survives. Poincaré said that his immediate sense of the correctness of the solution was rarely misleading. It usually withstood the essential proof-testing of the third, final stage. However, he noted that when he had let himself become too absorbed by the supposed elegance of his solution, he was more likely to be wrong!

Poincaré's observations seem to me highly relevant to the subject of this chapter, namely psychoanalytic clinical research in relation to its value in our understanding of dreams and dreaming. By psychoanalytic clinical research I mean that which relies solely on the use of the psychoanalytic method in the consulting room in order to make psychoanalytic observations. It uses no instruments or forms, yet is immensely valuable for making discoveries and for evaluating whether they are true or false. To some extent, dreaming is a special, rather difficult case. Can we show what justification there is for claiming to know anything at all about the meaning and function of dreams, since it cannot be taken for granted that dreams have meaning at all? Within dream consciousness, we have no capacity to know directly "meaning" of the kind that we ordinarily possess in waking consciousness. We then need to set out and justify the methods and principles psychoanalysis uses to interpret the meaning or significance of a given dream. We also need to have something to say in general about the possible functions of dreaming, spelling out what is involved when these sorts of questions are addressed. My hope is that I will eventually convey a certain kind of attitude to psychoanalytic clinical research: a confident questioning, possessing a balance of certainty and uncertainty, with some sense of what is not yet understood.

Poincaré's exceptional thinking brings vividly to life that sense of wonder, which he himself clearly possessed, at the quite remarkable intelligence of the mental operations involved in the unconscious processing needed to see beyond old formulas and to produce new ones. In Poincaré's case, the objects of his unconscious thinking were mathematical. Intriguing to us as psychoanalysts is the possibility that there may be some overlap between this and the kind of unconscious functions involved when, as I describe later, an otherwise uncurious analysand produces through the vehicle of a dream a complex scene or visual metaphor with the capacity to illuminate what is otherwise a totally confused set of elements. But, in addition, Poincaré had some very interesting things to say about science in general. I want to apply some of his thinking to the kind of clinical research that has been responsible for the central core of psychoanalytic knowledge about dreams and dreaming.

As far as I am aware, Poincaré did not refer explicitly to unconscious processing occurring in sleep or through dreaming, but it is strongly implied in his account. Again, as far as I can tell, his thinking about unconscious processing was quite independent of Freud's. It was not until 1920 that any of Freud's writings were translated into French (Quinodoz, 2010). *The Interpretation of Dreams* was published in Leipzig and Vienna in late 1899. By 1906 only 351 copies had been sold. The first French translation was not published until 1926. It was only slowly over the succeeding twenty years that *The Interpretation of Dreams (IoD)* was to assume its position as a defining part of the "spirit of its age".

In *The Interpretation of Dreams*, we find Freud proposing that everything conscious has an unconscious preliminary stage and that, "The unconscious is the true psychical reality." Even at that time he considered that unconscious mental functioning was vastly more extensive than waking consciousness. He wrote, "[I]n its innermost nature it is as much unknown to us as the reality of the external world, and it is as incompletely presented by the data of consciousness as is the external world by the communications of our sense perceptions." This remarkable conclusion came towards the end of *The Interpretation of Dreams*. Freud's italics indicate that he wanted to leave his readers in no doubt about the limitations of the view offered by our waking consciousness. He was stressing the severe limits that exist on the certainty of our knowledge of both *internal* and *external* reality. Interestingly, Poincaré also thought that reality, *the thing itself*, could not be directly or exactly known by us. For Poincaré, science could only approach nature through successive approximations.

However, Freud's conception of unconscious mental operations was more elaborate than Poincaré's and included more intentionality. Freud based his first conception of the unconscious almost entirely on what he thought he had understood about dreams. Displacement, condensation, mobility of cathexes, absence of negation, of doubt, of degrees of certitude, indifference to reality, and exclusive wishful subordination to the principles of pleasure and unpleasure were all held to be characteristic not only of dreams but of unconscious mental functioning in general. Freud used these features to distinguish a fundamental dichotomy between what he called primary and secondary forms of mental processing. Although dreams permit the gratification of infantile wishes, this is only their secondary function. Their primary purpose is to preserve sleep. The inhibition of the systems of voluntary movement in relation to thoughts or impulses, which would otherwise lead to action, means that the intense scenarios of dreams can be hallucinated without being put into external action.

What then is the current status of this conception of the processes involved in the formation of dreams, and, more generally, of the way that unconscious processing works? And if these were to be supplanted, what better account do we now have available to us? These are questions which run through this volume. Here, I consider the changes in these original views based upon the accumulating knowledge derived from the psychoanalytic session itself. Inevitably, my account has had to be compressed and selective. However, I will attempt to indicate a few of the many important points of contact with other bodies of empirical work. These bear upon the wider frame of knowledge within which psychoanalysts works. Finally, I will offer some speculative hypotheses derived from clinical work which might point to how empirical and clinical approaches to research might be able to be articulated with one another.

It seems fair to say that, almost from the very beginning, Freud and his collaborators realised that the founding theory provided an inadequate model for the range of the phenomena connected with dreams and the unconscious as these are encountered in the more ecological setting provided by the psychoanalytic session. We are familiar with the notion that in the analytic session the way that the patient uses the telling of the dream is often more important than its content. Again, almost from the beginning, it was clear that the method of free association was of limited value as an instrument of investigation in the clinical setting. But equally immediate to our theme is the non-trivial way that aggressive impulses, excessive arousal, anxiety, fear, and evidences of attempted problem solving form such large and meaningful parts of the manifest dream. Empirical research findings (see Palombo, 1978, 1984; Shredl, 2006; Kramer, 2007) are in line with these clinical observations. There are interesting issues here about the ways in which clinical thinking and empirical research develop. Do they do so interdependently or do they follow rather separate trajectories?

The status of Freud's original theory of dreams in relation to that of modern psychoanalysis is similar to that of Newtonian mechanics in relation to modern physics and astronomy. Newton's theory still works for aspects of celestial motion but not for the relativity of time and space, the origin of the universe, or at the quantum level generally. Freud's original theory of the formation of dreams and, by extension, of the nature of unconscious process, continues to offer a good fit for that limited part of the spectrum of psychoanalytic phenomena concerned with self-deception, hypocrisy, and to some extent the satisfaction of libidinal wishes, but not, I think, for others including Bion's influential idea that dreams have a role in the processing of different levels of thought and feeling.

Recently a number of authors, most notably Welsh (1994) and Blass (2001), have drawn our attention to the long period in which Freud's methods of justifying his conclusions about dreaming were exempted from major critique from within psychoanalysis itself. In essence, Freud had argued that the meaning—the latent dream thoughts he hypothesised—could be indirectly, but nevertheless validly, reconstructed through the vehicle of free association. But these associations arise in waking consciousness. It could be counter-argued that we may be finding in dreams only what we already know or suspect. According to this view, the putative latent thought may be present in the waking consciousness of the dreamer, but may not necessarily be crucial to the formation of the dream. In general, Freud's argumentation in support of his free association method was sometimes *ad hoc* or tendentious. Blass in particular demonstrates that Freud's method does not really convincingly support his conclusions.

Perhaps it was an uneasy awareness of the existence of these problems which led to a dormancy, or at least to a partial suspension of a collective psychoanalytic critical faculty. This phenomenon might indicate the operation of some factors in common with those which possibly underlie the latency or dormant period which some of Poincaré's mathematical discoveries seemed to require. Perhaps, much as is the case with individuals, science also needs a latency period before a deferred rethink finally becomes possible, or the full significance of existing observations can be realised.

Before moving on from *The Interpretation of Dreams* we should note how many crucial ideas it contained in addition to the headline theory that dreams derive from wish fulfilment. In this respect, Blass also showed how many of the theses in *The Interpretation of Dreams* can be justified by a method of proof which takes into account the whole set of the data which bear upon them. These include the overarching notion that dreams *are* meaningful, as well as the work's observations about the distinctive contents of the mind that we specifically associate with a psychoanalytic view of the human psyche. They include Freud's hypothesis that the infantile level continues to be a highly active motive force within the mind throughout life, operating throughout our entire thinking as well as our dreaming; and that in naked, as well as in disguised ways, we continue to desire the exclusive possession of one parent or of their substitute, and wish to kill or displace the rival, or *their* substitute. These theorems about our most private thoughts and motives possess characteristics which are necessary if a truth is to be a distinctively psychoanalytic truth. They must have the potential to upset the orthodoxy of the waking self. They must be able to stand outside taboos, including the incest taboo, and whatever other social or cultural norms that happen to be current at the time. This is partly why it would be mistaken to discard the classical theory of dreams and its method of free association.

To test the undiminished nature of the power of the classical theory, the reader is invited to follow for a few moments the haphazard line of any of his or her private thoughts, or to do the same with a recollected dream, and then to imagine how it would feel to be required to speak out loud these thoughts in a public gathering, even one of trusted friends. In this, as in so many things, we can still lean on Freud's valour. He risked revealing his dreams and private associations in order to communicate what he had understood about the universality of the devices of the unconscious part of the mind. One example came from what he called a relatively simple dream. In it there was a:

> ... company at table or table d'hôte ... spinach was being eaten ... Frau E. L. was sitting beside me; she was turning her whole attention to me and laid her hand on my knee in an intimate manner".... Freud continued, "I was struck by the contrast between my wife's behaviour at table and that of Frau E. L. ... my wife and me at the time at which I was secretly courting her .... The caress which she gave me under the table-cloth was her reply to a pressing love letter. In the dream, however, my wife was replaced by a comparative stranger—E. L. ... I was aware of intense and well-founded affective impulses [*as I associated*] ... the thoughts themselves fell at once into logical chains ... I might draw closer together the threads in the material revealed by the analysis ... they converge upon a single nodal point, but considerations of a personal and not of a scientific nature prevent my doing so in public. I should be obliged to betray many things which had better remain my secret, for on

my way to discovering the solution of the dream all kinds of things were revealed which I was unwilling to admit even to myself. (Freud, 1901)

Perhaps this has reminded the reader of his or her own version of the uncomfortable state of mind to which Freud's description refers. I want to speculate further that the uneasiness, identified above in relation to the tendentious quality of some of Freud's reasoning about dreams, may have also played some part in a more general tendency to inhibit the critical faculties which are needed for there to be rigour in psychoanalytic clinical research. It is dangerous to be thought to be casting the first stone.

Poincaré thought that to be a step towards a scientific theory a given description must enable the subject to go beyond *brute facts* to what he called *the soul of the fact*. By this he meant our understanding of the way that the thing in question works. Scientific or mathematical truth, while always an approximation, always aims to be as close an approximation as possible. In psychoanalysis, versions of Poincaré's three stages of discovery are also necessary. The first is hard disciplined clinical work, and here, as we know, there is often a sense of failure. However, it is only on the basis of this that, like the mathematician, the creative psychoanalytic clinician can proceed to the second phase—often after a break (such as that between sessions) in which he or she engages in unrelated activities—of valid intuitions about the phenomena with which he is dealing. We do not go very far without these. But such intuitive understanding then has to be tested by the production of an assessable and contestable line of observation and reasoning, in other words by a kind of proof with a form and content appropriate to the discipline of psychoanalysis. Finally, there is the testing of the predictions and the extrapolations which a scientific theory should make possible.

In this context, it is interesting to find, in a favourable review of Eissler's 1965 book *Medical Orthodoxy and the Future of Psycho-Analysis*, great frustration with the lack of encouragement given to these sorts of critical procedures in the course of psychoanalytic training. The reviewer, Wilfred Bion (1966), writes:

Eissler quotes a procedure adopted by Aichhorn, whose clinical acumen he praises highly, for watching strangers whom he is close to for a period with a view to forming a conjecture about their next act. As he describes it Aichhorn was playing a game not unlike that of a boy imitating Sherlock Holmes. He speaks of it with approval, attributing to it some of Aichhorn's flair for understanding instantly and accurately the personality of the delinquents with whom he dealt. But he deprecates the possibility of making any parallel procedure part of a formal training course. But why not? I welcome the introduction into training of Baby Observation; I think it would be all the better for an injection of the good humour of the "Holmesian" technique. The baby should be observed with all the enthusiasm of Holmes on the track of a desperate criminal. Eissler pessimistically doubts the success of any approach, even Aichhorn's, to the delinquent. I suggest that the lack of success will continue so long as the investigation is carried out with a predisposition to see the object of the investigation as a "delinquent" no matter what his life may have been, and to do so with the humourless attitude which seems to be inseparable from having suffered a psycho-analytic training course.

For Bion's "baby" or "delinquent" we could equally well substitute "dream" or "clinical theory". Perhaps it is no coincidence that this more challenging, intellectually vigorous position is found in someone who was, by general consent, one of the most eminent of the small number of clinical researchers who have substantially advanced psychoanalytic thinking since Freud's day. A reading of Bion will find him developing a notion of prediction specific to the nature of psychoanalytic data. Thus the analyst's intuition should be based upon early, barely noticeable signs of feeling in the patient, which nevertheless are observable in principle. This analytic form of clinical intuition is employed in a *predictive* way, to anticipate what is about to happen. Such an analytic hunch—which might well be based upon an element in a patient's dream—might suggest that the patient is on the verge of feeling something mentally painful. But should the analyst describe only what is already fully formed, he/she will be simply stating the obvious—or in Poincaré's terms, stating only *brute facts*.

In the 111 years since Freud's first account, the accumulation of our knowledge of the transference/countertransference relationship, and the discovery of the power and function of projective identification, mean that clinically we now have sources of information which were not available when Freud began. These developments, including a number of Freud's own, have meant that our ideas about the nature of dreams have changed. To illustrate something of this change, I use a clinical vignette to show the theory of dreaming that I find myself using, and of my approach to intuition in the clinical setting and to its proper evidencing. The clinical material is disguised while preserving the essentials. The patient is one who rarely brought dreams.

> When about fourteen years ago E began his analysis, he was a 22-year-old student of mathematics finding it very difficult to work. This was getting him into trouble. He happened to belong to one of the wealthiest families in the UK. Generally, his beautiful mother seems to have sustained little interest in her children. She would dip in and out of any engagement with E in a seductive way. When he was 14-months-old she went away for six months leaving him to be looked after by a succession of nannies. Some of them were disciplinarians and tended to use punishment. As E grew up his early promise was not realised. His intelligence disappeared from view. Perhaps it was consumed in his near-perfect capacities to disappoint, and waste time. He persisted with solutions connected with a central project of finding a girl, but their inevitable failure aroused no curiosity in him. In a sense, E was also a delinquent because he subverted the rules of academic or personal procedures, and provoked hostility and criticism while erasing from his mind any record of his subversiveness.
>
> The following exchange occurred towards the end of a period of lassitude lasting many months.

A: It affects you as a lack of energy, but it is meant to create a deadly, and I think, violent fight between us.

E: I agree that what you say seems to fit. But I don't know it. All I know is that I just feel defeated every time I leave here …

A: I think that just now you gave in to the temptation to defeat me. And of course it deals with other things … [By this I meant the way that his inhabiting a world provoked by his complaints enabled him to avoid more direct contact with many of his more subtle feelings of vulnerability.]

E: I get embarrassed at the thought that I might respond …. It's very strange, because I actually had a violent dream last night … I don't feel violent … Anyway … *It was on a bus and people were getting off at the front. In fact that doesn't happen, people get off in the middle. There was this black woman with a round face trying to get off at the front and I found myself oppositional. I kept obstructing her. Every time she tried one way I would stop her* [implying with increasing physicality]. *Anyway some way or another she got off. I then noticed that it was my stop too and I thought that when I got off she might be there waiting for me and would attack me ...'*

A: I think you could remember this dream because you felt I wasn't getting caught up in feeling blocked by you and then attacking you. Your dream matches what has been going on here. In your dream you were wanting to block and trap the woman, but at least there *was* a woman in your dream. We don't know why she was black. But this is taking place at the front of the bus, presumably by the driver, a bit like your opposition to me earlier was intended to distract me as someone like a driver who might be trying to go somewhere.

E: (as if puzzled by a nonsensical remark) I don't understand what you mean. [It was now within a minute or two of the end of the session.]

A: If what I say doesn't make sense it offers the prospect of a disagreement. And as we are near the end of the session I think that you try to detain us with a disagreement.

Later, I thought that E's ability to have this dream seemed similar to a slight shift towards a more cooperative attitude he had shown a few days earlier. There was some insight into the captivity in which he and I, and indeed all his objects, were kept. This insight was matched by the dream's imagery. I used it to signify the way E had been acting in the session because I had had months of first-hand experience of the pull and push of his oppositional way of proceeding. This provided me with sure ground for my comments. I felt much more uncertain about the significance of the other elements in E's dream, most particularly the black woman with the round face. But the fact that there was a woman in E's dream seemed in itself new. A couple of months later E began by saying:

E: Last night I went to my gym class .... I tried to stop getting angry with this woman who goes there. She insists on standing in front and blocking my view of myself in the mirror. She always does it.

A: I think you are trying to make me think that you are tempted to pick an argument because of your self-absorption [he has recently emphasised how often he becomes absorbed in looking at himself in the mirror] but I don't think this would be quite right. I think you are seeing if I will take this unsympathetic view of you.

Then you could argue that I was blocking a proper view of you. I think that this is how when someone whom you might think is good and important to you isn't "in the way", you sidestep any need to know that you might have thought them good.

E seemed interested and although the session was nearing its end he could go on to say:

I have noticed that some people are more lively than me. For the last couple of months there's been this black woman who some- times sits opposite me in the library. She's married and has got a child but although she's got troubles she just gets on with things.

Concluding comments

How is this final sequence to be understood? When E mentioned the woman blocking his view of himself in the mirror I was put in mind of the dream of the blocking encounter with the black woman. Unresolved, this had stayed with me. I had the same immediate feeling of recogni- tion when at the end of the session he spoke of "the black woman in the library". Such things may be attributed either to a long-extended kind of free association, or to an analyst's over-valued idea. However, neither of these explanations quite does justice to the reverberative qualities of what had passed backwards and forwards between the dream and the dreamer, between the analysand and the analyst, and between analysis and E's life over these days, months, and years.

My line of thought concerning my patient's dream was that it repre- sented an exceptional moment in terms of his relationship with insight. My speculation is that E's encounter with the "woman in the library" had led to two types of reaction: the first, a diffuse and unsymbolised arousal (the physiological reaction of fight/flight rather than sexual arousal); the second, an interest tinged with hope. This latter pro- vided enough of a good internal object to allow him to sleep to a depth where he could dream. At this point, when there was just enough of an experience of a good object within E, it allowed him a wish that was effective internally, in that he could hallucinate and/or remember the "woman" who was the cause of his divided reaction. It even extended as far as an image of roundness.

How do these things happen? I will close with a wider, bolder speculation. A process such as this may take advantage of the fact that man's dominant sense is vision. The processing of visual experience is developmentally earlier, and is less subject to the kind of emotional difficulties that have to be managed in the developmental task of linking infantile affects with language and verbal thought. The visual images and scenarios that are generated through dreaming may offer the kind of relief associated with something's *having happened*, compared to the kind of anxiety which accompanies something which has *not happened*. As a consequence, and other things being equal, the primitive physiological reactions of fight/flight are dissipated or relieved on the one hand, and some symbolic thought generated on the other. These processes at the neuropsychological level may play a part in the developmentally crucial integration of visual and auditory forms of experience.

Today, there are several contenders to account for the function of dreaming. These include wish-fulfilment/sleep preservation, problem solving/information processing, selective mood regulation, memory, and some notion of "debugging". To proceed any further it is necessary to specify more precisely what we mean by these terms. Under the impact of new knowledge, and perhaps after a period of relative dormancy, our understanding of dreams and their function may be about to enter a new and productive period of unresolvedness. Much new knowledge will derive from neuroscience, semiotics, and cognitive science. It is also important we acknowledge the important work of researchers such as Ellman & Weinstein (1991), Holt (2009), Kramer (2007), Palombo (1978, 1984), Shredl (2006), Solms (1997), and Weisstein (1999), plus several others, whose empirical investigations have shown that the psychoanalytic view that dreaming has both intrinsic meaning and its own functional importance is highly likely to be a correct one. In this chapter, I have argued that contestable psychoanalytic research in the clinical setting is equally vital if we are to peel back the layers to reveal the intimate connections that exist between dreams and our deeper selves and motives.

Note

1. In respect of automorphic functions, formerly known as Fuchsian functions, Poincaré used non-Euclidean geometry to develop the theory of the general transcendental automorphic function. Those with mathematical knowledge might wish to consider $f(z) = K/(cz+d)^r \ f(az+b/cz+d)$ where I[z] > 0. See Weisstein, E. W. (1999) at http://mathworld.wolfram.com/Poincare-Fuchs-KleinAutomorphicFunction.html or Birkhoff, G. (1920) at http://projecteuclid.org/euclid.bams/1183425178

References

Ayoub, R. G. (2004). *Musings of the Masters: An Anthology of Mathematical Reflections*. Washington, DC: Mathematical Association of America, p. 88.

Bion, W. R. (1966). Review of *Medical Orthodoxy and the Future of Psycho-Analysis*, by K. R. Eissler. *International Journal of Psychoanalysis*, 47: 575–579.

Birkhoff, G. B. (1920). The work of Poincaré on automorphic functions. *American Mathematical Society*, 26(4): 164–172. Available at http://projecteuclid.org/euclid.bams/1183425178

Blass, R. (2001). The limitations of critical studies of the epistemology of Freud's dream theory and clinical implications: A response to Spence and Grünbaum. *Psychoanalysis and Contemporary Thought*, 24: 115–151.

Ellman, S. J. & Weinstein, L. (1991). REM sleep and dream formation: A theoretical integration. In: S. J. Ellman & J. S. Antrobus (Eds.), *The Mind in Sleep: Psychology and Psychophysiology*. New York: Wiley.

Freud, S. (1901). On Dreams. *S. E.*, *5*. London: Hogarth, pp. 629–686.

Holt, R. R. (2009). *Primary Process Thinking: Theory, Measurement & Research*. Lanham, MD: Jason Aronson , p. 153.

Kramer, M. (2007). *The Dream Experience: A Systematic Exploration*. New York: Routledge.

Palombo, S. R. (1978). The adaptive function of dreams. *Psychoanalysis and Contemporary Thought*, 1: 443–476.

Palombo, S. R. (1984). Deconstructing the manifest dream. *Journal of the American Psychoanalytic Association*, 32: 405–420.

Poincaré, H. (1908). *Science et Méthode*. In: S. J. Gould (Ed.), *The Value of Science: Essential Writings of Henri Poincaré* (pp. 357–558). New York: Random House.

Quinodoz, J. M. (2010). How translations of Freud's writings have influenced French psychoanalytic thinking. *International Journal of Psychoanalysis*, *91*: 695–716.

Shredl, M. (2006). Factors affecting the continuity between waking and dreaming: Emotional intensity and emotional tone of the waking-life event. *Sleep & Hypnosis*, *8*: 1–5.

Solms, M. (1997). *The Neuropsychology of Dreams: A Clinical-anatomic Study*. Mahwah, NJ: Erlbaum.

Welsh, A. (1994). *Freud's Wishful Dream Book*. Princeton, NJ: Princeton University Press.

Weisstein, E. W. (1999). *The Poincaré-Fuchs-Klein Automorphic Function*. From MathWorld-Wolfram Web Resource, http://mathworld.wolfram.com/Poincare-Fuchs-KleinAutomorphicFunction.html

CHAPTER TWO

Dreams and play in child analysis today

Margaret Rustin

To approach the topic of children's dreaming in a psychoanalytic context the links between dream and play have to be our starting point. While in adult analysis there can be continuing robust debate about the centrality of dreams for understanding unconscious life, we are working in a different register with children. Klein's early papers about analysing children (1932) record her recognition of the need to find a technique appropriate to the child's natural forms of communication and activity. Lying on a couch and free associating was not something one could meaningfully propose to any child, whereas an invitation to draw and play in the presence of an attentive adult who would take seriously what the child's imagination revealed seemed to Klein, and remains for us, the starting point for an analytic space to be created. Her initially experimental provision of a selection of small toys with which the child could construct personal scenarios demonstrated to her that it was possible to provide a setting for child analysis which had the necessary characteristics of simplicity, replicability, continuity over time, and recognisable difference from the child's everyday world. The available toys and other materials were to provide a vocabulary with which the child could convey what was on his mind, and were thus to be objects which did not determine the direction of the child's activity, but instead ones which could be used in many different ways, depending on what the child's imagination suggested. Thus, fundamentally, her technique proposed that playing of this particular sort was the child's equivalent of free association and provided the observing analyst with the necessary material.

So what is the place of dreams in this scheme of things? Watching children inventing fantasy scenes with small dolls and animal figures or fashioning complex idiosyncratic constructions or drawing can sometimes feel like a window into the world of unconscious phantasy which has great similarity to listening to a dream narrative. But children do also have night dreams and sometimes these can be a part of the clinical material of sessions. In my own practice, asking a child to tell a dream if he has one in mind has often been a part of my initial technique of assessment, and certainly I explain at the beginning of an ongoing therapy that I am interested to hear about dreams as part of our finding out together about all the thoughts and feelings in the child's mind (Rustin, 1982).

However, when I started to ponder on the place of dreams in contemporary analytic work with children, my first troubling thought was that I had not in recent years worked with a child who brought dreams to his sessions, in stark contrast to my work with adolescents and adults. Nor had I much to draw on in my numerous supervisions of intensive child psychotherapy. What was going on?, I wondered. Somehow my memory of my earlier years of clinical practice was of more frequent dream material. I decided I must investigate this impression more carefully, and began to ask around.

An interesting and broadly similar picture has emerged from my literature search which included *The Journal of Child Psychotherapy* and other international journals, and a wide range of the best-known books about child analytic work of the last thirty years. The unmistakable trend is for fewer reports of children's dream material, and this seems true both for the Kleinian and post-Kleinian tradition with which I am most familiar and for the Anna Freud tradition, so well documented in *The Psychoanalytic Study of the Child*.

There seems to me to be a number of matters to consider in exploring possible factors at work. Probably the most significant of all is the changing composition of the patients seen for child analysis. When I trained in the late 1960s, we trainees expected to see at least two and often three neurotic patients among our three training cases—an under five, a latency child, and an adolescent. We saw these patients five times a week, and we also had a good range of children seen for assessment, for brief work, and for one or two times a week therapy, most of whom had neurotic difficulties in the classical sense. At that point, some work with severely psychotic children had also begun to take place, and there was a huge interest in autistic states. The psychotic patients by and large brought material that made one long for them to be able to dream their terrors and not to have to live them day and night.

In my own experience of long-term work with two psychotic patients, I found myself for years struggling in a world in which internal and external reality (phantasy and reality) were poorly distinguished. When one of these patients could clarify that something she had described was a dream from which she had awoken, or that something was in her mental life and had not actually happened, I felt that crucial developments in her mind were underway. The autistic patients, when they became able to communicate verbally, also spoke of mental events which they felt to be quite real, not dreams at all. One such child playing with an old-fashioned glue bottle which she had filled with water and was using as a baby bottle suddenly screamed at me one day, "The bottle has bitten my nose off," holding her hand over her nose and conveying vividly that she believed it was gone, and that only a bleeding hole remained.

The patients now seen for child analysis in the UK in NHS clinics include children on the autistic spectrum and with developmental delay, but the larger number have histories of severe maltreatment in their early years, including both deprivation and neglect, and physical, emotional, and sexual abuse. These children are now often in the care of the state, placed in group residential or foster care or living with adoptive parents. Some have been placed with kinship carers, a solution favoured by statutory agencies because it combines sustaining links with the child's birth family, which is an aim of public policy, with less demand on the public purse.

Reviewing my recent supervisory experience, I found that out of the last thirteen intensive case supervisions, six were children with such early lives. A further two had mothers who had abused drugs and alcohol during the pregnancy and in their infancy and a further two involved serious domestic violence culminating in the father abandoning mother and her children. Among the adolescents, one had been ill for five years with numerous episodes of self harm and inpatient admissions, and the other two had witnessed marital breakdown and the loss of one parent in the early years. Only one of these thirteen could be said to manifest a neurotic level of difficulties.

Checking informally with colleagues and also consulting a recent audit of the intensive cases seen by child psychotherapy students undertaking the Tavistock training confirmed this picture. Children with such damaging early experiences tend to have difficulties in symbolic activity. Instead of imaginative play, we often see either physical enactment (the hyperactivity sometimes leading to diagnosis of ADHD) or restricted repetitive forms of play. The underdeveloped capacity for play seems likely to be echoed in an inhibition in dream life.

A second factor may be the changing nature of parent–child relationships over the last two generations. There are two different features I have in mind here. The first is the greater openness of many parents to their children's emotional lives. It is difficult to make this point with any certainty, and such a generalisation is dangerous territory, but I think there are unmistakable trends. Broad contemporary social attitudes in the Western world include the idea that children are not little adults, that play is important, that self-expression is valuable, that harsh and repressive punishment is wrong, and that children's healthy growing up requires adult support and attentiveness. Such values are by and large represented in educational practice and in the background legal framework of states. The overall message of the numerous books, magazines, and radio and television programmes aimed at helping parents implies that children need to be understood as well as provided with clear boundaries, given appropriate help as well as faced with behavioural expectations. There is an interest in children's minds, and the impressive array of children's books and other cultural opportunities (sports, dance, music, film, theatre, and so on) is evidence of this, though one cannot ignore the problematic aspects of the potential market exploitation of the child as consumer.

My impression is that many children talk and express themselves in other ways more freely than in earlier generations. One might say that the Freudian century had this as one of its consequences. Dreams are the place where we can explore our unconscious emotions, so what may be the impact of the enlargement of conscious intimacy between parents and children? Is there perhaps less pressure to find a form in dreams for what might now be acceptable in day-to-day family life? The open expression of hostility to a new baby, of the fears stirred by first days at nursery or school, and of Oedipal rivalries, for example, all seem everyday expectations among many modern parents.

This picture of expanded tolerance and awareness does, however, have another side to it. There is a shift in the conception of what is private, at times involving a disturbing sense that there is little idea that there should be a distinction between what should and should not be expressed. A private inner space in which primitive infantile thoughts and feelings can be contained sometimes seems to be missing both in public discourse of various kinds (the elaboration of pornography, for example) and in the self-awareness of the children we see. Everything can hang out and be acted out. The conjunction of lessened repression and restraint and the absence of confident adult maintenance of necessary boundaries seems to provide an unfortunate basis for antisocial or unsocialised states of mind. The failure to develop internal mental space is a consequence of this kind of deprivation.

A third phenomenon which may be at work is the impact of the intensely visual quality of contemporary culture. Dreams are a world of personal images, intensively suffused with emotion. I wonder what effect it has on children's capacity for interior visual imagination that their visual fields are so replete with pictures created by others? The hours of television today's children watch and the opportunity to play computer video games and to possess toys representing so many specific characters offer a different experience from that of earlier generations dependent on their own invention to a greater degree. Young children's books, too, are full of illustration and do not leave the child mostly to picture things for himself. This stimulation of the eye may of course lead to the development of visual imaginative capacities rather than to its hypertrophy, and I am sure this is a complex phenomenon which has all sorts of outcome, but it may be worth wondering whether the balance between the inner and the outer landscape of the eye could be changing. The idea that there are cultural factors to take into account in thinking about the place of dreams in children's lives seems at least plausible. My child psychotherapy colleague Sheila Miller, who worked extensively for a number of years in South Africa, commented that she found black African children spoke much more naturally and readily about their dreams than their more economically and educationally privileged white peers (Miller, S., 1999). Some similar observations have been reported of Afro-Caribbean immigrants to the UK in the past.

The kinds of dreams children do report seem to fall into two categories, as Freud noted. First of all there are the often touchingly or amusingly, to the adult listener, transparent dreams of wish fulfilment: the dreams of platefuls of delicious food or of rearrangements of family relationships to match the child's desire, for example, recounted with innocent joy. By contrast are the bad dreams or even nightmares some children are tormented by, very often recurrent, and sometimes dreaded to the point of causing disturbance in being able to fall asleep. There is usually a very limited narrative, just an image of a monster behind the curtains, under the bed, or trying to open the door. Such childhood monsters can have an evolving significance through many years and often have some kind of traumatic origin. This is an idea described in classic works of literature—Jane Eyre's nightmare in the red room is a striking instance, as is Bion's remarkable delineation of Arf Arfer (his childhood version of "Our Father") in *The Long Weekend* (1982). The child's experience of terror which is both overwhelming and incomprehensible— beyond comprehension—is at the heart of a nightmare.

Before looking in more detail at some clinical material, I will touch on what emerged from my explorations of recent psychoanalytic writing about dreams. I found that papers discussing children's dreams are few and far between in recent decades. I detected an obvious reduction in the topic from the early 1980s onwards. I was interested to discover that a research paper by Lempel and Midgley (2007), "Exploring the role of children's dreams in psychoanalytic practice today: a pilot study", reported the same trend. On the basis of studying published papers and clinic records and interviewing a range of therapists at the Anna Freud Centre, they concluded that the importance attributed by therapists to dreams had diminished. They suggested two main explanations for this. First, that dreams initially highly valued as the "royal road" in analytic work because they were seen as providing access to unconscious material have been replaced by closer attention to object relations, particularly the transference relationship to the therapist. Second, that ego strengthening has become such a central therapeutic focus. They go on to discuss significant debates about techniques for working with dreams in the here and now—is the manifest or latent content the therapist's concern? Can we see children's play as providing the free associative material which is absent from their verbal communication? How do we look at a dream in the context of the evolution of the transference? Few contemporary therapists, they found, actively enquire about children's dreams.

I think the way that child analysts and psychotherapists now approach dreams has been, as would be expected, greatly influenced by the wider analytic discourse. The works of Segal, Bion, and Meltzer, and more recently Ogden and Ferro, in differing ways all take us in the direction of viewing dream life as a container for vital creative aspects of the dreamer's relationship to his own mind, of dreams as life experiences of great importance. Segal's grasp of the central developmental role of the capacity for symbolic representation of experience—enabling cognitive, aesthetic, and ethical growth to take place—was pivotal in the evolution of dream theory. She noted in her discussion of the nature of play and dream that "play has roots in common with the night dream" but added that the function of the dream is to achieve a phantasy solution to a phantasy problem. It belongs to the domain of the inner world, phantasy and private experience. By contrast, play can build links between phantasy and reality. She writes, "Two cannot dream together, but two or more can play together" (Segal, 1991, pp. 101–109). I wonder how far we can hold to this distinction, bearing in mind that once an analytic process is underway, the patient's dreams become entwined with the evolution of the transference.

Ferro's concept of the analytic field (1999) and Ogden's view of the functioning of the analyst's reverie and the "analytic third" (2001) underline that dreams within an ongoing analysis involve both analyst and patient working together. Both Ferro and Ogden are also drawing on Winnicott's understanding of creativity (1971), and implicitly investigating aspects of what he had defined as transitional phenomena, the not entirely private area of me and not-me. But whether we find the theory of transitional space useful or not, there seems to me a view shared by these theorists that dreaming is fundamentally an internal conversation with ourselves in sleep, in which a voice can be given to the hitherto inarticulate. This is what Meltzer argued in his monograph on dreams (1983). A dream is thus evidence of and the outcome of our ongoing desire to understand ourselves. Its symbolic nature can also be linked to Bion's (1962) distinction between what he called the beta and alpha elements of our mental life: the beta elements that achieve symbolic representation in a dream become thereby thinkable thoughts, that is alpha elements. There is a moving paper by Alex Dubinsky (1986) in which he describes work with two severely physically disabled adolescent boys whose dreams enabled him to work with them on the terrible phantasies they had created to explain their disabilities. The thinking this work initiated freed them from inner domination by a sadomasochistic vision of parental intercourse, and provided space for more ordinary adolescent sexual development within the confines of their painful limitations.

The idea of the dream as a container for emotionally significant thoughts was vividly brought home to me when hearing about a fourteen-year-old boy (Miller, L., 2010) whose psychotic anxieties included a sense that the furniture of the room was not stably situated on the floor but continuously drifting around outside the pull of gravity. His mother remarked with astonishment that she remembered that as a little boy of three he had a recurrent nightmare that the furniture of his room was all over the place and not where it should be. This suggests that the image of disordered furniture could for this boy at times be contained in a dream and distinguished from external reality and at others deteriorate into the disorder of psychotic confusion between internal and external, exposing him to the terror of living in a world full of "bizarre objects", in Bion's terminology. As long as the images are in a dream, there is the implicit potential of waking up and setting things in order, like the arrival of the sorcerer in *The Sorcerer's Apprentice* who can bring things under control again. If the experience of chaos has no dream-container, it is truly terrifying. As Klein remarked, "Some of the relief dreams provide derives from the fact that psychotic processes find expression in them" (1961).

The remembered dream has the particular potential for expanding the mind's awareness of itself, for being used as an aid to thought and insight whether within or outside an analytic setting. It can also, however, be used in quite different ways, for example to evoke admiration or excitement in the dreamer or analyst rather than as a form of contact with the inner world. The narcissistic overvaluation of dreams takes away their value as a stimulus to mental development and reduces them to functioning much more like day-dreams, playthings for the mind to distract itself, functioning in the sphere of omnipotence, not of creative thought. The contemporary focus on the use to which dreams are put in the analytic process, to the reporting of a dream in a session as potential acting-out meant to have an effect on the analyst rather than contribute to the analytic work, is another important feature of current clinical practice, and it is particularly useful in working with adolescents and adolescent states of mind where narcissistic investment in dreams can sometimes hold up the analytic work to a frustrating degree.

In summary, my assessment of the place of dream-analysis in contemporary work with children and adolescents is that while dreams have a continuing large place in work with adolescents, including both severely disturbed patients and others with normal-neurotic levels of functioning, with younger children there is comparatively little reporting of work on dreams. Frances Tustin's patient John, who was an eloquent child, said: "I have my nasty dreams with Tustin" (Tustin, 1981). This may be quite a good summary of what often happens. However, our child patients continue to play, though sometimes in rather primitive fashion, and this takes me to the question of how to take further the understanding of the links between dreaming and playing.

Before tackling this, I want to look briefly at Melanie Klein's way of working with a child's dreams since one of the rare examples of sustained detail of a child's dreams is of course Klein's *Narrative of a Child Analysis* (1961). Richard's dreams were not prolific, but it is of great interest to study them, particularly since he is a pre-pubertal child, and it is for this age group that so little published material is available.

Richard introduced the matter of dreams in his ninth session asking what he said was "an important question": "Can you help me not to have dreams?" He explained this was because they were always frightening or unpleasant. This is very much in line with the generally held view that it is children's bad dreams or nightmares which are brought to analysis. Klein responded to his mentioning several bad dreams with an interpretation based on Richard's behaviour while he recounted the dreams: he was turning the electric fire on and off, and he remarked on the red inside the fire when he turned it on. She linked the red inside the fire to Richard's thoughts about something inside Mummy which he wanted to stop as he showed when he turned the fire off, but that then he felt faced with a black, empty, dead Mummy of whom he was afraid. She then spoke of his suspicions of her as a Mrs Klein with a bad Hitler father inside, relating this to earlier material about Hitler and Austria and herself. This interpretation was developed at length to elaborate Richard's feelings about a bad parental couple and his wish for protection from them.

Klein drew on all three dreams he had told her in what she said to him. What interests me here, as well as Klein's characteristic boldness with Richard in tackling things head-on, is to note how she saw his fiddling with the fire as his free association to the dreams. She also saw the sequence of dreams he told her as presenting an associative line in themselves.

In a note to session fourteen, she commented on the fact that patients often include in their first dream in analysis much of deep significance. She suggests that Richard's immediate plunge into play activity (responding to the contents of the room, starting to draw and to play as soon as she produced the materials) was an example of how her play technique gave her the greatest access to his inner world. What she did not comment on so explicitly was Richard's very immediate and intense positive and negative transference to her, though she discusses the issue of timing of transference interpretation and the importance she places on giving serious attention to the child's feelings about his current family relationships. Overall, the treatment of his dreams does not suggest that she placed special emphasis on the evidence they provided of his internal conflicts. Rather it is the overall situation, the "total transference", Klein's seminal idea developed in contemporary theory by Joseph (1985), that she is after.

She is however very interested in Richard's relationship to his dreams and always describes his way of telling them. She occasionally asks if he had one, noting that this can be useful when there is evidence of unconscious resistance—the dream may provide access to the conflict being held at bay. Richard sometimes complained about dreaming all night, unpleasant dreams he did not want to talk about, and only being able to remember the nasty bits. Choosing to tell or not tell a dream allows a patient some sense of control, and Klein suggests that drawings "which can in some sense be equated to dreams" are also up to a point under a child's control because he can always move on to another drawing. She believed that play with the small toys she provided more easily represented deep infantile anxieties, especially in Richard's case his anxieties about his destructiveness. The broken toys caused him great anxiety. He was able to return to play with the toys after a long gap when he felt more hopeful that damage might be able to be put right. Klein links this to the way that adult patients can return to old dreams and do more work on their meaning at a later stage of analysis.

While I would agree with Klein that the use of the toys provided for the child are a vital focus of clinical observation (and of course this may amount to noticing the child's incapacity to play), I think that the somewhat wider vertex of observation suggested by the concept of the total transference is more at the heart of contemporary clinical practice.

This viewpoint includes all aspects of the child's behaviour and communications in the room, play with toys, pretend play and physical activity, all that the child says, free associations, stories, dreams, and so on, and, importantly, attention to the non-verbal bodily communication to the analyst and to countertransference experience. It is bringing all these together that provides analytic conviction, the testing of one sort of evidence against others in the process of interpretation which first has to take shape in the analyst's mind.

If we understand the "playing" of the child in the broad sense of his total use of the room, the toy materials, and some aspects of his analyst (that is, her willingness to enable his play to proceed, which can depend on her willingness to join in limited ways), I think we can see what Klein meant by the equivalence she postulated between the child's playing and the adult's free associations. Our conceptualisation thus has to make space for the "dreaming" activity in the child often to take the form of enactment in play rather than night dreams reported in the session.

Here is a description of the first moments of a child's session, as an instance of this idea. This little boy is five years old and was adopted three years ago after appalling early neglect in his first year of life. He has three times a week sessions and this is a Monday session. The therapist was told in the waiting room by his escort, who usually brings him, that his mother is working abroad this week. Charlie interrupted her to say he had fallen over at school. On entering the room, he took possession of the therapist's chair, turned it upside down and asked if he could climb on it. The therapist spoke about his not feeling safe today and went on to refer to his fall at school and his Mummy's absence. "A whole week is a long time," she remarked, after he had dismissively stated "I won't miss her." Charlie then pulled the cushions off her chair, unzipped the cushion cover and pushed his head inside, as far as it would go. The therapist spoke of his wish to get right inside today after the weekend when she was away. "Maybe one way not to feel lost and out in the cold is to find a way right inside," she said. Charlie wandered round the room sightlessly with his head in the cushion cover. She added that being deep inside means that he cannot see where he is going and might hurt himself. This is a problem.

Charlie lay down at her feet, pressing himself against her legs. He then pulled himself out of the cushion cover, much dishevelled. She felt an impulse to cuddle him and spoke about his wish to get close to her today. He then took out the cushion pad so that he could get his whole body fully inside and curled up into a ball. A conversation followed in which they first explored the idea that inside-the-cushion would represent no weekend separation ("Then I would not miss you," he said); and then, when Charlie wanted to be completely zipped-up inside, the claustro-agoraphobic dilemma he faced: the therapist felt preoccupied with his not being able to breathe inside, but Charlie explained, "No! I won't be able to breathe outside!"

This fascinating sequence is a powerful exemplification of Klein's thesis about children's playing. It is so easy to bring to mind weekend dreams of older patients resorting to intrusion into the internal object as a means to evade separation and any sense of separateness or dependence on an absent object which follow the same lines as Charlie's behaviour. The phantasy represented in this play sequence has been evoked by the conjunction of the analytic weekend and the mother's absence at home.

In the later part of the session Charlie used the small doll figures to show the relationship between what he called "soft baby" and "unravelling boy" which his therapist understood as parts of himself. There is great danger to both doll figures and doubt about whether either can survive the dangers they encounter. A fight to the death between them ensues. The boy hates baby, Charlie explained, because baby has a Mummy and Daddy and the boy doesn't. "He is on his own," he stated.

Analytic work with young children sometimes does move very fast, as in this session, where Charlie's phantasy about his early neglect begins to be explored. He was, indeed, the boy "on his own", overwhelmed with rage and hatred, we might suggest, at the baby he felt must have taken all the space in his mother's mind leaving him to "unravel". There was no actual other baby but an imagined other, vividly real to Charlie in his attempt to make sense of his experience of neglect and of a mother whose mind was always elsewhere. But within the session he is also in touch with a baby self that does have a mother and father when he experiences his therapist's sensitive understanding of him. At breakneck speed we can observe something more of the defensive function of the claustro-agoraphobic position I described earlier.

Let me now try to place the kind of playing we observe in a child psychotherapy setting in a broader framework of thinking about the nature of play. In *Beyond the Pleasure Principle*, Freud (1920) described a form of play by his grandson which he understood as an attempt to master an experience—to give it shape, to turn the experiencing of something painful into pleasurable activity under the control of the child, which could be happily repeated. This analysis makes it plain that the child's play is an attempt to come to terms with an emotional event, with psychic turbulence. Play is thus a form of thought expressed in action.

Very small children's play often reveals their conviction of their omnipotent powers to control their world and their objects. If they cannot see, they do not believe they can be seen, a belief we all joyfully collude in when we engage in the first games of peep-bo with infants. Gradually the child's developing mind expands to make it possible for games to provide symbolic representation of all kinds of experience, and once this stage is reached children can move from parallel play to the enjoyment of playing with other children. This transition involves the move from play which is fundamentally located in bodily experience, or in using objects which are barely differentiated from bodies (like Charlie's use of the chair and cushion in the sequence I described earlier), towards the capacity to use toys in symbolic ways, as true symbols and not symbolic equations (Segal, 1957).

Symbolic play functions as a bridge between phantasy and external reality and its elaboration and interpretation in child analysis is one central way in which the analyst helps to support the growth of the child's capacity to think. Play in itself, just like dream, can reduce levels of anxiety by providing them with a form and by allowing for the differentiation between phantasy and reality (playing at mayhem and murder is not the same as actual killing). It also offers opportunities for the child's sense of frustrating limitations to be modified—we can play at mothers and fathers or doctors and nurses or superheroes and monsters and within the game acquire actual skills as well as the comfort of make-belief powers.

Developed symbolic play of this sort is, however, something of a treat for many of today's child psychotherapists, or a hard-won achievement after a lengthy exposure to a child's difficulties in being able to play, and painstaking work aimed at developing capacities for symbolic expression. This clinical reality has led to much debate about technique. How active should we be in showing a child how to play? Should we provide more of the kind of toys today's children are used to? How willing should we be to take the role of playmate? Is it part of child analysis to simply provide a sequestered time and place for playing, with a theory which emphasises the therapeutic function of play as such rather than one which views children's play as the language of the unconscious, and our task as the understanding of internal object relations, with the child's play activity as a resource with which to grasp transference and countertransference dynamics?

These are some of the elements of ongoing contemporary dialogue about the theory and technique of psychoanalytic psychotherapy with children which should also be of interest to the wider psychoanalytic community.

References

Bion, W. R. (1962). *Learning from Experience*. London: Heinemann.

Bion, W. R. (1982). *The Long Weekend*. Abingdon, UK: Fleetwood.

Dubinsky, A. (1986). The sado-masochistic phantasies of two adolescent boys suffering from congenital physical illnesses. *Journal of Child Psychotherapy*, 12(1): 73–85.

Ferro, A. (1999). *The Bi-Personal Field: Experiences in Child Analysis*. London: Routledge.

Freud, S. (1920). *Beyond the Pleasure Principle. S. E., 18*. London: Hogarth.

Joseph, B. (1985). Transference—the Total Situation. *International Journal of Psychoanalysis, 66*: 447–454.

Klein, M. (1932). *The Psychoanalysis of Children*. London: Hogarth (reprinted as *Writings of Melanie Klein Vol. 2*).

Klein, M. (1961). *Narrative of a Child Analysis*. London: Hogarth (reprinted in *Writings of Melanie Klein Vol. 4*).

Lempel, O. & Midgley, N. (2007). Exploring the role of children's dreams in psychoanalytic practice today—a pilot study. *Psychoanalytic Study of the Child, 61*.

Meltzer, D. (1983). *Dream Life*. Perthshire, UK: Clunie Press.

Miller, L. (2010). Personal communication.

Miller, S. (1999). Home thoughts from abroad: psychoanalytic thinking in a new setting: work in South Africa. *Journal of Child Psychotherapy, 25(2)*: 199–216.

Ogden, T. (2001). *Conversations at the Frontiers of Dreaming*. London: Karnac.

Rustin, M. E. (1982). Finding a way to the child. *Journal of Child Psychotherapy, 8(2)*: 145–150.

Segal, H. (1957). Notes on symbol formation. *International Journal of Psychoanalysis, 38*: 391–397.

Segal, H. (1991). Imagination, play and art. In: *Dream, Phantasy and Art* (pp. 101–109). London: Routledge.

Tustin, F. (1981). *Autistic States in Childhood*. London: Routledge & Kegan Paul.

Winnicott, D. W. (1971). *Playing and Reality*. London: Tavistock.

CHAPTER THREE

The manifest dream *is* the real dream: the changing relationship between theory and practice in the interpretation of dreams[1]

Juan Pablo Jiménez

Introduction

Some 110 years after the publication of *The Interpretation of Dreams*, a foundational text of our discipline, the theoretical and practical panorama of psychoanalysis is complex and variegated, not to say worrisome. Ever since Wallerstein (1988, 1990) declared over twenty years ago that the theoretical and technical diversity is the rule and that there is no unique theoretical truth or practical approach, various works have come out in succession alerting about the fragmentation of knowledge (Fonagy, 1999) and the chaotic appearance of contemporary psychoanalysis (Thomä, 2000). The problem is that beyond a welcome pluralism what really exists is a mere plurality or, even worse, a fragmentation that makes a theoretical and practical dialogue among colleagues increasingly difficult. What is lacking is a methodology which can be applied systematically to compare the various theories and technical approaches. Thus, the menace spills over the *scientific discipline* nature of psychoanalysis. Wilson (2000) warns us that today's "pluralism", which has managed to remedy yesterday's authoritarian monism, "can easily evolve into tomorrow's nightmare, unless some guiding principles chart an ever evolving integrative course" (2000, p. 412). According to Charles

31

Hanly, the standing president of the International Psychoanalytical Association (IPA), "At present, psychoanalysis has an abundance or even superabundance of theory and a paucity of theory-testing observations" (2010a). In order to tackle this problem, the IPA recently set up two work groups aimed at proposed strategies that would remedy the problems related to the theoretical and practical diversity in psychoanalysis. The task of a first such group consists in exploring means to define the so-called "clinical evidence"; in other words, "to explore how clinical observations are being used, how they can be used and how they can best be used to test interpretations and theories" (Hanly, 2010a). The task of a second such group is to search for methods to better integrate the psychoanalytical theoretical edifice. One of its purposes is "to clarify theoretical differences where logically irreconcilable differences exist and to explore directions in which their resolution might be found and to find and clarify real agreement, when it exists, despite apparent difference and even contradiction" (Hanly, 2010b). Whether or not these groups will make progress on any of these fronts is something that remains to be seen. The truth is that during the last decades many have attempted to clarify the complex relationship between theory and practice in psychoanalysis (Bernardi, 2003; Canestri, Bohleber, Denis & Fonagy, 2006; Fonagy, Kächele, Krause, Jones & Perron, 1999; Jiménez, 2006, 2008, 2009; Kächele, Schachter & Thomä, 2009; Strenger, 1991; Thomä & Kächele, 1975).

In a recent paper (Jiménez, 2009), I stated that two main obstacles yet stand in the way to explore convergences and divergences in psychoanalytic practice: first, the epistemological and methodological problems in relation to the construction of theory in psychoanalysis and especially the inaccessibility, in any reliable way, of what psychoanalysts really do in the intimacy of their practice. I proposed to separate, at least in part, theory from practice in psychoanalysis, in an attempt to grasp and consider psychoanalysts' practice on its own merits. All things considered, however, the fact that psychoanalytic theory and practice have a certain degree of autonomy and that the degree of correspondence between each other is much less that is believed, it does not mean that theory and practice do not interact, albeit this interaction is not as simple as it seems.

An area in which this interaction can be studied is the area of the theory of dream formation in relation to the technique of dream interpretation. What I stated back in 1990 continues to be valid today: namely, that "Few analysts will agree with the absolute emphasis Freud gave to the theory of wish fulfilment as an explanation for dream formation and dream work. However, alternative theories have had, in general, little success" (Jiménez, 1990, p. 445).

Lansky (1992) and Reiser (1997) highlight the fact that Freud's primary objective in *The Interpretation of Dreams* was to explain how the mind works when producing dreams. His interest was not placed on the psychoanalytical process or the place that working with dreams has in it.

For over 50 years, *The Interpretation of Dreams* was the most potent theory to explain the dreaming phenomenon. As a neurologist, Freud built his theory based on the neuroscience of his time and, although present-day neuroscience has substantially modified the parcel of knowledge available in Freud's time, his interpretation continues to be an unavoidable benchmark in scientific controversies about the act of dreaming, either to counter his points of view or to defend his "classical" theory of dreams as "wish fulfilment" (Boag, 2006; Nir & Tononi, 2009; Colace, 2010). To be sure, it is not my intention to get into that controversy here.

The split between the theory of genesis of dreams and the technique of their interpretation

In this chapter I attempt to show how the technique of dream interpretation has *de facto* assigned increasing importance to the so-called manifest dream, contrary to Freud's systematically repeated explicit warning that one should not fall into the temptation of regarding the manifest content as a *genuine* psychical product.

The following is representative of a large number of relevant passages:

> It is natural that we should lose some of our interest in the manifest dream. It is bound to be a matter of indifference to us whether it is well put together, or is broken up into a series of disconnected separate pictures. Even if it has an apparently sensible exterior, we know that this has only come about through dream-distortion and have as little organic relation to the internal content of the dream as the façade of an Italian church has to its structure and plan. (Freud, 1916/1917, p. 165)

The practice of dream interpretation has nevertheless followed a different path. Since the pioneering work of Erikson (1954), there has been a steady flow of publications stressing the important part the manifest dream can and does in fact play in the clinical use of dreams (Blechner, 2001; Brooks Brenneis, 1975; Curtis & Sachs, 1975; Ehebald, 1981; Fosshage, 1983; Grunert, 1984; Jiménez, 1990; Reiser, 1997; Robbins, 2004; Spanjaard, 1969; Stolorow, 1978; Stolorow & Atwood, 1982; Thomä & Kächele, 1987). In 1954, Erikson described the situation in the following terms: "Unofficially, we often interpret dreams entirely or in parts on the basis of their manifest appearance. Officially, we hurry at every confrontation with a dream to crack its manifest appearance as if it were a useless shell and to hasten to discard this shell in favor of what seems to be the more worthwhile core" (p. 17). This trend appears to have intensified during the last fifty years. Thus, Robbins states that, currently, "Much of dream interpretation in everyday practice involves reflection about the dream as a primary gestalt expression of mind that is unique, rather than a cover-up for something else" (2004, p. 357).

It could be said that in the technique of dream interpretation a split has arisen between the theory of the genesis of dreams, which was upheld by Freud to the end of his life and which supports the so-called "classical" technique, and the technique that takes the manifest content seriously. This time, the development of practice has preceded that of theory: to this day there is no universally accepted overall theory of dream formation that bears out the *de facto* technical opinion that there is an "organic relationship" between the manifest and the latent content, i.e., between the manifest dream and the rest of the individual's mental life. All things considered, Greenberg and Pearlman (1999) are of the opinion that current neurobiological findings suggest:

> that dreams serve an integrative and adaptive function and that we can see this illustrated in the manifest dream without resorting to ideas about disguise. This leads to the idea that the language of [the manifest] dream is different from the language of waking life and that it needs translation rather than interpretation. Dreams can be understood as dealing with problems that are active at the time of dreaming but that are problems because of their connection with earlier unresolved problems. (p. 762)

Similar ideas were put forward by French and Fromm (1964), who suggested that the manifest dream expresses a focal conflict and an attempt to solve that conflict. Much earlier, Jung (1934) had suggested that "The manifest dream picture is the dream itself and contains the whole meaning of the dream ... we would do better to say that we are dealing with something like a text that is unintelligible ..." (p. 149). To be fair, *The Interpretation of Dreams* contains a second theory about dream formation, which purports that dreams are the expression of the primary mental process that differs qualitatively from waking thoughts and, because of that, they are incomprehensible from the perspective of the secondary mental process (Robbins, 2004). Seemingly, such would be a sort of protolanguage (*Ursprache*) requiring translation, but not interpretation. Matte Blanco (1988) states that the translation of such language should consider the existence of a different logic, which combines in different ways with the Aristotelian or bivalent logic that is akin to the secondary mental process (Jiménez, 1990).

All things considered, the so-called classical technique, proposed by Freud, is based on the assumption that all dreams are an expression of the hallucinatory satisfaction of repressed desires. The predominant contemporary trend—especially among the British school—is to understand dreams as the expression of a representation of the here-and-now transference of the psychoanalytic session. For some psychoanalysts, especially those influenced by the ego psychology, such manner of interpreting dreams neglects the recovery of memories: an important factor of the change process (Loden, 2003). For Morton Reiser (1997, p. 895):

> The manifest dream reflects mind/brain processes as they attempt to resolve current life problems and conflicts, including the forms in which they are expressed in the transference. The meaningful content of the dream is related to these current life problems, as well as to the past. The manifest dream images are drawn both from the current life context and from images registered during earlier conflictual experiences relevant to the present.

But, this topic leads us into another controversy; i.e., the one about the possibility of recovering memories during the therapeutic process and the therapeutic value of it. For Mauro Mancia, the dream has symbol-generating functions which provide an outlet by which affective experiences and fantasies and defences stored as part of an unrepressed unconscious in the implicit memory can be represented in pictorial terms, then thought and rendered verbally (2004, p. 530). All things considered, Fonagy thinks that implicit memories would only be accessible via the analysis of the transference (1999).

Of course, any theory of the genesis and interpretation of dreams inevitably runs up against the same core problem: the actual experience of dreaming is not accessible and can be deduced only from the record of the dreamer's recollections. We resort in this case to the "hypothesis of distortion-consistency" (von Zeppelin & Moser, 1987), which postulates that the fundamental structure and dynamic of the dream as dreamt remains intact in spite of the lacunae and distortions to which the process of remembering gives rise. In this sense, I understand by manifest dream the account given by the patient of the dream, which may or may not be enriched with subsequent associations.

The construction of the meaning of dreams in the psychoanalytical process

In the clinical material that I will submit next I intend to show how the joint work between the patient and the analyst with the manifest dream, within the context of a vigorous psychoanalytical process, builds meanings that contribute towards deepening the therapeutic process and thus facilitate the recovery of archaic memories and the integration of split parts of the self. I suggest that what Freud calls latent content is the product of the joint construction of meaning between patient and analyst. In this manner, we turn around the Freudian model. Based on the manifest dream, namely, of the patient's dream narration, the analyst-patient dyad not only recovers implicit or repressed meanings, but also builds new meanings that become an integral part of the old ones. In other words, interpreting a dream consists not only of redirecting the patient to alleged original sources in latent thought, but continuing with the meaning-creating process that the brain is continuously working on.

In a previous paper (Jiménez, 2009), I suggested that the analyst's task consists in a continued process of validation that includes observation, conversation, and interaction. Thus, the knowledge achieved in the process is a social and linguistic construct of an intersubjective reality between the patient and the analyst. This means that the interpretation of a given dream must be "negotiated" with the patient within the context of the patient's emotional history, of the history of the analytic process, and of the here and now of the session. All things considered, the communicational validation does not suffice. If we are to take seriously the nucleus of the psychoanalytic theory about therapeutic change—which purports that investigation and cure go hand in hand— then the construction of the narrative truth must also be validated by the curative effect of its rhetoric force (Spence, 1982). In this manner, the interpretation of a given dream is validated with the changes observed in the patient. I would expect these concepts to become clearer with the clinical material that I will present to you next.

Carmen's dreams

Carmen is just beginning her sixth year of analysis, with a frequency of four sessions per week. She came to consult me on her fortieth birthday, because she could no longer tolerate the depressive pain that had been afflicting her for many years. She had been involved in the resistance to the Pinochet dictatorship, during which she had been exposed to dangerous situations and suffered traumatic losses of companions of both sexes in the struggle. Fifteen years earlier her husband had been killed, and this had plunged her into profound mourning. He inhabited her, like a living dead. After his death, Carmen had felt (and continued to feel) empty, dead, immensely alone, with no emotional contact with her small children. One year later, she consulted a psychotherapist, but after some months, this relation came to a traumatic end after a session in which caresses became sexual intercourse. The feeling of void and the longing for nearness that she developed in the transference process was only comparable to her intense resentment for the therapist after this episode. She never went back, although at times she entertained the fantasy of confronting him which what she feels was a rape. After some years, there was a second marriage, this time to Pedro Pablo, with whom she had a child. According to her, this relation "helped her to survive". Another reason for consulting me was the symptom of being invaded by fantasies of disease and death whenever her children were away. On those occasions she had to fight against the impulse to call the police to report an alleged misadventure whenever one of her already teenage children was even a few minutes late in coming back home after the agreed time.

She has two brothers and is her parents' only daughter. She described her father as quite depressive and a workaholic, violent to his children when they were young. When referring to her mother, she made it a point to say that she always thought that her mother preferred her brothers. Carmen is afflicted by amnesia episodes, and whole periods of her life have been blanked away as a result of repression. It was only after years of analysis that she could bring up the topic of her sexuality and her difficulty to attain pleasure. An interesting fact is that after about two years of analysis she surprised me with her recollection of having met me at the end of the 1960s at university.

The first years of analysis, in which there prevailed an atmosphere of brittle patience, were used up by the analysis of the mourning, her guilt feelings, and the idealisation of Roberto. The result was the progressive appearance of strong aggressiveness and an urge to compete. Carmen's apparent modesty and meekness broke down a couple of times with episodes of intense rage against me, during which she toyed with the idea of abandoning the treatment. As a rule, these episodes were unleashed by situations in which she could no longer fail to acknowledge that I was a different person, with independent opinions of my own: her intense rage emerged from the painful experience of humiliation. The idealisation of the analyst was hiding feelings of envy and resentment against men, especially her father. When idealisation decreased, there appeared a threatening erotic transference which, as an expression of a fantasy of erotic and narcissistic fusion, proved to be a defence against the awareness of her wish to be a man and of her deep feelings of worthlessness because of being a woman, all of which had recently clearly appeared in her dreams.

Shortly before the session that I am presenting, the last of the week, Carmen spent a week abroad for work reasons. The session takes place a few days prior to a break for a week and a half on my account. So it is a session between two breaks, one of them of four sessions and the other of six, this one on my account. The session was reproduced from memory immediately after the sessions.

P: Last night I had a dream: I was with Pedro Pablo [her husband] and there were three other men dressed in black. One of them lifted his shirt and showed an area of his skin, red, covered in eczema, oozing some excretion and this made an impact on me. Another man said, "At long last I find somebody who has the same I have," and lifted his trouser leg up to his knee and also showed some inflamed skin, which was oozing some kind of juice. There was something the matter with the other man, but I can't remember. I didn't like all that and told Pedro Pablo that we should leave. We had to go across some desolate stony place: it was like those shots of the aftermath of a nuclear disaster in science fiction movies set in the twenty-first century. We came across a group of people, this time women, all of them also wearing black. It was necessary to go across a place that was like a dam, a gully, but it was very dangerous to do so because at intervals the water gushed in and flooded everything. We were thinking of crossing over, but one of the women, M., an old acquaintance of mine, told me that it was extremely danger-ous, that she had decided not to come along, because there were just a few minutes to find a place where to cross before the water came. Pedro Pablo and I began our crossing, but in a weird direc-tion. Instead of walking across, we walked along lengthwise. It was a place full of caverns, creepy. Eventually, there were some broad stone stairs that we could climb to get to the other side. I said, "This way we shall be saved," and we began to climb the stairs. But Pedro Pablo did something, some kind of movement that suddenly raised me, together with the stairs, and left me hanging, about to fall into a very deep gully. I panicked, felt the wind on my face and didn't want to die. I begged Pedro Pablo to please bring me down, that I could fall and die at any moment. I woke up terrified, at around five o'clock in the morning, and had trouble going back to sleep. I was afraid of going on dreaming the same dream.

After her account of her dream, long minutes elapsed. The dream itself had been described in a slow way, with dramatic intensity, in a cautious way, as if she was choosing every word. The narration engaged me, aroused my curiosity and immedi-ately prompted my own fantasies. Fleeting ideas crossed my mind. I thought that today was Thursday, before the weekend break and a few days before a six-session break because of me. Pedro Pablo … Is it me, Juan Pablo? Could this movement that leaves her hanging at the edge of the gully be related to my absence? And those men, could they be castrated beings displaying their wounds? The men and women in black, and the dismal setting made me think of the prolonged pathological mourning, Carmen's chronic depression and the analytic crossing. Men and women apart, a couple attempting to negotiate the crossing along a landscape already devastated by a nuclear catastrophe ... What type of primitive tragedy was being staged in the dream? Oedipal? The account had taken about fifteen minutes, and I had the feeling that in it, what had not been said was much more than what had been voiced, that what was important was silenced. For this reason, I opted for a circumspect and expectant attitude. Naturally, I had many elements to use as the basis to break the long silence that followed the account, for example, to ask for associations or ask her about what might have made M. take the decision not to cross to the other side. Yet, I waited for some more long minutes. I kept thinking and observing how she snuggled up on the therapy couch, pulling the blanket over her. What a difference between now and when she started analysis, already five years ago. Then, on coming in or leaving, she barely looked at me and the expression on her face was always sullen and afraid. It had been very difficult for her to make up her mind to lie down on the couch: it was a couple of months before she gave up the face-to-face mode. Now, on the contrary, she greeted me with a wide smile, looking straight into my face and after taking the blanket, she wrapped herself in it and lay down smoothly on the couch.

[She interrupts my thoughts.]

P: The dream has to do with my sexuality. Umm ... It's terribly difficult for me to talk about it. Umm ... In spite of being in analysis for years, I feel shame, fear. I don't know. Why so much difficulty? Why can't I speak more freely and simply tell you things? ...

[After a new silence.]

A: Tell me things that you already know about your dream, but that you don't mention, that you leave unsaid in your silences, and pauses, and in the slow and cautious narration. For example, I believe that you know why M. appears in your dream, you must know what type of difficulties prevented M. from going across the dam.

P: Umm ... M. is homosexual, she is enormously afraid of men. [Silence.] Sure, this fear to talk about my sexual fantasies. I always tend to throw them out no sooner they appear, as if I was terrified of acknowledging them.

A: Terrified of getting excited? That's quite dangerous. Crossing over the gully, getting into the caverns, sex. Apparently, you've got to have sex but without getting excited, with no pleasure, no enjoyment. Excitement and pleasure lead you to the edge of the gully. The dam may fail and you may suddenly be flooded with dangerous pleasure.

P: Umm … Well [in a resolute tone] … yesterday there was something that I omitted. In Italy I was assigned a wonderful room, with a spectacular view. I had taken along some books, my favourite music, and I enjoyed lying down to read and listen to music. It was an enormous pleasure. For three nights I had intense erotic dreams about the delegate from Mexico, the enfant terrible of the seminar: that man was the star, as you said yesterday. The same one. Umm …

A: Lying down, snuggling up, and beginning to feel good here, to feel pleasure. There appear fantasies, talking to me about them here … That is very dangerous.

P: All these days I have been thinking that I must go far away, to Europe, and meet an attractive and intelligent fellow, to be able to have sexual fantasies safely, with no catastrophe taking place. But, umm … I realise that the Mexican man is a substitute for you. This thing's got to do with you. I feel quite ashamed and, what's more, afraid. As if I was a girl and you were to punish me severely for these thoughts.

I cannot help thinking that not only the Mexican but also Pedro Pablo in the dream are Juan Pablo substitutes, that is, substitutes for me. I feel enveloped in erotic idealisation. I allow myself to be brushed by it and think of the boundaries between analysis and life. Many times Carmen gives me the impression of "living" me as a primal experience, not as transference but as a first experience, something new. There is something fused together, undifferentiated in my relationship with her. A thought crosses my mind: how far can a transference interpretation go? If in an interpretation I was to identify with her husband, saying something like "It's you and I as a couple that are going across the dam, and therefore it is I that excites you, etc. …", wouldn't I be triggering iatrogenia? The catastrophe, to go to bed with one's analyst? I realise that Carmen is indeed right to perceive the danger. It must have been like this when she ended up by having sex with her first therapist. I must tread the narrow path between accepting taking the place of her man, but without going over the line of seduction. I think of the taboo of incest. How shall I go about it? I decide to approach the erotic transference fantasies with caution.

A: However, it appears to be evident that yesterday and today you feel more secure on the couch because little by little you are making me get closer to your sexual fantasies. Obviously, the problem is that as you snuggle here, wrap yourself in the blanket …

P: Yes, sure, I get ideas that I dare not voice.

A: Not only is it necessary that you should travel to Europe, but there should also be another step, something happening here, a bridge between your trip and my interruption of next week. There is no danger there. You can talk today, Thursday. Then there's a three day break; afterwards, next, a few more days and you won't be seeing me for six sessions.

P: Yes, that must be what reassures me here …

A: That no catastrophe can take place. In any case, there are many points in your dream, much information that we won't have enough time to analyse today. There are just a few minutes before our time is up. You've been taking your time; everything has been very slow, cautious. It's as if you were revealing yourself and not revealing yourself.

I stop there, although I would have liked to go on saying something along these lines: What is it that is hidden? Is the eczematous, juice-oozing, inflamed skin a painful, searing, sexual excitement? What are we talking about? About mutilated men within you? Of something of yours that you see in men? What's this thing about homosexuality? In addition, you have always shown a Pedro Pablo who is little interested in sex, not very attractive to you, who even makes you suspect that he might be a homosexual. Yet in the dream, that Pedro Pablo is capable, with just a little movement to excite you to the point of panic and death anxiety. Could this dream possibly be submerged until here, during the analysis, there may be another combination of circumstances that will make you feel secure?

[As I was thinking this last thought, she surprised me by saying:]

P: I hope that this issue won't get submerged. Because I realise that it is crucial and important. Many things depend on my understanding my sexuality. I'm different, many things have changed. I am not terrified by the things of the past. I feel more self-confident in life, at work, with myself. Some very important things, which I can't quite understand, took place within me during this trip. It seems that I feel I can do things in a different way, that I can indeed lead a different kind of life, with more enjoyment, taking more pleasure in life.

Upon resuming the analytic work after my absence, Carmen frequently alluded to topics that had appeared in the dream. I was especially intrigued by the reference to homosexuality, although its meaning escaped me. I had the impression that there was something erotised but, above all, confused in her relationship with me. This state of affairs became gradually clearer in the weeks that followed. Now, some of the key points in the process:

A few weeks after this session, Carmen brought a dream in which she appeared in a white '69 Peugeot car (she herself associated that it was the same colour as the walls of my office). She associated it with a summer in her adolescence when she and three girlfriends went "cruising" in a car of the same make but of a different colour, in some seaside town. This was in 1969, the year when she first met me at the university. Throughout the associations she suddenly remembered another dream. She was in her gynaecologist's office, in the gynaecological position and the doctor said to her she had an infected anal fistula that should be lanced immediately because the pus was pressuring the frontal area, contaminating her genitals.

The unconscious situation became clear in a flash and I interpreted: "We must talk openly of a type of hidden relationship you have with me, that you, in your fantasy, have concealed in your body, precisely, between the anus and the vagina. In this fantasy you and I are engaged in a sort of permanent sexual intercourse, a 69, in which you suck my penis and I suck your vulva, and thus, you get to convince yourself that the penis is at times yours and at times mine. It is a confusing relationship that is causing you great distress; it is exerting a lot of pressure, and contaminating your sexuality. If we persist in not speaking of this openly, the contamination of your sexuality as a woman will continue." She strongly rejected this interpretation and the connection I had made with the (anal) control that she exercised over me during the sessions.

However, some days later she brought the following dream: "I am inside a roofed gymnasium; there are lots of people engaged in athletics. Suddenly I feel an itch in the genital area and I ask S. (a co-worker with whom she competes) to go with me to the toilet where I ask her to look what I have down there. I pull my knickers down and, much to my surprise and fear I find that I have an enormous penis, with something like an allergy on the glans." Later she added that what was going on in the gym was an athletics competition for women: there were only women involved.

In an incidental way, these episodes shed light on the unconscious motives underlying her sexual acting out with her former therapist. They also made it possible to understand the great rage and subsequent disillusion: the unconscious fantasy of at least sharing the longed-for penis with the therapist was drastically belied by reality; after which she felt more empty and incomplete than ever.

In the period that followed, Carmen questioned and was perplexed about her gender identity. She thought she had lived her entire life thinking of herself as a man not a woman and this had led her to making big mistakes in life. After this period, the early maternal transference appeared with much more clarity and the erotisation disappeared completely. I then understood that the homosexuality in the first dream was an expression of confusion in her sexual identity caused by the potent phantasy of being equipped with a phallus, probably, in turn, a defence against her devalued self-esteem.

Discussion

Most likely, all clinicians would agree with me in that the therapeutic value of the interpretation of dreams varies with the very diverse clinical situations. There are patients that rarely bring a dream to their therapy sessions without damaging the process because of it; and yet, there are others, such as is the case of Carmen, good dreamers, who, in turn, have a special access to their internal world, who are able to communicate their dreams constructively to therapists. Using the couch or not and the frequency of the weekly sessions are also factors that bear an influence and there are therapists who are more bent on using clinically the dreams than others. It is also true that the technique of eliciting associations remains valid. In this discussion I shall attempt to outline the technical principles that—I believe—guided my work with Carmen.

In the first place, I want to emphasise the willingness to listen to the narration of the dream in the session that I transcribed in detail above. I believe that such disposition matches Ehebald's (1981) recommendation of listening to the patient's narration in a manner of "dreaming with her" (*mitträumen*), internally experiencing the emotions and occurrences that the dream awakens in oneself, within the context of the transference-countertransference. In this case, the focus was placed on the action of narrating the dream (Tuckett, 2000), especially the manner in which Carmen was telling it, while observing her manner of accommodating on the couch (transference enactment?). The images and emotions that the narration awoke in me—basically, erotic fantasies and emotions—were also framed within the patient's history, which brought to my memory her traumatic episode with her previous therapist.

The second noteworthy aspect of this case is that it is the patient herself who underlines the main theme of the dream, namely, "The dream has to do with my sexuality". I wish to highlight this point, because it shows what I understand as the co-construction of meaning.

Among the multiple meaning possibilities—of such an apparently bizarre dream—the patient points out a very clear one: it has to do with her own sexuality. At first, I could not understand how the dream imagery could relate to Carmen's sexuality, although for a long time I had been increasingly suspicious about the erotic transfer.

It is precisely at this point where I believe the manifest dream work begins. Cautiously, I keep confronting Carmen with dream images, relating them with her erotised manner of narrating the dream; always guided by my countertransference. She responds with associations that evidence the huge anxiety aroused by her sexual desires towards me. It is interesting to note, however, that this is an oblique dialogue: we never speak directly about the subject, even if we both know what we are talking about; our strict adherence to the manifest dream seems to keep us on safe ground. At any rate, the idea is to leave open the meaning horizon and not to saturate it with interpretations. In the construction of meaning, the patient has a much more important role than that granted by the classical technique. On this point, I believe I have followed Isakower's recommendation—as mentioned by Reiser (1997, p. 903)—in terms of committing the patient's interest in "getting back into the dream".

The dreams brought by Carmen to subsequent sessions went on to clarify the central conflict and resolve the erotic transference that had interfered with our analytic work for a long time. The manifest content of such dreams revealed, in an extraordinarily precise manner, profoundly repressed childhood sexual fantasies.

Note

1. Dedicated to Helmut Thomä on his ninetieth anniversary.

References

Bernardi, R. (2003). What kind of evidence makes the analyst change his or her theoretical and technical ideas? In: M. Leuzinger-Bohleber, A. U. Dreher & J. Canestri (Eds.), *Pluralism and Unity? Methods of Research in Psychoanalysis* (pp. 125–136). London: IPA.

Blechner, M. (2001). *The Dream Frontier*. Hillsdale, NJ: Analytic Press.

Boag, S. (2006). Freudian dream theory, dream bizarreness, and the disguise-censor controversy. *Neuropsychoanalysis, 8*: 5–16.

Brooks Brenneis, C. (1975). Theoretical notes on the manifest dream. *International Journal of Psychoanalysis, 56*: 197–206.

Canestri, J., Bohleber, W., Denis, P. & Fonagy, P. (2006). The map of private (implicit, preconscious) theories in clinical practice. In: J. Canestri (Ed.), *Psychoanalysis: From Practice to Theory* (pp. 29–44). New York: Wiley.

Colace, C. (2010). *Children's Dreams. From Freud's Observations to Modern Dream Research*. London: Karnac.

Curtis, H. & Sachs, D. (1975). Dialogue on "The changing use of dreams in psychoanalytic practice". *International Journal of Psychoanalysis, 57*: 343–354.

Ehebald, U. (1981). Überlegungen zur Einschätzung des manifesten Traumes. In: U. Ehebald & F.-W. Eikhoff (Eds.), Humanität und Technik in der Psychoanalyse. *Jahrbuch der Psychoanalyse* (Beiheft Nr. 6, pp. 81–100). Berne, Switzerland: Hans Huber .

Erikson, E. (1954). The dream specimen of psychoanalysis. *Journal of the American Psychoanalytic Association, 2*: 5–56.

Fonagy, P. (1999). Memory and therapeutic action. *International Journal of Psychoanalysis, 80*: 215–221.

Fonagy, P., Kächele, H., Krause, R., Jones, E. & Perron, R. (1999). *An Open Door Review of Outcome Studies in Psychoanalysis: Report Prepared by the Research Committee of the IPA at the Request of the President*. London: University College.

Fosshage, J. L. (1983). The psychological function of dreams: A revised psychoanalytic perspective. *Psychoanalysis and Contemporary Thought, 6*: 641–669.

French, T. & Fromm, E. (1964). *Dream Interpretation. A New Approach.* New York: Basic.

Greenberg, R. & Pearlman, C. A. (1999). The interpretation of dreams: A classic revisited. *Psychoanalytic Dialogues, 9*: 749–765

Grunert, U. (1984). Selbstdarstellung und Selbstentwicklung in manifesten Traum. *Jahrbuch der Psychoanalyse, 14*: 179–209.

Hanly, C. (2010a). *Project Group on Clinical Observation—Mandate.* Unpublished.

Hanly, C. (2010b). *Project Group on Conceptual Integration—Mandate.* Unpublished.

Jiménez, J. P. (1990). Some technical consequences of Matte Blanco's theory of dreaming. *International Review of Psycho-Analysis, 17*: 455–469.

Jiménez, J. P. (2006). After pluralism: Towards a new, integrated psychoanalytic paradigm. *International Journal of Psychoanalysis, 87*: 1487–1507.

Jiménez, J. P. (2008). Theoretical plurality and pluralism in psychoanalytic practice. *International Journal of Psychoanalysis, 89*: 579–599.

Jiménez, J. P. (2009). Grasping psychoanalysts' practice in its own merits. *International Journal of Psychoanalysis, 90*: 231–248.

Jung, C. (1934). The practical use of dream-analysis. In: R. C. F. Hull (Trans.), *Collected Works: Vol. 16*. Princeton, NJ: Princeton University Press, 1968, pp. 139–162.

Kächele, H., Schachter, J. & Thomä, H. (2009). *From Psychoanalytic Narrative to Empirical Single Case Research.* London: Routledge.

Lansky, M. R. (1992). The legacy of the interpretation of dreams. In: M. R. Lansky (Ed.), *Essential Papers on Dreams*, (pp. 3–31). New York: New York University Press.

Loden, S. (2003). The fate of the dream in contemporary psychoanalysis. *Journal of the American Psychoanalytic Association, 51*: 43–70.

Mancia, M. (2004). The dream between neuroscience and psychoanalysis. *Archives Italiennes de Biologie, 142*: 525–531.

Matte Blanco, I. (1988). *Thinking, Feeling, and Being.* London: Routledge.

Nir, Y. & Tononi, G. (2009). Dreaming and the brain: from phenomenology to neurophysiology. *Trends in Cognitive Sciences, 14*(2): 88–100.

Reiser, M. F. (1997). The art and science of dream interpretation: Isakower revisited. *Journal of the American Psychoanalytic Association, 45*: 891–905.

Robbins, M. (2004). Another look at dreaming: Disentangling Freud's primary and secondary process theories. *Journal of the American Psychoanalytic Association, 52*: 355–384.

Spanjaard, J. (1969). The manifest dream content and its significance for the interpretation of dreams. *International Journal of Psychoanalysis, 50*: 221–235.

Spence, D. (1982). *Narrative Truth and Historical Truth. Meaning and Interpretation in Psychoanalysis.* New York: W. W. Norton.

Stolorow, R. (1978). Themes in dreams: A brief contribution to therapeutic technique. *International Journal of Psychoanalysis, 59*: 473–475.

Stolorow, R. & Atwood C. (1982). The psychoanalytic phenomenology of the dream. *Annual of Psychoanalysis, 10*: 205–220.

Strenger, C. (1991). *Between Hermeneutic and Sciences. An Essay on the Epistemology of Psychoanalysis.* (Psychological Issues. Monogr. 59.) Madison, CT: International Universities Press.

Thomä, H. (2000). Gemeinsamkeiten und Widersprüche zwischen vier Psychoanalytikern (Commonalities and contradictions between four psychoanalysts). *Psyche—Z Psychoanal, 54*: 172–189.

Thomä, H. & Kächele, H. (1975). Problems of metascience and methodology in clinical psychoanalytic research. *Annual of Psychoanalysis, 3*: 49–119.

Thomä, H. & Kächele, H. (1987). *Psychoanalytic Practice. Vol. 1: Principles.* Berlin: Springer.

Tuckett, D. (2000). *Dream Interpretation in Contemporary Psychoanalysis.* Unpublished paper presented at the English-speaking Conference of the British Psychoanalytic Society, London, October.

Wallerstein, R. (1988). One psychoanalysis or many? *International Journal of Psychoanalys, 69*: 5–21.

Wallerstein, R. (1990). Psychoanalysis: The common ground. *International Journal of Psychoanalysis, 71*: 3–20.

Wilson, A. (2000). Commentaries to Robert Michels' paper. *Journal of the American Psychoanalytic Association, 48*: 411–417.

Zeppelin, I. v. & Moser, U. (1987). Träumen wir Affekte? Teil 1: Affekte und manifester Traum. *Forum der Psychoanalyse, 3*: 143–152.

CHAPTER FOUR

Changes in dreams—from a psychoanalysis with a traumatised, chronic depressed patient

Marianne Leuzinger-Bohleber

> "It is like a deeply engraved, though entirely irrational program: that alone and without protection, love and security I am unable to survive in this world …"
>
> (Mr W)

Preliminary remarks

Established by Freud, the psychoanalytic extended case report continues to be one of the most important forms of communication in international psychoanalysis, albeit in more recent years such reports have rarely been published in international journals of psychoanalysis. Among others, the partial disappearance of this erstwhile tradition in psychoanalysis as "clinical science" may be linked to the heated controversies in which various authors have questioned the very validity for science of such case reports (cf. e.g., Thomä & Kächele, 1987). A discussion of these controversies would exceed the constraints of the present contribution (cf. also, Leuzinger-Bohleber, 2007, 2010; Leuzinger-Bohleber, Rüger, Stuhr & Beutel, 2002, 2003). I myself contend that, to date, no credible alternative to the case reports has been developed for adequately and "legibly" presenting the "narrative truths",[1] as acquired over the course

49

of lengthy psychoanalysis, to the psychoanalytic and non-psychoanalytic communities. Indeed, while precise reports of sessions (either verbatim, or else based on analysts' notes) may be indispensable for many clinical and conceptual discussions, they nevertheless remain insufficient for conveying the total impression of a treatment and the results thereof. By contrast—and naturally as best exemplified in Freud's own literary extended case studies—the comprehensive case report succeeds in conveying both to students and to a broad public "what psychoanalysis is", the goals it pursues, and the types of transformations it effectuates within patients etc. Hence, as empirical psychoanalytical researcher and as clinician, I do not confine my admiration exclusively to the work and legacy of Freud: it also encompasses writers and poets as a whole to the extent that the latter succeed in giving masterful articulation to their insights in complex, psychic processes of transformation of the unconscious, and in mediating the results to their readers. For these reasons, I concur with leading narrative researchers who postulate that many "truths can only be told and not be measured".

And it is precisely because of this esteem for the clinical case reports that I am an active member of the Project Group for Clinical Observation of the IPA (Chair: Marina Altmann) in its endeavours to improve the quality of clinical research. The drawbacks associated with this tradition are well known. These range from the arbitrary status of clinical observations for buttressing a given theoretical stance or hypothesis; the hazard of hermetically closed viewpoints; narcissistic confirmation, in lieu of the (self-) critical reflection of an observation; a gravitation towards "positively resolved" star cases, in contrast to the absence of poorly performed treatments; the danger of (unconscious) "fabrication"—especially in training cases; repetition or conformity to mainstream discussions within the psychoanalytic community and, as a consequence, the disappearance of innovative, unconventional ideas, and much else. The various methods elaborated for dealing with such drawbacks of "clinical research" also comprise the object of critical discussion. One such drawback will be presented for discussion in what follows: it is an attempt to critically approach the arbitrariness and condensation in the presentation of clinical materials, in theoretical assessment as well as in the interpretation of clinical observations with the aid of so-called *clinical expert validation* (cf. among others, Leuzinger-Bohleber, Engels & Tsiantis, 2008, p. 153 ff. Leuzinger-Bohleber, Rüger, Stuhr & Beutel, 2003). In summary: in periodic clinical conferences, this psychoanalysis was presented by way of a patient suffering from chronic depression—carried out as part of the LAC

Study on Depression[2]—such that the colleagues were already well familiar with the course of the treatment. This was documented systematically and in detail. The "truth content" of the following summary was similarly presented to colleagues for mutual deliberation. Based on the Hampstead Index, we furthermore elaborated a means for systematising the compression of complex clinical observations, without, moreover, restricting the creativity of the narration as a consequence. One of the aims of our "clinical research" is to provide a comprehensive, systematic collection of case histories on psychoanalyses and psychoanalytic long-term therapies of chronically depressed patients. The following case history is the first of such attempts I am presenting here for discussion. I hope to motivate other groups of clinicians to write such systematic, expert validated case studies on other groups of patients. The method proposed here is very close to clinical practice. Supervision and intervision groups, as well as courses with candidates or IPA members, could be systematically used to expert validate ongoing psychoanalyses and document the gained knowledge in extended case reports with different theoretical foci. In my view this would be a contribution to improved clinical observation and its public communication in contemporary psychoanalysis.

As is discussed in this volume, dreams have long since been considered the "via regia" to the unconscious. Hence considerable importance has been and continues to be attributed to them in the clinical observations in psychoanalysis. In the following case study the transformation of manifest dream content, as well as the analytical work with dreams, serves as an indicator for the unconscious reactions of the analysand to the therapeutic process.[3] In this narrative, all relevant clinical observations are compressed, summarised, and "recounted" by "validated experts" with the greatest possible precision. Here, a compromise is sought when summarising the entire treatment "narratively": to mediate, on the one hand, the above-mentioned, total impression of the psychoanalytical process as it occurs, along with the transformations in the inner object world of the analysand, while at the same time the selection of central sequences of consecutive sessions is to be reproduced verbatim, at least in part though without thereby rupturing the narrative structure of the summary.[4]

Depression and trauma: focus of the case study

In psychoanalytic literature reference is frequently made to the connection between depression and trauma (Blum, 2007; Bohleber, 2005;

Bokanowski, 1996; Bose, 1995; Bremner, 2002; Denis, 1992; Kernberg, 2000). However, we found it astonishing not to have discovered in the LAC studies on depression currently being conducted almost any among the patients suffering from chronic depression who had not experienced cumulative traumatisation. The first systematic analysis of all the patients who are in treatment in our Frankfurt group shows that 84% of chronically depressive analysands indicate an explicitly cumulative history of trauma. For this reason, one of the results of this extensive, comparative psychotherapeutic study will be to provide a detailed empirical, as well as analytical, reappraisal of this connection. As mentioned, the Frankfurt group of the LAC Depression Study is working on a publication with comprehensive case reports illustrating both the influence of early traumatisation on the emergence of chronic depression, and a range of consequences relevant to treatment of these findings. The following case study represents one of these narrative summaries of a lengthy psychoanalysis with a chronic depressed patient. The following observations will be presented for discussion here:

a. Unresolved traumatic experiences may lead to chronic depression.
b. The traumatic experiences are buried in the body as "embodied memories"[5] (Leuzinger-Bohleber & Pfeifer, 2002; Pfeifer & Leuzinger-Bohleber, 2011), and unconsciously determine present thinking, feeling and action.
c. A sustained transformation of a depressive complex of problems can only be introduced to the analyst by an understanding of the enactment of the specific trauma within the transference situation.
d. The "historic reality" of the trauma must be acknowledged. To this also belongs the fact that although the effects of traumatisation may be alleviated in the process of working through the analytical relationship, they cannot be erased. Recognition of the destruction of the basic sense of trust in good, helpful inner objects through the traumatic experience appears to be a prerequisite for recognising the enactment of the trauma, and thus for containing its effects (see Leuzinger-Bohleber, 2008).
e. The traumatic experience may also manifest itself in dreams. For this reason, psychoanalytic work with dreams may contribute to the symbolisation and mentalisation of the trauma.

In that this contribution places emphasis on the communication of clinical observation, the following theoretical deliberations must remain fragmentary.

"There is no unitary concept of depression ..." Theoretical remarks on the genesis of depression, psychoanalytical and epigenetic reflections

Contemporary psychoanalysts and psychiatrists agree that only a multifactor model is capable of doing justice to the complex and always very individual causes leading into a depression. "There is no unitary concept of depression ..." (McQueen, 2009, p. 225). The psychiatric model by Schulte-Körne and Allgaier (2008), for example, postulates that various factors have an influence on the genesis of depression although to different degrees and intensities. Many replication studies have investigated the influence of genetics on the neurotransmitter system. At the same time, the influence of early traumatisations by physical and sexual abuse on later depression has been shown in many studies that hint at the biographical as well as the societal factors just mentioned. The interaction between genetic and environmental factors can now be considered as a valid model of explanation in psychiatry as well as in psychoanalysis, although, as will be discussed in the following case report, the influence of early trauma on depression still seems to be underestimated.

Psychoanalysis adds another dimension to such models: we postulate that there are many different *unconscious* determinants, which finally may lead to a depressive symptomatic. All our experiences, from the very beginning, are retained by the unconscious and determine—as secret, unknown sources of our psyche—the affects, cognition, and behaviour in the present. Particularly traumatic experiences as well as other developmental conflicts and fantasies have left their specific marks and characteristics in the *dynamic unconscious* of each person (see Leuzinger-Bohleber, 2001). Hence, "normal" and "pathological" psychic and psychosocial functioning is always the product of a distinct biography.

In short, psychoanalysts working with depressed *case studies* seek to discover the unique unconscious roots of his or her depressive functioning: each patient has complex individual pathways which lead to a specific form of depression.; each depression possesses its own unique features. Depression is not a closed category, but is considered as an ongoing process.

Bleichmar (1996, 2010), a senior clinical psychoanalytic researcher on depression, has developed a model which recognises the multiple paths through which a person proceeds from one circuit, as dominated by one factor, to another when becoming depressed. Bleichmar describes these different, though not exclusive pathways, by means of the graph below.

For Bleichmar (1996, p. 77 ff.) Freud's paper *Mourning and Melancholia* continues to be the fundamental text for our psychoanalytic understanding of depression. Freud characterised depression as a reaction to the loss of a real or an imaginary object, and thus defined depression as a reaction which is not only connected to the "real loss" of an object, an idea, a self-image, etc., but depends on how the loss is codified by unconscious fantasies and conscious thoughts. In *Inhibition, Symptoms and Anxiety* (1926), Freud underscores the "insatiable cathexis of longing" of the depressed after the loss of an object: instinctual satisfactions, attachment wishes, and narcissistic wishes as well as wishes related to the object's well-being are no longer satisfied by the real or fantasised object. Corresponding to the sense of hopelessness about the fulfilment of wishes, the depressed patient experiences himself to be *powerless, helpless, and impotent*. The emotions tending towards the object of desire are deactivated: apathy, inhibition, and

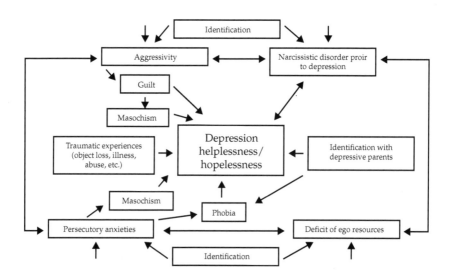

passivity are some of the consequences. Many psychoanalysts have hinted at the central role of helplessness and powerlessness in depression (see, e.g., Bibring, 1953; Bohleber, 2005, 2010; Haynal, 1977, 1993; Jacobson, 1971; Joffe & Sandler, 1965; Klein, 1935, 1940; Kohut, 1971; Leuzinger-Bohleber et al., 2010; Steiner, 2005; Stone, 1986; Taylor, 2010). Rado (1928, 1951) has observed coercive rage as one attempt to recover the lost object. He also described the defensive self-reproaches meant to decrease feelings of guilt and to recover the love of the superego by self-punishment (see top right hand of the graph).

> When the pain of depression is prolonged, the restorative mechanisms prove insufficient for maintaining the illusion that the wish can be fulfilled. The psyche's final defensive strategy may consist of mobilizing defenses against mental functioning itself, attempting to abolish wishing, thinking and feeling altogether. This might be the case with mental states described by Spitz (1946) as the final phases of hospitalism, or in the severe detachment process that takes place after an important loss not compensated by an adequate substitute object (Bowlby, 1980). Ogden (1982) describes an extreme form of defense in certain schizophrenic patients who have faced conditions of prolonged unbearable suffering, a defense which he calls the "state of nonexperience". (Bleichmar, 1996, p. 937).

Another consequence of extreme feelings of hopelessness and powerlessness are phobias and anxieties: the representations of the self as incapable, as weak and impotent establish a psychic state in which anything might appear as dangerous, and overwhelm the weak ego (dynamics on the bottom right of the graph).

It is thus possible to arrive at the sense of hopelessness for wish fulfilment which constituted the nucleus of every depressive state though multiple paths, none of which are obligatory conditions. Each one of these paths is driven by different factors or areas of pathology.

Many psychoanalysts have pronounced the central role of *aggression in depression* although there are still a number of controversial views about the nature and the function of aggressive impulses (Abraham, 1911, 1924; Blatt, 2004; Freud, 1917; Jacobson, 1971; Klein, 1935, 1940; Kohut, 1971, 1977; Steiner, 2005; Taylor, 2010).[6] Bleichmar (1996, p. 942 ff.) also stresses the connection between *depression and guilt* and mentions four conceptions of the origins of guilt.[7] Kohut (1971) and other psychoanalysts emphasise that often in depression it is not guilt but *shame and narcissistic suffering* which is the major topic. He talked about the "tragic man" in contrast to the "guilty man". Following Kohut, Ehrenberg (1998) and others postulate that the feelings of shame are more central in contemporary depressions than feelings of guilt (e.g., due to forbidden sexual desires as Freud noted in nineteenth century Vienna). Melanie Klein (1935, 1940) suggested that *persecutory anxieties* may lead to depression because they destroy mental functioning and disturb the development of the ego, object relations, sublimation, and reality testing. Contemporary mentalisation theories explain these inner processes in a new way, such as in depressions of borderline patients (see, e.g., Fonagy, in press; Rohde-Dachser, in press). Often the reality of the loss can not be accepted but is denied (see, e.g., Steiner, 2005).

Identification with depressed parents is also a well described pathway to depression (see also Anna Freud, 1965; Hellman, 1978; Leuzinger-Bohleber, 2001; Markson, 1993; Morrison, 1983). Any condition that produces *ego deficits* (inner conflicts, traumatic reality, parent's ego deficits, etc.) diminishes the possibilities for sublimation, for establishing satisfactory relationships, etc., and may thus be another pathway to depression.

Finally, Bleichmar (1996) mentions the influence of *traumatic external realities on depression* (see also Balint, 1968; Baranger, Baranger & Mom, 1988; Brown & Harris, 1989; Winnicott, 1965) as one of several possible pathways. But as I would like to discuss by way of the following case example, the connection between trauma and depression is far more dramatic than has been postulated in classical psychoanalytical literature. In my view, the role of trauma in causing depression often remains underestimated in the literature, as some authors have also discussed in recent papers (Blum, 2007; Bohleber, 2005; Bohleber, in press; Bokanowski, 2005; Bose, 1995; Bremner, 2002; Denis, 1992; Leuzinger-Bohleber, 2010, in press; Skalew, 2006; Taylor, 2010).

Interestingly, a growing body of interdisciplinary literature has come out in favour of this position. I will mention a few such authors. Hill (2009) summarised developmental perspectives on adult depression in a general paper. Numerous studies showed the increasing probability of developing adult depression after early neglect or the loss of a parent (Bifulco, Brown & Harris, 1987; Hill, 2009, p. 200 ff. Hill et al., 2001). Fergusson and Woodward (2002) reviewed the literature as to the role of childhood sexual abuse and showed that the association with depression in adulthood was substantial: a history of childhood sexual abuse increased the risk of depression approximately four times.[8]

Twin studies have established that unipolar depression is moderately heritable (Hill, 2009, p. 202 ff. Kendler, Gatz, Gardner & Pederson, 2006). New research in epigenetics, however, shows that even genetic vulnerability only leads into depression where the person also undergoes severe early traumatisation. Caspi et al. (2003) have been able to show that only severely negative environmental factors, such as early trauma, trigger the short allele of the 5-HHT gene which regulates relevant neurotransmitters and might afterwards cause depression. If no such trauma occurs, then no subsequent depression is observed.

These findings are of extreme importance for psychoanalysts, and support our clinical findings that early prevention and intervention programmes for depressed children, adolescents, and adults—even those from genetically burdened families—may be helpful and effective in strengthening the resiliency of those individuals at risk.

Epigenetic and neurobiological studies also give new relevance to the famous studies of René Spitz on anaclitic depression and hospitalism in the 1940s, which showed impressively how early separation trauma can determine severe depression already in infancy. Robertson and Robertson have replicated his findings in the 1970s with their impressive studies on early separation. Their observations correspond significantly with Harlow's famous experiments on monkeys. Thanks to modern research instruments, one of Harlow's successors, Steven Suomi (2010) was even able to demonstrate that early separation trauma has an enormous influence on neurobiological factors that determine the development of aggression, anxiety, and social integration, and thus to the survival of genetically vulnerable Rhesus monkeys. These findings are highly relevant for the following case study.

These influences of early trauma are transmitted to the next generation—a finding which corresponds in detail with many clinical psychoanalytical observations by many authors, including those of ours in the above-mentioned LAC depression study. Goldberg (2009) concludes his overview of more recent studies in these fields thus:

> These interactions between gene and environment, between behavior and genotype are important for the manner in which they provide explanations of how the many different features constituting the *"depressive diathesis"* arise. However, they have a much wider

significance. They provide a possible pathway by which *changing inter-personal and cultural factors across the generations* can be both cause and effect of genotype, and through which changes in human culture might possibly operate as an accelerator of evolutionary processes.

To sum up, we see that adverse environmental conditions are especially harmful to some particular genotypes, leaving the remainder of the population relatively resilient. Research in this area is expanding very fast—and we may expect many more advances in the years to come ...." (pp. 244–245)[9]

Another finding is especially relevant for us psychoanalysts. Suomi (2010) has shown that undoing the separation trauma in baby monkeys might "undo" the neurobiological and behavioural damages once again—clearly, a revolutionary finding for all forms of early prevention and for psychoanalytic treatments. As the following summary seeks to illustrate, the psychoanalysis of chronically depressive Mr W, so the understanding of the enactment of traumatic experience in the transfer, enables the analysand to recognize the continual repetition of the trauma, and to thus counteract it with a new and different psychic reality. The horror of the original experience of helplessness and of inundation through the trauma can be countered by an adult psychic reality, an active approach to the trauma. In this sense, while the memory of the trauma is not erased—its automatic, re-traumatising effect in the present can be "undone".

> ... being alone without any protection, love and security, makes it impossible for me to survive in this world .... (Mr W)

Summary of a psychoanalysis

Assessment interviews[10]

When meeting him for the first interview, Mr W at once reminded me of Little John, a child in the famous 1970s film series by the Robertsons.[11] I puzzled over why this countertransference phantasy has at all occurred to me, since Mr W is in his early fifties, a well-built, handsome man, though with a somewhat severe facial expression, melancholy eyes, and heavy facial neurodermatitis. He explained that he had been suffering from severe depression for the last twenty-five years, and that he is coming to us because after the last depressive breakdown he had submitted an application for retirement pension. The doctor who assessed his application concluded that he did not require a pension, but an "intelligent psychoanalysis", initially a response Mr W found highly insulting. He felt that he had not been taken seriously, especially his substantial physical symptoms: the unbearable pains covering his entire body, his acute eating disorders, as well as his acute suicidal tendencies. Furthermore, the patient suffered under acute sleep disorders. Often he is unable to sleep at all. As a rule, he wakes up after one and a half hours, or after three hours at the most. He feels physically exhausted and is barely able to concentrate his mind on anything.

Mr W had already undergone several unsuccessful attempts at therapy, including behavioural therapy, Gestalt therapy, "body therapy" as well as several indoor treatments in psychiatric and psychosomatic clinics. He is among that group of patients for the most part apparently unable to respond to psychotropic drugs, and whose relapses occur at ever shorter intervals and with increasing intensity. After many consultations with various psychiatrists and neurologists, he then discovered that only lyrica helped him to more or less deal with his states of physical stress and anxiety attacks.

Although four hours per week psychoanalysis is indicated, due to the distance from his place of residence Mr W has only been able to manage three hours per week throughout most phases of the treatment. Due to his extreme sleeping disorders, the thirty minute car journeys are often cause for concern.

Biography and trauma history[12]

The patient is an only child. One of the known details about his early history is that he was a "crybaby". Clearly, his parents most often felt helpless, and sought out a paediatrician who advised them to ignore the infant as much as possible, and to "let it cry itself out … this helps strengthen the lungs". Over the course of the first three months of psychoanalysis, the patient characterised his parents as loving, who showed him considerable care and attention. And yet over the course of time what increasingly became clear was that both parents showed a severely disturbed sense of empathy: the mother, moreover, suffered from migraines and from a pronounced compulsion to clean. The father also complained of a series of psychosomatic symptoms. Like Mr W he suffered a "nervous breakdown" in a situation of professional stress. Both parents had experienced the Second World War as adolescents and still retain vivid memories of how they had suffered as children under the straightjacket of National Socialist educational ideology (the children were to be as "hard as Krupp steel" etc.). One of the grandfathers had lost an arm in the First World War. He was violent-tempered and would frequently thrash his children.

When he was four years old Mr W's mother fell seriously ill. Mr W was admitted to a convalescent home for children, evidently founded on authoritarian, inhumane educational principles reminiscent of National Socialist ethos. Just how traumatic an experience was this stay in a home is something that became transparently clear during psychoanalysis. After a courageous aunt literally battled for and finally gained access to her nephew, she found him in a state of utter apathy, seriously ill, and in an isolated room. The official version as conveyed to the parents was that the boy was cheerful, that he played, and that he was generally doing well. The aunt sounded the alarm, and father collected Mr W immediately. Mr W's first childhood memories revolve around the following event: he recalls how his father took him by the hand and led him out of the home. He also recalls how a girl had been forced to eat her own vomit.

When asked, the mother recounted that after his stay at the home, Mr W had completely changed: he had become silent; he did not wish to go to kindergarten, and was a shy, daydreaming boy who felt best in the countryside. Over the course of psychoanalysis it became clearer that through the traumatic separation from the primary objects, he lost his basic trust to his inner objects, and that he has subsequently been living in a state of dissociation for years (see, e.g., Bohleber, 2000). In many of his dreams he feels himself to be in mortal danger having been left alone and full of panic-ridden anxieties and desperation (cf. below). Mr W experienced two further separations from his ill mother, but these incidents had proved less traumatic since he had been taken in by relatives. The family moved house when he was eleven years old. He recalls how he had protested against this move with everything he could muster, and his parents found his panic-ridden anxiety connected with the move incomprehensible. They perceived him as being tyrannical and strange.

In spite of the dissociative states and his social isolation, Mr W was a good pupil, who went on to complete his first apprenticeship training and later his university studies. During adolescence, he had a psychosomatic breakdown, which the parents diagnosed as a "crisis in growing up", and sought to help him by way of a vitamin cure. At the age of fifteen years, he met his first girlfriend. His condition improved. At the age of twenty-two he separated from his first girlfriend because he fell in love with another woman. Although the separation ran in his favour, he reacted very severely to it. A few weeks later, he could barely eat and suffered intestinal complaints. After enduring horrendous diarrhoea, he then suddenly felt better. He also initiated the separation from his second girlfriend, though suffered for weeks due to the separation. After entering another relationship he was dramatically overcome by a nervous breakdown during a party held by his new girlfriend: he had to be taken to hospital due to hyperventilation (panic attacks). "I have been unable to trust my body ever since that experience. I experience repeated panic attacks and a sense of being unable to breathe." He experienced another severe depressive collapse when this third girlfriend betrayed him with another man. He was unable to defend himself, and instead pleaded with her to stay with him in what he then felt to be a humiliating manner.

Although all his therapies alleviated him, "none of them cured him".

He is married to a woman from a non-European country, and has a son who was three and a half years of age at the beginning of his treatment. The last severe depression (one and a half years ago) was first triggered when his wife coldly, and without empathy, attacked him while he was in a state of exhaustion after a month-long two-fold burden in connection with the building of a house. Without any foundation, his wife accused him of endangering the life of his son because he had failed to stop the infant from crawling around dangerous objects. Mr W was incapable of defending himself against this unfounded attack. He awoke the next morning in a state of unbearable depression.

In spite of this, after a few weeks he attempted to start work again for the sake of securing the well-being of his family. However, after some time, he felt himself unable to persevere with his profession. He took a vacation. He then fell ill with acute bronchitis which developed into pneumonia. During his stay in hospital a tumour was discovered which had to be operated on. During the first interview he gave an impressive description of how he had wished to die during the operation "to escape the misery". At the same time, he hoped the tumour had been a contributory cause of his depressions, something that proved to be an illusion. It was for this reason that several weeks after the operation he very unexpectedly submitted his application for a pension.

On the course of the treatment: changes of the manifest dream content: an indicator for the enactment of the trauma in the analytical relationship?[13]

An intensive relationship between Mr W and me began to show itself already during the assessment interviews; I began struggling with the fantasy that it would no longer be possible for me to transfer him to a colleague so that the patient would have a choice as to which analyst he would wish to begin a treatment—as is my common assessment practice. During supervision it became evident that in my countertransference I would most likely experience myself as the "saving father", who took the patient away from the home, namely, an irreplaceable primary object. Mr W established an apparently almost symbiotic proximity to the object of love and experienced a separation from it as a life-threatening danger: this world of inner fantasies tallies with my countertransference fantasies being strongly absorbed from the outset of the treatment with the question as to whether or not we would manage to draw near to the core of the chronic depression. It seemed almost a fantasy of omnipotence to me such that, in contrast to many of Mr W's previous therapists, I could be successful in such an attempt.

> ... it was war ... (Mr W)

To my surprise, the first therapy sessions were filled by the most ferocious affects: Mr W was full of rage towards his wife and described the most terrible marriage scenes. His wife attacked him verbally and physically in front of his small son, with whom she would also become involved in the most heated affective confrontations. His child suffers from selective mutism: he talks only with his parents. Moreover, he continues to wear nappies.

It soon became evident during the sessions that due to his fear of being abandoned by her, Mr W is incapable of defending himself against his wife's onslaughts. He lives in an inner world of panic, desperation, and profound loneliness. When I sought to suggest a link between the affects and the trauma of separation he had experienced,

Mr W rejected this vehemently. "Other therapists would repeatedly make reference to my stay in the children´s home. I simply cannot believe that a three-week stay in a home at the age of four could exert such a long-term influence on me ... this just all seems very contrived ...." Another initial fierce conflict emerged after I cautiously enquired about whether he might not be inclined to seek solace from the present intolerable marital conflicts, and the demands of his work in depression. Mr W erupted in fury and went on to explain just how offended he had been when the doctor who made the original assessment had described him as "a sort of hypochondriac who had no desire to work and who wished to escape into illness". "He had no conception of the existential dimension of my anxiety and depression. I am not a shammer!" These scenes revealed to me how important it was for Mr W during psychoanalysis that I take seriously and grasp his unbearable psychological suffering. Furthermore, in retrospect I came to understand these scenes as an indication that in the transference he was struggling with the reactivation of the traumatic experience he had had with his non-empathetic primary objects. As mentioned, both parents had suffered from a seriously disturbed empathy and were incapable of understanding, supporting, and containing Mr W's affect outbreaks either during the latter's infancy or his early childhood in "good enough ways"—experiences of relationships which, in all likelihood, possessed a traumatic quality for Mr W (relationship trauma, type II, according to Terr, 1994). For this reason he appeared to carry within him an archaic, yet unappeased need for an (anaclitic) melting with a (symbiotic) primary object (cf. Blatt & Leuyten, 2009).

After the scenes as sketched in the above, Mr W recounted his initial dream in the tenth session:

> The context was war. I was in a concentration camp with my wife because she is a foreigner. I tried to protect her, but was overcome by a sense of panic.

The associations led to a present, though helpless and threatened love object which the self is unable to protect, a self which, in a state of panic and powerlessness, is subject to a situation of inner war and persecution. Later in the night, Mr W had a further dream:

> Several people had barged their way into the courtyard of our house. I flew into a terrible rage and yelled out: "What the hell do

you want here! Go away." ... They actually did vacate the garden.
My wife remarked how well I managed the situation.

In the psychoanalytic session we understand the second dream
as an investment of hope in psychoanalysis: he wished to acquire
the ability to apply his aggressive impulses for the protection of his
"house", of himself, and the objects of his love so as to actively encounter danger rather than being passively subjected to it and inundated
by anxiety and panic. This would empower his sense of autonomy and
masculine identity and, also, so he hoped, win the acceptance and love
of his wife who, in reality, would scorn and degrade him owing to his
depression.

The staging of the traumatic loss of the object of love and "embodied memories" in the existentially threatening physical state during the stay at the home ...

The subsequent weeks witnessed a dramatic escalation in the external
realities of the analysand: his wife had fallen in love with someone else.
Terrible scenes erupted, in one of which his wife revealed to the patient
that she had never actually loved him, and was presently experiencing
for the first time what a fulfilling sexuality really means.

For Mr W everything collapsed: he was flooded by a sense of panic
and desperation, and could barely sleep. He felt completely degraded
by the rival. It was shocking to observe the sheer extent to which he
identified with the degradation heaped upon him by his wife. The
sessions were filled by depressive self-accusations and ferocious self-
loathing such that I finally confronted him by saying: "You experience
this terrible slight and this abandonment probably in the same way you
experienced it then, during the stay at the home as a young child, and
you now see everything through the depressive spectacles you have
since been wearing. Instead of defending yourself as you do in your
second dream, you inwardly hand over house and home to your rival
without even putting up a fight. Clearly, your wife then confirms the
depressive self-image which you carry within yourself."

Thus, during this phase the sessions frequently took on the character of a crisis intervention: the traumatic separation anxieties shifted
to the core of the work and disclosed their existential attributes.
The massive rage and destructive aggression towards the love object

or the primary object were thematised. The perpetually recurring attempt during the sessions, to distinguish the inner objects from the painful experiences of loss and betrayal in the present reality, in the end enabled Mr W to overcome the paralysing passivity and sheer desperation. He booked a plane ticket for him and his son for a summer vacation to his wife's distant homeland. He left his wife behind with her lover. In spite of guilt feelings, he then had a surprising and fulfilling sexual encounter with an acquaintance, which he experienced as reconfirmation of his adult masculinity and, to a certain extent, as narcissistic restitution.

And yet the subsequent months signified a dire period for Mr W, and marked dreadful wounds and humiliations: his wife lived with her lover and left the son with the patient. Mr W managed to care for his child with the support of his parents. His overall bodily pains have increased substantially, to the extent that he often feels like an "open wound". We suspect that such signs that for him represent an almost life-threatening physical condition are related to the "embodied memories" of the life-threatening illness experienced during his stay at the home. A certain amelioration of the symptoms as an answer to the corresponding interpretations apparently confirms this hypothesis.

Mr W refers to heady nightmares: for example, that in the woods he observes at a distance how a blazing helicopter plunges to the ground. In addition, during the sessions his existential anxieties about being abandoned become clearly evident, as well as his pathological bond to his parents.

Astonishingly enough, during these months, his child displayed a relatively composed disposition and, in the words of the kindergarten nurse, was presently developing positively, gradually overcoming its selective mutism, now being able to visit the toilet alone and is cautiously beginning to find its way out of its social isolation.

The extent to which the patient continues to be tied to the wife was revealed when the wife demanded to have the child returned to her custody: against the advice of his parents and his friends, he was unable to use the situation to separate from her and to apply for custody of the child. He persisted in reacting in panic at the thought of divorcing from his wife, hoping, thereby, that in spite of the injuries the marriage could be maintained. Similar fantasies appear in connection with the treatment: Mr W expresses anxiety about his becoming so dependent on me as an analyst that he will not be able to bear it when the treatment finally comes to a close. Here we encounter his unconscious conviction that "nothing and nobody can really help me ...".

In the subsequent session, Mr W recounted the following dream:

> "I am in a wood close to X., and crawl through a long, dark tunnel. I then come to a hotel with a capacious terrace looking out across the Swiss Alps.[14] It is very pleasant and yet I am still gripped by the anxiety that I might topple from the terrace into the abyss. I thus do not dare stay on the terrace, and rather turn back, even though I know that at the other end of the tunnel, in my home village, things are no longer the way they were."

His associations prompt a deep-seated doubt within him as to the value in embarking on a course of psychoanalysis—to crawl through the dark tunnel of depression so as to be able to behold the light, the distant Alps of Switzerland, and to orient himself on them, but also to gaze into the abyss without falling into it, or whether it is preferable to return to the familiar, albeit gloomy "security" of depression, the home village. Most probably attached to the additional, secondary illness is also the fact that Mr W flees into depression instead of once again resolving to venture into a relationship with the attendant risk of being abandoned and rejected by the object of love. A further aspect is vehemently rejected by the patient during this period, namely, the conflict of loyalty connected with distancing himself from the home village, the inner world of representation of the depressive primary objects, of leaving this behind him, and divorce. The existential dimension of divorce triggers thoughts of an early conflict in individuation and autonomy.

"The revenge on the traumatizing primary object"

By this stage in the treatment, it became clear what severe consequences the reactivating of the separation trauma—of being directed by the panic-ridden anxiety of being abandoned—was capable of exerting on the narcissistic basic self-esteem: towards his wife he feels akin to a helpless, dependent child permitting itself to be humiliated, wounded, and attacked. In this connection he recalled the following dream:

> I catch sight of a man lying at the side of the road severely wounded—his intestines are spewing out, and everything is saturated in blood ... A helicopter appears. It is unclear as to

whether the man is still being shot at, or whether one should go to his aid. Someone appears claiming that the man has now passed away. I notice that the man is still alive and he really does open his eyes and enquires, 'Why is nobody helping me?' The woman hands him a saucepan lid which he should hold over the open wound .... I then wake up riveted by panic ....

In the figure of the woman of the manifest dream, who in a cold, unsympathetic, and unhelpful manner hands a saucepan lid to the man suffering from life-threatening wounds so that he may cover them, I see an indicator that in the transference Mr W now experiences me as an unsympathetic, unhelpful, indeed perhaps even sadistic primary object. Approached cautiously, it then also becomes possible to address his debasing aggressive fantasies towards me. He observes his massive anxieties; like his mother, I was not able to bear such aggressive impulses: until today, his mother has responded fiercely to criticism most often in the form of a migraine.

Recognition and working through aspects of negative transference

Only once it had become possible to directly address his mistrust and his aggressive fantasies, also towards the analyst, did it appear—gradually, in the second year of the treatment—that changes were occurring. Mr W became somewhat more self-confident. He began a new love relationship with a more empathetic woman than his wife. More secure self and object boundaries began establishing themselves. Furthermore, it was now that archaic feelings of guilt became accessible to therapeutic work: in one session, he discovered the fantasy in being unable to leave his wife since he was somehow convinced that, by doing so, he would destroy her. The analyst offered him an explanation based on developmental psychology:

"If parents are not in a position to calm a crying baby, the baby then becomes subject to a condition of acute desperation. Psychoanalysts assume that this can stimulate early fantasies, which contain within them untamable destructive impulses, since the extremely aggressive fantasies that a child perceives in such a situation of desperation cannot be caught and thereby alleviated by the parents. The child then experiences his parents as powerless and impotent (indeed, in much the same way you experience me in relation to your depression).

A further consequence is that the aggressive-destructive fantasies remain excluded by other psychological developments. They then occasionally appear in such unreal convictions as those you have just mentioned."

In the next session, Mr W reported the following dream:

> I dreamt that, full of anxiety, I was suspended over a deep chasm. Two women are above me; they do not come to my assistance, but instead proceed to cast a white ribbon across the chasm in a strange way. Clasping the ribbon, they then attempt to cross to the other side of the chasm. I cannot help being astonished about this stupid idea, and then witness how they really do fall into the chasm … I wake up in a state of utter panic.

A: You often complain of the "stupidity" of your wife—and the previous session focused on your sometimes having the impression that I am too limited and unhelpful to build a bridge across the chasm of depression. Do you think this was to some extent taken over into the dream? The women were unable to help you out of your life-threatening situation, but then also finally plummeted to their own deaths due to their own idiocy.

Technically, it is not easy to express the fact that these catastrophic dream images probably encapsulate his enormous rage towards women. Often humour proves helpful in such contexts. When, after the above-mentioned session, Mr W by chance discovered that I had a technical problem with my car, I then intuitively said, "Yes, perhaps I really am a stupid woman." Mr W responded with an outburst of laughter at this remark, most probably an indication that I had just hit the nail on the head.

The subsequent months centred over and again on his wrath towards women. Working through the unconscious fantasies and conflicts connected with this led to further transformations: the slack attitude improved substantially, such that the patient then dared to reduce his medication (dosage of Lyrica). He rediscovered an increased sense of joy in life, and developed more creativity in his work. Despite massive anxieties about failure, he took on an important private work contract, which, in his financial situation, was a ray of light, and which offered important narcissistic fulfilment.

"Taking the 'black dog' out on a lead"[15]

Over the following months, his struggles in dealing with his panic-driven anxieties of abandonment, and with not allowing the self to be passively inundated with this, increased. Occasionally, he succeeded in putting a leash on the "black dog", as he would refer to it. The content of his manifest dreams also visibly changed: the dream self became more active, and less susceptible to passive catastrophes and mortal dangers, but was often aggressive and involved in conflicts important for survival. We understand the following dream to be a key dream for this inner transformation:

> I am in the car with my father, but am barely able to control the vehicle. It drives faster and faster. Suddenly, a high tower stands in the middle of the road. The car drives wildly up the wall of the tower and down the other side again. Although I am terribly anxious, nothing happens to us. We are able to continue driving. We then notice how another man likewise races up the tower and, similarly, slumps down the other side again. Nothing happens to him, either … We follow this man and then get out. He then transforms into a man with a slippery surface, like Delta in Star Trek: Enterprise. I do not know whether he is man or robot. He had a black dog. It becomes bigger and bigger, rests its paws on my shoulders. I begin panicking; the dog could bite through my throat. And then I suddenly see that the dog has the face of a woman which also appears to be frightened. I then say to it that it is not as dangerous as I had thought and compliment it, which it clearly finds pleasing.

The associations to the dream lead to several references which Mr W takes up and pursues in the subsequent sessions: for example, in the identification with the father, the attempt to regain a piece of his masculine phallicism (dream pictures with the tower), the experience of dissociation and of not being quite anchored in this world (the robot man in the dream), his existential anxiety when in front of an affectionate object of love (dog-woman), etc. However, above all, it has to do with the active overcoming of his panic and anxiety. In the dream he does not disavow the dangers and the extreme feelings that are consequently released, but instead dares "to look the dog straight in the eye". He discovers the anxiety of the other by way of his own activity, and is no longer flooded by his own panic: namely, while the ego is unable to inhibit the reactivation of death anxiety and panic, it is able to actively counter it somewhat, by looking at it and by understanding. What I found interesting was that Mr W had been processing my own feelings of insufficiency in his dream (dog with woman's face, which is itself in need and is anxious); during this period, I was often gripped by doubt as to whether it really would be possible to modify the depression by means of our psychoanalysis: the "black dog" often assumed a disproportionately large size that it was barely possible to subdue.

To each of us, this dream thus assumes a symbolic function for the presently occurring therapeutic work—an attempt, together, within the psychoanalytic relationship, to look the terror of traumatisation in the eye, to not repudiate its reality, or dismiss it, but rather to psychically accept its existence: to actively counter it with something so as not to be flooded by panic, desperation, and anxiety, and hence to thereby allow oneself to be unconsciously determined by it.

After the reactivation of the trauma could be thematised, above all in outer reality (in relation to his wife, for example), it then become more possible for Mr W to experience and comprehend the traumatic separation anxiety directly in the transference. This was during the third year of psychoanalysis.

The reactivation of the trauma in the transference[16]

Mr W reacted with increasing vehemence to situations of separation from the analyst. During a vacation, he underwent a problematic orthodontic operation, which led to intolerable headaches. He was unfit for work for over two months, and unable to come to the analytic sessions. Finally, I telephoned him. Several crisis interventions then ensued by telephone, which saw him gradually emerging from "the black hole". Evidently, Mr W was acting out his early separation trauma and brought me, as analyst, into the situation of the "rescuing father object" (who took him away from the home). When I referred to this fantasy directly, in the next telephone call Mr W recounted the following dream:

> I am gazing at a group of people all smeared with clay and who are working together on the shell of a house. A cold wind blows—the work is torturous, arduous, and barely tolerable. And yet, in the dream I have the certain sense that the men will succeed: at some

point the house will be built and provide them with a warm home. I then turn to my wife and say: "You see, one can do it—one just has to stay together … ."

The associations led to a fundamental sense that "My house cannot be repaired: it will always remain a draughty, dangerous shell … but, perhaps a spark of hope remains in the dream: I am convinced that the building of the house will finally be completed." We draw a comparison to the way he depicted himself at the beginning: "I am like a fine house, though without a foundation."

Half a year later, just before a one-week vacation, he seemed really confident. And yet, afterwards, he appeared at an analytic session in a state of complete desperation[17]. He was convulsed by sobbing on the couch. "I am completely finished—my overall bodily symptoms are unbearable. I can't take it any more, I cannot live any more." He had overlooked to take his medication one evening, and broke down the next morning. "I noticed just how dependent I still am on medication—without them I am simply unable to live." The analyst also felt distressed, powerless, and helpless, and once again doubted her ability to really help Mr W

A: This relapse was certainly a bitter disappointment to you—and I was once again not available to you. Were you also tortured by thoughts that the psychoanalysis also amounted to nothing?

W: Yes, that's right: everything that we covered here in discussion seemed to me to be so far away, so theoretical …

A: Did you lose the inner connection to me?

W: Yes, I felt utterly alone—I was unable to imagine you any more: you were foreign to me and in some sense entirely unreal …

A: Probably similar to how Little John felt when his parents left him for several weeks in the home.[18]

At this point Mr W wept uninhibitedly and was in great distress throughout the duration of the session … The psychoanalyst also felt herself inundated by powerful emotions and a sense of helplessness and powerlessness.

The next day Mr W came to the session with greater composure.

W: In some way it did me some good to be able to weep here, in spite of the fact that I continue to feel very distressed. In the days before this incident, I felt myself as if in a cage—I felt absolutely nothing, everything was dead within me. At night my body began reacting chaotically—everything was painful and I was unable to sleep at all.

A: (After a pause): We frequently return to the thought that your body remembers the unbearable pains and fear of death, which you had experienced most likely during your stay at the home.

W: I am really unable to say whether this is true … in any case, the pain is utterly intolerable.

After a lengthy pause, during which I sense the analysand's distress and hopelessness, as well as my own perplexity, I then say: "Perhaps it is very important for you to show me here the full extent of your distress and sense of panic. Quite some time ago you said to me that you are convinced that nobody, but nobody at all, is capable of understanding you in your misery, and consequently you feel profoundly alone. You were also unable to really show your distress to your parents after the stay at the home—you simply went silent. As a result, your body was unable to relax; it could not be calmed. You remained alone."

Mr W silently wept for a long time.

During the next session Mr W still seemed distressed and in a state of panic.

W: I really have no idea. Last night I must have briefly dropped off to sleep. I had two dreams which bear no relation to my present state. I first dreamt that a woman fell in love with me. I wondered, and I was unsure about whether or not I felt attracted to her. And yet she said that this was not important and that everything would turn out well …. I then dozed off again and continued to dream. I was seated in a lecture hall. An especially desirable looking woman began caressing my thigh. This I found extremely agreeable. She revealed to me that she was in love with me; that I am so charming and so calm. I was very fond of this woman. However, in the dream I then thought that I ought to tell her that I am not calm, but rather depressive and that she ought to know this.

A: Yes, here you have often mentioned that you no longer wish to act a part—neither in a love relationship nor here during psychoanalysis.

W: Yes, this is true. Do you really think that the dream might contain a spark of hope?" Mr W now remains silent for quite some time and appears relaxed.

Over the following ten days, he appeared visibly relaxed, though to some extent particularly ill at ease. Mr W oscillates between hope and profound desperation also during the sessions.

A: The depressive dog seems to be defending itself against any form of change, attempting to make the spark of hope disappear again.

W: And then the depressive holes and the bodily pain seem to become far more difficult to endure.

After the weekend, Mr W explained that he had had two anxiety dreams, but that he could only recollect one since his wife had woken him up owing to his terribly loud yelling.

W: The dream resembled a horror film. Strangely, I had a brother who mutated into a dangerous and ominous entity that would kill other people. I observed all this aghast, thinking to begin with that since he was my brother I would be spared the same fate. But I then discovered that my execution had, indeed, not been overlooked. I was filled by terrible anxiety, and ran away as fast as possible, finding myself in a square. I then gazed upwards into a building to my mother's window. I yelled and yelled, but she still did not hear me. The dream was interrupted at this point by my wife awaking me.

After a lengthy silence, Mr W made the following associations: "The first thing that occurred to me was the home and the yearning I felt for my mother, who was unable to hear me when I yelled out and felt distraught …. Strange that I had a brother here."

A: Who mutated into a dangerous, ominous entity.

W: And triggered a fear of death.

A: And as you noticed in the case of John, the inner picture of your parents also changed during the stay at the home—they probably became dangerous and threatening; Little John could no longer keep hold of the loving inner image of his parents, which, shattering, now revealed itself as a "murderous", persecuted inner image—a terrifying, life-threatening experience.

W: Yes, and afterwards nothing was what it once was.

A: The trust in your parents was repeatedly broken—although you apparently seemed to be normal again.

W: Though nothing was normal again … like with my body—nothing was right, everything hurt.

In the next session Mr W reported, almost amused, that he had dreamed of his neighbours and a concrete mixer:

"Like me, my neighbour had also been extending his house, and I would often hear the noise of his cement mixer during the summer. I had often had occasion to admire him since he appeared to have an abundance of energy, and that he was somehow successful in his family life. Perhaps I do have a spark of hope after all, and I'll be able to get my cement mixer working again."

This sequence in the psychoanalysis could mark a turning point in the treatment: had Mr W re-experienced his trauma in the transference, and consequently been able to, at least in part, understand and psychically accept it?

In any case, after the Christmas break he returned and in the first session reported that during the separation he had struggled fiercely against the "black dog", and with varying degrees of success. He had had, he found, an astonishing dream:

"I dreamt of a couple—they were most likely not lovers, and yet their relationship was genial. They had a business with flowers in Africa … (it then occurred to me that the day before I had watched a television programme about a couple in Africa who planted and cultivated Christmas stars and had established a successful business from this). I felt particularly attracted towards the two people and their charming manner and asked them fervently to allow me to take a share in their business. They accepted me—and the woman even embraced me. I sold my house and dared to make a new beginning … I was so happy when I awoke that all I wanted to do was to go back to sleep and continue the dream … Perhaps something is changing in me after all."

Discussion

The close connection between early traumatisation and severe, chronic depression became clear in the course of psychoanalysis with Mr W It was especially the separation trauma suffered at the age of four years during his stay at a children´s home and without an empathetic substitute relationship that had, to a large extent, remained unresolved, and which then triggered depressive reactions after the separation from his love persons. These reactions were significantly exacerbated following the separation: the depression became increasingly chronic. It was striking to note during treatment how the traumatic experiences had been retained within the body: decoding these "embodied memories" led to a certain alleviation of the symptoms, through which Mr W was able to actively approach his condition without making them disappear altogether. For quite some time Mr W refused to acknowledge the "historical reality of the trauma" as a part of his own biography: that this exerted a sustained effect on his depression, as well as inducing a fundamental mistrust towards close persons of reference due to the traumatic collapse of his basic trust (*Urvertrauen*) in "good helping, inner objects". Only once this profound mistrust and the unconscious truth, that "nobody, but nobody, can really understand and reach me in my psychic misery and so contribute to alleviating my intolerable condition", had become tangible and to some extent understandable in the transference to the analyst, was the "power of the trauma" relativised and no longer determined present thinking, feeling, and action as a dominating, unconscious belief system. This initially revealed itself in the transformation of the manifest dream content, which, as indicated, constituted keys for successively understanding the unconscious fantasies and conflicts—as reaction to the analytical work.

The transformations in the manifest dream content and their latent (unconscious) dream thoughts were selected as Ariadne's thread for this case report since, in my view (as also in the case of other indicators), they are able to provide clues about whether the work of analytic interpretation was unconsciously understood by the analysand, and experienced as "true". This was illustrated both in the narrative summary of the treatment, as well as by way of the detailed sequences from four consecutive sessions.

As touched upon in the preliminary remarks, with this case report, I sought to formulate a defence for the revaluation of the narrative tradition of psychoanalysis as a unique, valuable form for communicating the results of clinical-psychoanalytic research. With the aid of the *method of psychoanalytical expert validation*, the quality of such narrations can be enhanced, whereby it is possible to systematically encounter the danger of subjective distortion in clinical observations as indicated at the outset. This can be achieved, moreover, without destroying the advantages of the clinical case report (the compression of observations and "truths", the communication of unconscious semantic structures by readable "histories", as well as the proximity to metaphor, literature, and art).

However, in the contemporary age of the internet, the difficulties relating to attitudes to discretion and the protection of privacy—something which has always been connected to comprehensive case summaries—are tending to become greater. As is often the case in the context of the LAC depression study, the analysand is able to sufficiently identify with the analyst's research interests such that through the codified summary of his treatment he has the impression of being valued and taken seriously. Several of the analysands declared themselves prepared to read and comment on the case report. This is a unique opportunity for (externally) validating the "truths" by the analysand himself.

However, owing to ethical and psychoanalytic considerations, it is not always possible to acquire former analysands for this cooperation. In such cases, one might attempt casting the summary of the treatment report in relatively abstract terms and with active codification, and assign greater weight to the depiction of sequences of sessions (cf. the last section of this case report). Often adding additional biographical data which does not distort the "narrative truth" (e.g., number of siblings, similar but not "real" professional positions, etc.) may help to protect the anonymity of the analysand. Naturally, the reader must be adequately informed of this attempt in order to be convinced of the author's wish that, while protecting the intimacy of the psychoanalytic treatment belongs to the specific professional ethics of the analyst, it is also one of the outstanding characteristics of psychoanalysis as a clinical science to convey experience and knowledge to the scientific community, the essential aspects of which "can only be narrated and not measured".

Notes

1. There is an extensive discussion on "narrative", "historical", and "empirical" truth in psychoanalytical literature (see, e.g., Leuzinger-Bohleber, 1989, 2001, 2010; Spence, 1982; Thomä & Kächele, 1987).

2. LAC stands for the short- and long-term results of psychoanalytical as compared to cognitive-behavioural long-term therapy among sufferers of chronic depression: a prospective, multi-centric therapy effectiveness study which is currently being conducted (project directors: M. Leuzinger-Bohleber, M. Beutel, M. Hautzinger, and U. Stuhr), supported by the DGPT, the Heidehofstiftung, the Research Advisory Board of the International Psychoanalytical Association, and Dr M. Von der Tann. See www.sigmund-freud-institut.de

3. Horst Kächele summarises in his contribution in this volume my empirical study investigating the changes of the manifest dreams as well as the psychoanalytic work with dreams in five psychoanalyses comparing the first and the last hundred sessions of the psychoanalyses (see Leuzinger-Bohleber, 1987, 1989). In my chapter I am concentrating on my clinical observations. The changes of the manifest dream contents of Mr W are also investigated by extraclinical research methods. Tamara Fischmann et al., in their chapter in this volume, will report some of the first results of this empirical study.

4. Detailed summaries of sessions from the assessment period, the first, second, and third year of psychoanalysis, also have been presented at the workshop of the Project Group for Clinical Observation in order to illustrate our "Three Level Model" for Clinical Observation (see website of the IPA).

5. The concept of "Embodied memories" takes up Freud's original idea that the trauma is "engraved in the body" but offers a new, interdisciplinary explanation for Freud's clinical observations. The embodiment of psychic processes has been fruitful in many different contemporary scientific disciplines after having been empirically tested in the so-called "embodied cognitive science" (see e.g., Edelman, 1987; Pfeifer & Bongard, 2006; Pfeifer & Leuzinger-Bohleber, 2011). To make a long story short: due to "embodied cognitive science", memory does not result from an activation of "statically stored contents somewhere in the brain" but is the result of sensomotoric coordinations in the here and now of a current interactional situation—memory thus has a dynamic, creative, and "constructive" quality as was illustrated by concrete clinical cases elsewhere (see Leuzinger-Bohleber, 2008; Leuzinger-Bohleber & Pfeifer, 2002; Pfeifer & Leuzinger-Bohleber, 2011).

6. Bleichmar (1996, p. 940 ff.) differentiates between three forms of aggression in depression:

    a. Aggression and deterioration of the internal object: the subject feels as though he destroyed the object. The most speculative theory in this context is Freud's concept of the death drive which is seen to be responsible for the fact that the patient does not return to life after a loss of an object, but remains attracted by death (see also Steiner, 2005, p. 83). Mr W's self-observation of having been depressed ever since he can remember would describe the phenomena Freud has in mind: for years he has been absorbed by suicidal tendencies, the "longing for death".

   b. Aggression directed at the external object: the subject not only displays aggression against the representation of the object, but also acts it out in the external world (destroying friendships, family relations, etc.).

   c. Aggression directed against the self: due to a rigid superego, aggression is turned towards the self (see, e.g., role of masochism in depression or in introjective depression: one of the two basic types of depression described by Sidney Blatt (2004)).

   d. Guilt through introjection of aggression against the object: the self is reproached in the conscious, the object in the unconscious.

   e. Guilt due to the quality of the unconscious wish: guilt may be the product of the existence of certain sexual and hostile desires.

   f. Guilt due to the codification of wishes: the (sadistic) superego codifies the wishes as aggressive and destructive for the object.

   g. Guilt through identification: there is an unconscious belief of a global identity of being bad, of being aggressive, of a self of being harmful.

7. Although it is fascinating to note how new epigenetic research adds a new dimension to this knowledge, the results of the epigenetic studies remain controversial. "In sum, we conclude that the totality of the evidence on G x E is supportive of its reality, though more work is needed to properly understand how 5-HTT allelic variations affect response to stressors and to maltreatment" (Rutter, 2009, p. 1288).

8. Thus I agree with Goldberg's (2009) formulation: "It is time that the dialogue of the deaf between psychiatric geneticists and psychotherapists came to an end: exciting progress has been made in understanding the interaction between our genetic constitution and social environment that either allows genes to manifest themselves in the phenotype, or suppress them altogether" (p. 236). His conclusions, having provided an overview of the contemporary state of research in this field, are highly relevant: "In humans, the effect of maternal care on hippocampal developments have so far been demonstrated (in females, but not in males). The effects of the environment in promoting gene expression appear to be supported by work showing that the extent of abnormalities in a particular gene responsible for the metabolism of an important inhibitory neurotransmitter (serotonin), can be shown to be responsible for the sensitivity of the adult to external stress. This gene is also related to the likelihood

of secure attachment. Thus the abnormalities observed in the rat also appear to apply to the human. Similarly, abnormalities in another gene responsible for the neurotransmitter monoamine oxidase A are associated with the sensitivity of the infant to the harmful effects of physical punishment: with the normal gene, the relationship is fairly weak, though when abnormal antisocial behaviour results …" (pp. 244–245).

9. Following the Hampstead Profile, staged observations and important scenes drawn from the first interview, transference–countertransference reactions as well as the symptoms, the motivation behind treatment, and the socio-economic context examination are presented here. Mr W agreed to publish material from his psychoanalysis. In order to protect confidentiality some biographical and socio-economic data are actively changed, although without destroying the "narrative truth".

10. Robertson and Robertson published films observing children during early separation, e.g., John during a ten day stay in a children's home due to the birth of his sibling.

11. Again following the Hampstead Profile, important information on early object relationships, important biographical events, the socio-economic background on the dynamic structural assessment of the conflict, the developmental level, etc. are summarised in narrative form).

12. In the case study the attempt is made to provide in narrative form a highly plastic impression of the analytic process and the course of treatment, and yet also to depict several clinical key scenes as close as possible to the concrete interaction in the analytic session. In these narrative summaries, the clinicians of the LAC survey select various foci (e.g., handling suicidality of the patients, the role of medication, the "psychic retreat" of the analysands, etc.). They all have been trained by David Taylor applying the "Tavistock Manual for Depression". Here, emphasis is placed on the transformations in the dream content or the acquisition of knowledge by way of the analytical work with dreams in the transference to the analyst.

13. I am a Swiss national!

14. Mr W caught sight of the impressive illustrated book by Matthew Johnstone (2005) entitled *I Had a Black Dog* lying in my office, and purchased a copy. Occasionally, reference is made to the book in the psychoanalysis.

15. As is known, in the specialist psychoanalytic literature of recent years an interesting controversy is taking place on the question as to how the life-threatening truth of the trauma bears in on the analytic process (cf. Bohleber, 2010; Fonagy & Target, 1997; Leuzinger-Bohleber et al., 2010).

16. The specific interactions between analyst and analysand in the following are, in part, recorded verbatim.
17. Mr W has meanwhile watched the CD of John from the above-mentioned Robertson films, which we had discussed in earlier stages of the treatment.

References

Abraham, K. (1911). Notes on the psychoanalytic investigation and treatment of manic-depressive insanity and allied conditions. In: *Selected Papers on Psychoanalysis* (pp. 137–156). New York: Basic, 1953.

Abraham, K. (1924). A short study of the development of the libido, viewed in the light of mental disorders. In: *Selected Papers on Psychoanalysis* (pp. 418–501). New York: Basic, 1953.

Balint, M. (1968). *The Basic Fault. Therapeutic Aspects of Regression*. London: Tavistock/Routledge, 1989.

Baranger, M., Baranger, W. & Mom, J. M. (1988). The infantile psychic trauma from us to Freud: pure trauma, retroactivity and reconstruction. *International Journal of Psychoanalysis*, 69: 113–128.

Bibring, E. (1953). The mechanism of depression. In: P. Greenacre (Ed.), *Affective Disorders. Psychoanalytic Contributions to their Study* (pp. 13–48). New York: International Universities Press.

Bifulco, A. T., Brown, G. W. & Harris, T. O. (1987). Childhood loss of parent, lack of adequate parental care and adult depression: A replication. *Journal of Affective Disorders*, 12: 115–128.

Blatt, S. (2004). *Experiences of Depression. Theoretical, Clinical and Research Perspectives*. Washington, DC: American Psychological Association.

Bleichmar, H. B. (1996). Some subtypes of depression and their implications for psychoanalytic treatment. *International Journal of Psychoanalysis*, 77: 935–961.

Bleichmar, H. (2010). Erneutes Nachdenken über krankhaftes Trauern-multiple Typen und therapeutische Annäherungen. In: M. Leuzinger-Bohleber, K. Röckerath & L. V. Strauss (Eds), *Depression und Neuroplastizität* (pp. 117–137). Frankfurt, Germany: Brandes u. Apsel.

Blum, H. P. (2007). Holocaust trauma reconstructed: Individual, familial, and social trauma. *Psychoanalytic Psychology*, 24: 63–73.

Bohleber, W. (2000). Editorial on trauma. *Psyche—Z Psychoanal*, 54: 795–796.

Bohleber, W. (2005). Zur Psychoanalyse der Depression. *Psyche—Z Psychoanal*, 59: 781–788.

Bohleber, W. (2010). Editorial. *Psyche—Z Psychoanal*, 64: 771–781.

Bokanowski, T. (1996): Freud and Ferenczi: Trauma and transference depression. *International Journal of Psychoanalysis, 77*: 519–536.

Bokanowski, T. (2005). Variations on the concept of traumatism: Traumatism, traumatic, trauma. *International Journal of Psychoanalysis, 86*: 251–265.

Bose, J. (1995). Trauma, depression, and mourning. *Contemporary Psychoanalysis, 31*: 399–407.

Bowlby, J. (1980). *Loss: Sadness and Depression. Attachment and Loss, Vol. 3.* London: Hogarth.

Bremner, J. D. (2002). *Does Stress Damage the Brain? Understanding Trauma-related Disorders from a Mind-body Perspective.* New York: W. W. Norton.

Brown, G. W. & Harris, T. (1978). *Social Origins of Depression.* London: Tavistock.

Caspi, A., Sugden, K., Moffitt, T. E., Taylor, A., Craig, I. W., Harrington, H., McClay, J., Mill, J., Martin, J., Braithwaite, A. & Poulton, R. (2003). Influence of life stress on depression: Moderation by a polymorphism in the 5-HTT gene. *Science, 301*: 386–389.

Denis, P. (1992). Depression and fixations. *International Journal of PsychoAnalysis, 73*: 87–94.

Edelman, G. M. (1987). *Neural Darwinism: the Theory of Neural Group Selection.* New York: Basic.

Ehrenberg, A. (1998). Das erschöpfte Selbst. Depression und Gesellschaft in der Gegenwart. Frankfurt, Germany: Campus, 2004.

Fergusson, D. M. & Woodward, L. J. (2002). Mental health, educational and social role outcomes of adolescents with depression. *Archives of General Psychiatry, 62*: 66–72.

Fonagy, P. (2010). Attachment, trauma and psychoanalysis: Where psychoanalysis meets neuroscience. In: M. Leuzinger-Bohleber, J. Canestri & M. Target (Eds.), *Early Development and its Disturbances. Clinical, Conceptual and Empirical Research on ADHD and other Psychopathologies and its Epistemological Reflections* (pp. 40–62). London: Karnac.

Fonagy, P. & Target, M. (1997). The recovered memory debate. In: J. Sandler & P. Fonagy (Eds.), *Recovered memories from abuse. True or false?* (pp. 183–217). London: Karnac Books.

Freud, A. (1965). *Normality and Pathology in Childhood.* New York: International Universities Press.

Freud, S. (1917). *Mourning and Melancholia. S. E., 14.* London: Hogarth, pp. 243–258.

Freud, S. (1926). *Inhibitions, Symptoms and Anxiety. S. E., 20.* London: Hogarth, pp. 87–174.

Goldberg, D. (2009). The interplay between biological and psychological factors in determining vulnerability to mental disorder. *Psychoanalytic Psychotherapy, 23*: 236–247.

Haynal, A. (1977). Le sens du désespoir. Rapport XXXVIe Congrès de Psychanalystes de Langues Romanes. *Revue Francaise de Psychanalyse, 41*: 5–186.

Haynal, A. (1993). *Psychoanalysis and the Sciences: Epistemology—History.* Berkeley, CA: University of California Press.

Hellman, I. (1978). Simultaneous analysis of parent and child. In: J. Glenn, (Ed.), *Child Analysis and Therapy* (pp. 473–493). Northvale, NJ: Jason Aronson, 1992.

Hill, J. (2009). Developmental perspectives on adult depression. *Psychoanalytic Psychotherapy, 23*: 200–212.

Hill, J., Pickles, A., Burnside, E., Byatt, M., Rollinson, L., Davis, R. & Harvey, K. (2001). Sexual abuse, poor parental care and adult depression: Evidence for different mechanisms. *British Journal of Psychiatry, 179*: 104–109.

Jacobs, K. S. (2009). Major depression: revisiting the concept and diagnosis. *Advances in Psychiatric Treatment, 15*: 279–285.

Jacobson, E. (1971). *Depression. Comparative Studies of Normal, Neurotic and Psychotic Conditions.* New York: International Universities Press.

Johnstone, M. (2005). *Mein schwarzer Hund. Wie ich meine Depression an die Leine legte.* Munich, Germany: Kunstmann, 2008.

Joffe, W. G. & Sandler, J. (1965). Notes on pain, depression and individuation. *Psychoanalytic Study of the Child, 20*: 394–424.

Kendler, K. S., Gatz, M., Gardner, C. O. & Pederson, N. L. (2006). A Swedish national twin study of lifetime major depression. *American Journal of Psychiatry, 163*: 109–114.

Kernberg, O. F. (2000). Mourning and melancholia. Eighty years later. In: J. Sandler, R. Michels & P. Fonagy (Eds.), *Changing Ideas in a Changing World: The Revolution in Psychoanalysis—Essays in Honour of Arnold Cooper* (pp. 95–102). New York: Karnac.

Klein, M. (1935). A contribution to the psychogenesis of manic-depressive states. In: *The Writings of Melanie Klein, Vol. I* (pp. 262–289). London: Hogarth, 1985.

Klein, M. (1940). Mourning and its relation to manic-depressive states. In: *The Writings of Melanie Klein, Vol. I* (pp. 344–369). London: Hogarth, 1985.

Kohut, H. (1971). *The Analysis of the Self.* New York: International Universities Press.

Kohut, H. (1977). *The Restoration of the Self.* New York: International Universities Press.

Leuzinger-Bohleber, M. (1987). *Veränderung kognitiver Prozesse in Psychoanalysen, Band I: eine hypothesengenerierendeEinzelfallstudie*. Ulm: PSZ-Verlag.

Leuzinger-Bohleber, M. (1989). *Veränderung kognitiver Prozesse in Psychoanalysen, Band II: Fünf aggregierte Einzelfallstudien*. Ulm: PSZ-Verlag.

Leuzinger-Bohleber, M. (2001). The "Medea fantasy". An unconscious determinant of psychogenic sterility. *International Journal of Psychoanalysis, 82*: 323–345.

Leuzinger-Bohleber, M. (2007). Forschende Grundhaltung als abgewehrter "common ground" von psychoanalytischen Praktikern und Forschern? *Psyche—Z Psychoanal, 61*: 966–994.

Leuzinger-Bohleber, M. (2008). Biographical truths and their clinical consequences: Understanding "embodied memories" in a third psychoanalysis with a traumatized patient recovered from serve poliomyelitis. *International Journal of Psychoanalysis, 89*: 1165–1187.

Leuzinger-Bohleber, M. (2010). Early affect regulations and its disturbances: Approaching ADHD in a psychoanalysis with a child and an adult. In: M. Leuzinger-Bohleber, J. Canestri & M. Target (Eds.). *Early development and its disturbances: Clinical, conceptual and empirical research on ADHD and other psychopathologies and its epistemological reflections* (pp. 185–206). London: Karnac.

Leuzinger-Bohleber, M. (in press). Preventing depression: Transgenerational trauma—an unexpected clinical observation in extra-clinical studies. Paper given at the Meeting of the Canadian Psychoanalytical Association, June 2, 2010.

Leuzinger-Bohleber, M., Engels, E.-M. & Tsiantis, J. (Eds.) (2008). *The Janus Face of Prenatal Diagnostics. A European Study Bridging Ethics, Psychoanalysis, and Medicine*. London: Karnac.

Leuzinger-Bohleber, M. & Pfeifer, R. (2002). Remembering a depressive primary object? Memory in dialogue between psychoanalysis and cognitive science. *International Journal of Psychoanalysis, 83*: 3–33.

Leuzinger-Bohleber, M., Rüger, B., Stuhr, U., Beutel, M. (2002). *"Forschen und Heilen" in der Psychoanalyse. Ergebnisse und Berichte aus Forschung und Praxis*. Stuttgart: Kohlhammer.

Leuzinger-Bohleber, M., Stuhr, U., Rüger, B. & Beutel, M. (2003). How to study the "quality of psychoanalytic treatments" and their long-term effects on patients' well-being. A representative, multi-perspective follow-up study. *International Journal of Psychoanalysis, 84*: 263–290.

Leuzinger-Bohleber, M., Bahrke, U., Beutel, M., Deserno, H., Edinger, J., Fiedler, G., Haselbacher, A., Hautzinger, M., Kallenbach, L., Keller, W., Negele, A., Pfenning-Meerkötter, N., Prestele, H., Strecker-von Kannen, T., Stuhr, U. & Will, A. (2010). Psychoanalytische und kognitiv-verhaltensthera-peutische Langzeittherapien bei chronischer Depression: Die LAC Depressionsstudie. *Psyche—Z Psychoanal. 64*: 782–832.

Markson, E. (1993). Depression and moral masochism. *International Journal of Psychoanalysis, 74*: 931–940.

McQueen, D. (2009). Depression in adults: Some basic facts. *Psychoanalytic Psychotherapy, 23*: 225–235.

Mills, J. (2004): Structuralization, trauma and attachment. *Psychoanalytic Psychology, 21*: 154–160.

Morrison, H. L. (Ed.) (1983): *Children of Depressed Parents: Risks, Identification and Psychotherapeutic Technique.* Northvale, NJ: Jason Aronson, 1991.

Ogden, T. H. (1982). *Projective Identification and Psychotherapeutic Technique.* Northvale, NJ: Jason Aronson.

Pfeifer, R. & Bongard, J. (2006). *How the body shapes the way we think: A new view of intelligence.* Cambridge, MA: MIT Press.

Pfeifer, R. & Leuzinger-Bohleber, M. (2011). Minding the traumatized body—clinical lessons from embodied intelligence. Unpublished paper given at the Neuropsychoanalysis Congress, "Minding the Body", June 25, (see www.sigmund-freud-institut.de).

Rado, S. (1928). The problem of melancholia. *International Journal of Psychoanalysis, 9*: 420–438.

Rado, S. (1951). Psychodynamic understanding of depression. *Psychosomatic Medicine, 13*: 51–55.

Reerink, G. (2003). Traumatisierte Patienten in der Katamnesestudie der DPV. Beobachtungen und Fragen zur Behandlungstechnik. *Psyche—Z Psychoanal, 57*: 125–140.

Rohde-Dachser, C. (in press). Depression bei Borderlinepatienten. *Psyche—Z Psychoanal, 64*: 862–889.

Rosenfeld, H. (1964). On the psychopathology of narcissism: a clinical approach. In: *Psychotic States. A Psychoanalytic Approach* (pp. 169–179). London: Maresfield Reprints, 1984.

Rutter, M. (2009). Gene-environment interactions. Biologically valid pathway or artefact? *Archives of General Psychiatry, 66*: 1287–1289.

Schulte-Körne, G. & Allgaier, A.-K. (2008). Genetik depressiver Störungen. *Zeitschrift für Kinderund Jugendpsychiatrie und Psychotherapie, 36*: 27–43.

Skalew, B. (2006). Trauma and depression. *International Journal of Psychoanalysis, 87*: 859–861.

Spence, D. (1982). *Narrative Truth and Historical Truth: Meaning and Interpretation in Psychoanalysis.* New York: Harper.

Spitz, R. (1946). Anaclitic depression. *Psychoanalytic Study of the Child, 2*: 313–341.

Steiner, J. (2005). The conflict between mourning and melancholia. *Psychoanalytic Quarterly, 74*: 83–104.

Stone, L. (1986). Psychoanalytic observations on the pathology of depressive illness: selected spheres of ambiguity or disagreement. *Journal of the American Psychoanalytic Association, 34*: 329–362.

Suomi, S. (2010). Trauma and epigenetics. Unpublished paper given at the 11th Joseph Sandler Research Conference: Persisting Shadows of Early and Later Trauma. Frankfurt, Germany, February 7.

Taylor, D. (2010). The Tavistock Depression Manual. *Psyche—Z Psychoanal, 64*: 833–861.

Terr, L. C. (1994). *Unchained Memories: True Stories of Traumatic Memories, Lost and Found.* New York: Basic.

Thomä, H. & Kächele, H. (1987). *Psychoanalytic Practice. Volume 1: Principles.* Berlin: Springer.

Winnicott, D. W. (1965). *The Maturational Processes and the Facilitating Environment.* London: Hogarth and the Institute of Psycho-Analysis.

PART II

EXTRACLINICAL RESEARCH ON DREAMS

CHAPTER FIVE

Dreams as subject of psychoanalytical treatment research

Horst Kächele

An overview of the various functions of dreams distinguishes six (Strunz, 1989):

1. Dream as by-product of the biological phenomenon of sleep
2. Adaptive functions
3. Creative functions
4. Defensive functions
5. "Negative functions", e.g., in the repetition of a trauma in a nightmare, and
6. So-called "demand functions", e.g., dreams during a therapy.

This paper will focus on the last of the six functions and shall—by providing three empirical illustrations—point to the rather meagre attention given to dream reports in treatment research. When we speak about dreams in psychoanalytic therapy, we tend to think of a specific dream; rarely enough is it considered that the repeated communication of dreams belongs to the core features especially of psychoanalytic therapies. How else could one understand that an expert panel of North American psychoanalysts places this feature on the first rank of a list of features that discriminates a "psychoanalytic prototype" from prototypes of other psychotherapies (Ablon & Jones, 2005).

Table 1.   Rank ordering of Q-items by factor scores on ideal psychoanalytical process factor. Eight of the twenty most characteristic items of an
ideal psychoanalytical treatment (Ablon & Jones, 2005).

PQS	Item description	Factor score
90	P's dreams or fantasies are discussed.	1.71
93	A is neutral.	1.57
36	A points out P's use of defensive manoeuvres (e.g., undoing, denial).	1.53
100	A draws connections between the therapeutic relationship and other relationships.	1.47
6	A is sensitive to P's feelings, attuned to P; empathic.	1.46
67	A interprets warded-off or unconscious wishes, feelings, or ideas.	1.43
18	A conveys a sense of non-judgmental acceptance.	1.38
32	P achieves a new understanding or insight.	1.32

From the psychoanalytic literature of the middle of the last century
I want to remind us of two documents that illustrated the usefulness
of the systematic study of complete dream series. The one document is
Alexander Mitscherlich's book on *The Origin of Addiction* (1947) where
the author tried to convey "what the patient was able to communicate
about her unconscious attitude expectation" (Mitscherlich, 1983, p. 285).
From his third case he provided a complete list of all 103 dreams in
the appendix. The other document—also widely forgotten—is Thomas
French's three volume opus *The Integration of Behavior* (1952, 1954, 1958).
As the introduction to the second volume he wrote:

> In this volume we shall try to show that every dream has also a
> logical structure and that the logical structures of different dreams
> of the same person are interrelated, that they are all parts of a single
> intercommunicating system (French, 1954, p. V).

* * *

Let me mention one more example from the beginnings of psychoanalytic dream-related treatment research. The founder of cognitive therapy,

Aaron Beck, at that time still psychoanalytically oriented, reported with his colleague Hurvich (1959) about the psychological correlates of depression. They investigated the frequency of "masochistic" dream contents based on a sample of patients from private practices. Looking back later, Beck motivated his moving away from psychoanalysis with the findings from this study.

* * *

I shall now report on three studies on dreams that I was able to undertake, collaborating with a number of colleagues.

* * *

Study I: patients' dreams and the theory of the therapist
(based on Fischer & Kächele, 2009)

An often repeated opinion within clinical quarters is the critical statement, that patients' dreams correspond to the theory of their therapists. If any, some kind of proof could be based on the famous study by Hall and Domhoff (1968) that compared Freud's and Jung's own dreams with the content-analytic system developed by Hall and van de Castle (1966). My doctoral student Christoph Fischer and I decided to examine this issue (Fischer, 1978; Fischer & Kächele, 2009).

Thirty dreams from each of eight patients—four in Freudian therapy and four in Jungian therapy—were compared both in terms of kinds of content and in terms of changes over time. The patients were matched in diagnosis, age, sex, and social background.

To analyse the dream materials we used the content constellations that Hall and Domhoff had identified as "Freud" and "Jung" syndromes. In the first third of the dream series, Freudian patients dreamt more "Freud-syndrome" dreams, and Jungian patients dreamt more "Jung-syndrome" dreams, producing a significant difference. In the last third of the dream series the difference was no longer statistically significant. These findings support the hypotheses that the theoretical orientation of the therapist exercises an initial influence on the dreams of the patient, and that this influence diminishes as the treatment progresses and the patient becomes more independent of the therapist.

Study II: Relationship patterns in dreams *(based on Albani, Kühnast, Pokorny, Blaser & Kächele, 2001)*

Twenty-two years ago the study group of Lester Luborsky reported that in reported dreams and relationship narratives the most frequent components of the CCRT-method agree, as well in terms of content as in terms of the valence of the reaction components; both in dreams and in the narratives negative reactions prevail. In the view of these authors this confirms that there is a core relationship pattern, which is expressed in dreams in the same way as in relationship episodes (Popp, Luborsky & Crits-Christoph, 1990).

To check this claim we studied the 330-session-long psychoanalytic therapy of the 27-year-old patient Franziska X (see Thomä & Kächele, 1994, chap. 2.2.2), who had received the diagnosis of "anxiety hysteria with obsessional, phobic features".

Franziska X suffered from intense bouts of anxiety attacks that were tied to situations where she had to display her professional competence. Her training as a lawyer had been very successful and she could expect to start a good career if she could get over these anxieties. With her husband, whom she had met during her studies, she enjoyed a satisfying psychological and social relationship in which sexual demands did not play a major role.

Her development was complicated as Franziska X at the age of six had been confronted by the sequelae of her mother's eclampsia in the context of giving birth to a younger sister. Franziska remembers only a mother unable to talk in a clear way. The father had had to take care of the children, but she always was afraid of him.

We were able to analyse one third of all the sessions: there were 113 transcribed sessions spread out evenly across the whole treatment. We identified fifty-seven dreams in which twenty-one relationship episodes were located.

In the dreams we found positive reactions of the subject (SO) above chance, yet in the immediate relationship episodes after a dream, more negative reactions above chance. The same was true also for the reactions of the object (RO), that in the dreams the positive reactions dominate, although this could not be statistically confirmed.

The wishes in dreams and in the narratives are widely congruent; however, anticipated reactions of the object and the subject clearly diverge. In her dreams the patient is connected to friendly objects, and feels respected, which is in clear contrast to the frustrating reaction expressed in her relationship narratives.

Sexual wishes dominate most of the dream episodes and she dreams of the fulfilment of these wishes. In the relationship episodes after a dream, sexual wishes are more infrequent. So this study contradicts the claim by Luborsky's group for this single case. The expectations towards significant others clearly are at variance between dreams and narratives. In her narratives the patient feels rejected.

We also noted that in the majority of the relationship episodes excerpted from dreams or narratives, "men" are the prevailing partner of interactions (e.g., doctors, "boys", music teacher), the analyst most frequently among them. In her dreams the husband does not show up at all. There are few very relationship episodes with the father; the patient talks a lot about him, and clearly the father is an important object but the episodes were often incomplete and thus could not be used in the formal evaluation. It seemed to us that the "object father" was a relevant topic but not the relationship to the father. We found very few relationship episodes about the mother, which demonstrated the psychological absence of the mother figure; only late in the treatment the relationship to the mother became a salient topic; as the treatment was interrupted prematurely due to external circumstances, the study was not able to observe change in this pattern to the mother. Our findings confirm that the salient aspect of dream and dreaming resides in the "modeling of affective-object related references", as Ilka von Zeppelin and Ulrich Moser have pointed out (1987, p. 122).

Summarising the findings of the study we can say that the differences between dream episodes and narratives do not result from different topics. In dream episodes as well as in the first narratives after a dream the topics are congruent, but the organising relationship patterns are quite divergent. These findings do not corroborate the claims by Popp et al. (1990). The core relationship patterns in dreams and narratives do not correspond in this case. In the dreams of the patient positive expectations towards objects and the self prevail. This means that the patient reverses her frustrating experiences in her dreams. In contrast to this in her narratives the patient presents her factual relationship experiences in quite substantial negative qualities.

This signifies that the manifest dream content is therapeutically relevant. It represents her internalised, relationship experience. Therefore a contrast between narratives about daily experiences and dream reports may have a diagnostic and a communicative function, as Mark Kanzer (1955) has already pointed out.

* * *

Study III: Dream series analysis as a measure of process
(based on Kächele & Leuzinger-Bohleber, 2009)

This study in close collaboration with M. Leuzinger-Bohleber explored the issue of how development over the course of treatment can be portrayed by the study of dreams. Particularly for the long-term treatments, what kind of models do we have to map the process? In our work in the long-term processes we have seen different courses for different variables (Kächele & Thomä, 1993); however, we assume that a linear trend model for changes in basic cognitive functioning is the most plausible.

To test this assumption we need data covering the course of the analysis from the beginning to the end phases of a treatment. By using a single case design we might find out which of the descriptors are most likely to follow the linear trend model.

The study uses the instruments developed in an earlier study by Leuzinger-Bohleber (1987, 1989) on cognitive changes, that had examined the beginning and end phases of this treatment.

Now we utilised the total dream materials that we could identify in the transcribed sessions of the psychoanalytic treatment of patient Amalia X (see Thomä & Kächele, 1994, chap. 2.4.2).

At the time when we performed this study we had a large number of transcribed sessions: out of 517 recorded sessions 218 had been transcribed for various studies. In these sessions a student rater (M.E.) identified all dreams. A total of 93 dream reports were identified with some sessions containing multiple dreams; so the total number of dreams used in this replication study was 111.

The reliability study

Three raters—two of them medical students (M. E. and M. B.) and one of them a psychoanalytically experienced clinical psychologist with more than ten years of clinical experience (L. T.)—were intensively trained to understand Clippinger's and Moser's models of cognitive processes.

In several pre-tests they were acquainted with the kind of material to be rated. The training was very time-consuming; the inter-rater reliability achieved was quite impressive: the three raters jointly judged one third of all identified dream reports (38 out of 111 in 93 sessions):

Item B2.1, B2.2, C4:	Kappa 0.82–0.89
Item A1, A2, C1, C3:	Kappa 0.90–1.0
Item A3.1, A3.2, B1, C2:	Kappa 0.47–1.0

It is noteworthy that 84% of all values are beyond a kappa value of 0.7.

Guided by principles of Moser's dream theory and special hypotheses detailed by Leuzinger-Bohleber's study, the investigation focused on the various aspects of dream content which will be commented upon now.

Expressed relationships

A1. How does the dreamer appear in the dream action?
Most frequently during the whole course of the treatment the dreamer is actively involved in the action. This is somewhat surprising since the patient came with a depressive basic mood to analysis.

A2. Do dream partners occur in the dream?
Again the patient is heavily involved with more than one partner all the time. A clinician might "see" in the data a slight increase of dyadic relationship, probably reflecting the patient's gain in intimate relationships, of which one is the relationship with the analyst.

A3.1. What kind of relationship occurs between dreamer and dream partner?
Statistically there are more loving, friendly, respectful relationships and less neutral relationships. We see this as a shift to the development of more pronounced positive qualities in relationships.

To summarise the findings we use a graphical illustration to make our point that the overall impression of these items, along the course of the analysis, allows quite straightforward conclusions. There is less dramatic change and more stability, as the findings from an earlier study, comparing beginning and end sessions only, had suggested (Figure 1):

Dream atmosphere

B1.1. Does the dreamer comment about the atmosphere of her dreams more often?
No obvious change.

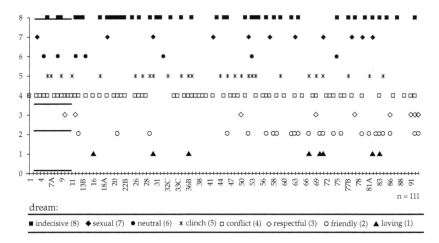

Figure 1. What kind of relations do you find between the dreamer and the dream partner in the manifest dream content?

B1.2. If yes, how does she comment?
The findings are presented as a ratio of neutral:positive in relation to the total amount of sentences where she comments about the atmosphere in the dream in Table 2.

There is a definite increase in the second half of the analysis of neutral:positive comments in regard to the dream atmosphere. From our clinical knowledge we find this is in good correspondence with the development of her personal life.

B2.1. How do you judge the atmosphere of the manifest dream?
By Spearman rank correlations of time and bipolar adjective list we find rather impressive systematic changes in time in some of the bipolar adjectives like pleasurable/non-pleasurable (–0.56), euphoric/depressive (–0.64), harmonic/disharmonic (–0.42), hopeful/resigned (–0.70), happy/sad (–0.58), easy-going/painful (–0.61), peaceful/dangerous (–0,52), happy/desperate (–0.68); all of these correlations are below <0.001 p value.

By Spearman rank correlations we also find rather impressive systematic changes over time in some of the unipolar adjectives such as anxiety ridden (–0.43), neutral (–0.26). However, aggressive atmosphere remained the same, shifting from very low to very high level along the treatment.

Table 2. Atmosphere in the dreams.

Phase/Sessions		Dreams	Sentences with neutral: positive to total	Percentage
I	1–99	1–18	1/11	9%
II	100–199	19–34	3/14	21%
III	200–299	35–54	5/16	31%
IV	300–399	55–70	6/8	75%
V	400–517	71–111	6/10	60%

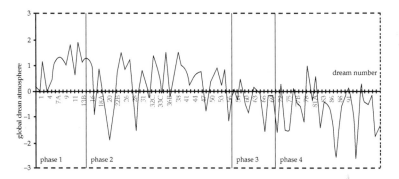

Figure 2. Global dream atmosphere. General factor: negative (high) versus positive (low) emotions.

By factor analytic technique we identified a strong general factor that demonstrated the development of dream atmosphere over the course of treatment from negative to positive (Figure 2).

Keeping in mind the diverse findings on the level of single items, an orthogonal varimax rotation was performed. The outcome of this operation pointed to two components. The factor "negative me" using Dahl's system of classification of emotions (Dahl, Hölzer & Berry, 1992) incorporates the self emotion states and displays a decreasing trend whereas the factor "negative it" assembles the aggressive and anxious states that are object-oriented showing an up-and-down across treatment.

Problem solving

C1. Are there one or more problem solving strategies?
One or two problem solving strategies are equally distributed across the treatment. There is no substantial change.

C2. Is the problem solving successful?
The percentage of successful problem solving strategies is increasing and the unsuccessful strategies are decreasing; furthermore, partially successful solutions tend to be increasing.

C3. What problem solving strategies do you find?
The patient throughout the analysis is actively seeking solutions of problems; there is a slight increase in deferred actions. A clinician might be surprised by this result.

C4. Are the problem solving strategies reflected upon?
There is a powerful increase of the reflection upon these strategies continuously taking place over the course of the analysis. This finding is well presented in a graphical representation (Figure 3). The changes occur in a continuous non-dramatic fashion along the continuum of treatment.

The overall hypothesis of this study focused on the issue of whether the changes can be modelled as linear trends or whether other, non-linear models are necessary. Here the findings are very unequivocal: either we find stationary processes with variations in intensity (such as in aggressive or anxious feelings) or the changes that are patterned along the time axis in a linear fashion incline or decline.

Some surprises in the findings have to do with the patient's particular capacities that she already brought to the treatment. From the start she brought the capacity to actively organise relationship patterns in her

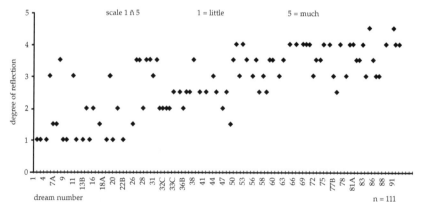

Figure 3. Reflection of problem solving.

dreams; however, change occurred in the quality of these relationships: they became more friendly and caring.

The impressive findings concern the systematic change in dream atmosphere along the time axis: "negative me" emotions decreased, but "negative it" emotions display a stable variability. Another impressive finding is the systematic tendency for the capacity to shift from unsuccessful to successful problem strategies along the analysis.

Our conclusion is that the process of change in this psychoanalysis, in basic psychological capacities—in so far as they are represented by the capacity to organise a dream space, takes place all along the way. If the textual material that dreams are made of is considered a valid extract from the patient's psychic life, then this study has demonstrated the following:

a. Psychic change does occur
b. Psychic change mainly takes place in a linear trend
c. Relationship, atmosphere, and problem solving in dreams are valuable dimensions of capturing a patient's psychic change process.

I have tried to illustrate with three studies that formal research on dream reports can be a useful tool to investigate certain phenomena which usually escape clinicians' attention, their curiosity being more often directed to the single dream which makes clinically perfect sense. The function of formalised treatment research thus occupies a different space from the clinical work and has another task.

References

Ablon, J. S. & Jones, E. E. (2005). On analytic process. *Journal of the American Psychoanaytic Association*, *53*, 541–568.

Albani, C., Kühnast, B., Pokorny, D., Blaser, G. & Kächele, H. (2001). Beziehungsmuster in Träumen und Geschichten über Beziehungen im psychoanalytischen Prozeß. *Forum der Psychoanalyse*, *17*, 287–296.

Beck, A. T. & Hurvich, M. (1959). Psychological correlates of depression. I: Frequency of "masochistic" dream content in a private practice sample. *Psychosomatic Medicine*, *21*, 50–55.

Dahl, H., Hölzer, M. & Berry, J. W. (1992). *How to Classify Emotions for Psychotherapy Research*. Ulm, Germany: Ulmer Textbank.

Fischer, C. (1978). *Der Traum in der Psychotherapie: Ein Vergleich Freud'scher und Jung'scher Patiententräume*. Munich, Germany: Minerva-Publikation.

Fischer, C. & Kächele, H. (2009). Comparative analysis of patients' dreams in Freudian and Jungian treatment. *International Journal of Psychotherapy*, *13*, 34–40.

French, T. M. (1952). *The Integration of Behavior. Volume 1: Basic Postulates.* Chicago, IL: University of Chicago Press.

French, T. M. (1954). *The Integration of Behavior. Volume 2: The Integrative Process in Dreams.* Chicago, IL: University of Chicago Press.

French, T. M. (1958). *The Integration of Behavior. Volume 3: The Reintegrative Process in a Psychoanalytic Treatment.* Chicago, IL: University of Chicago Press.

Hall, C. S. & Domhoff, B. (1968). The dreams of Freud and Jung. *Psychology Today 2*: 42–45, 64–65.

Hall, C. S. & van de Castle, R. L. (1966). *The Content Analysis of Dreams.* New York: Appleton-Century-Crofts.

Kanzer, M. (1955). The communicative function of the dream. *International Journal of Psychoanalysis, 36*, 260–266.

Kächele, H. & Leuzinger-Bohleber, M. (2009). Dream series as process tool. In: H. Kächele, J. Schachter, H. Thomä & The Ulm Psychoanalytic Process Research Study Group (Eds.), *From Psychoanalytic Narrative to Empirical Single Case Research* (pp. 266–278). New York: Routledge.

Kächele, H. & Thomä, H. (1993). Psychoanalytic process research: Methods and achievements. *Journal of the American Psychoanalytic Association, 41*: 109–129 Supplement.

Leuzinger-Bohleber, M. (1989). *Veränderung kognitiver Prozesse in Psychoanalysen. Band 2: Eine Gruppen-statistische Untersuchung.* Berlin: Springer.

Mitscherlich, A. (1947). *Vom Ursprung der Sucht (The Origin of Addiction)* Stuttgart, Germany: Klett. In: A. Mitscherlich (Ed.), *Gesammelte Schriften* (pp. 141–404). Frankfurt, Germany: Suhrkamp, 1983.

Mitscherlich, A. (Ed.) (1983). *Gesammelte Schriften* (pp. 141–404). Frankfurt, Germany: Suhrkamp.

Popp, C., Luborsky, L. & Crits-Christoph, P. (1990). The parallel of the CCRT from therapy narratives with the CCRT from dreams. In: L. Luborsky & P. Crits-Christoph (Eds.), *Understanding Transference* (pp. 158–172). New York: Basic.

Strunz, F. (1989). Funktionen des Traums—Teil 1 und 2. *Psychotherapie, Psychosomatik, Medizinische Psychologie, 39*: 282–293, 356–364.

Thomä, H. & Kächele, H. (1994). *Psychoanalytic Practice, Volume 2: Clinical Studies.* Paperback edition. Northvale, NJ: Jason Aronson.

Von Zeppelin, I. & Moser, U. (1987). Träumen wir Affekte? Teil 1: Affekte und manifester Traum. *Forum der Psychoanalyse, 3*: 143–152.

CHAPTER SIX

The work at the gate—discussion of the papers of Juan Pablo Jimenez and Horst Kächele

Rudi Vermote

Juan Pablo Jimenez's paper is a beautiful illustration of dealing with and thinking about dreams in psychoanalysis. The psychoanalytic research by Horst Kächele shows how the use of a strict methodology and statistical analysis of the data of a long-term analysis can offer new and thought provoking findings, which are not visible from within the sessions.

The common points between both papers are striking. Both papers focus on the manifest dream. In the research of Kächele and colleagues, this is the story of the dream; to Jimenez it is the narration of the dream and the associations that go with it.

Both authors further focus on the divergence between dream content and what happens in life at a conscious level. From this divergence, we might gain the impression that they are two separate worlds. This is challenging because most psychoanalytic models on dreams are based on a link between dreams and actual experiences: the Freudian approach linking dreams to inner conflicts and wish-fulfilment, the Kleinian interpretation linking dreams to the transference-countertransference in the here and now of the session, and the Bionian interpretation where dreams are seen as a processing of thoughts and feelings by the dream work alpha, which comes close to what Mauro Mancia hypothesises from a neuroscientific approach.

Also in clinical practice dream life seems to influence what happens in conscious real life or vice versa, but at times dream life and waking life seem two worlds apart.

Let me give three short clinical vignettes:

- The first is of a patient who was for a long time in analysis and came back because of suffering a severe vital depression with weight loss of more than 10 kg, lack of interest and libido, motor retardation, anxiety, sleep disturbance with early waking, dark thoughts, hopelessness, but no crying. Psychiatric treatments like combinations of antidepressant drugs did not help. At his request I started again with sessions in a psychoanalytic frame, on the couch. The result was peculiar: amid the misery which invaded his body and mind and while remaining as depressive as in the beginning, the patient started to dream about a nice atmosphere, about a place like my office that expanded over different streets; he dreamt of feeling good and even of falling in love. For a long time there was no apparent effect on the severe depressive mood disorder. Two completely different worlds in the same person.
- Another patient, who had not been dating for years, started to have erotic dreams linked to the transference. In her dream life she had new experiences and this was followed by meeting as if by coincidence several men who were attracted to her. It was her dream life that offered her new experiences and preceded what happened in real life.
- Another example of the intriguing relationship between a manifest dream and reality is about a patient who was referred because of a complete anhedonia. He was examined in the somatic department because nothing inspired him: food, love, sex, going out, friends, work. My colleagues from the internal medicine and neurology departments thought that there was something somatic, but could not find anything. Depression was ruled out by a psychiatrist colleague. After offering the patient the psychoanalytic device, he said that for the first time since long before he had a dream. He dreamt that his belly became a field of tulips. The dream was a point of entrance to a psychic emotional world that was out of reach for him till then.

What is this intriguing difference between real life and dream life? I am excited by the paper of Horst Kächele, especially the first study, of a long-term analysis. This study shows no relation in content, nor in CCRT themes—the dream seems to be for a great part an independent creation.

In our approach to this phenomenon we should also focus on the dream function, besides its content. It reminds me of a story about dreams and the unconscious in Matte Blanco's (1988) *Thinking, Feeling and Being*. A man enters a club and walks over the wall, over the ceiling with his head down, again over the wall to the bar and asks the bartender for a glass of milk. The question that is on the analyst's mind is: why a glass of milk?, instead of wondering how it is possible to walk over the ceiling to the bar. This wondrous dream function is probably a pictorial form of thinking, different from conscious thinking. Freud discovered the language of this *Alice in Wonderland* kind of world which is not bound to time and logical links.

In contrast to Freud who saw the dream as protector of sleep, we now agree that we sleep to dream. It is strange that evolution spared so many hours a day to sleep and be in a vulnerable position, what seems at first sight dangerous and inefficient. Something must happen in our brain that is vital and that forms a neuroscientific point of view goes with a de-activation of the prefrontal cortex and an activation of the amygdala. Are the dreams a random side product of this necessary brain activity? Or are they a kind of creative defragmentation and making new links?

Our analytic experience puts us in favour of the last hypothesis, that it is a creative functioning (quoting Borges and Grotstein, (1979): a dreamer who dreams the dream) and that bringing patients into contact with this automatic process within them is often one of the most therapeutic happenings in psychoanalytic work.

It is probably wrong to see this as a primitive function, for the same reason as Damasio showing that there are no primitive emotions in the limbic system and sophisticated thoughts in the neocortex. The contrary is true: the one cannot function without the other.

Here we may come back to Horst Kächele's text. If we hypothesise that dreaming is indeed a creative function that is necessary and probably healing, then we may hope that this creative function does not change during the psychoanalytic process into something integrated, balanced, as was the original hypothesis of the study by

Leuzinger-Bohleber (1987/1989). In this sense it is not unexpected that his research shows that during psychoanalysis the amount of love and conflict (Figure 1) does not change and that the aggressive atmosphere keeps shifting from low to very high. If the dream function is creative it should keep all its forces and negative powers in the way Green (1999) discussed. In this respect I do not understand the linear increase of a problem solving attitude in the dreams in the study. From my experience dreams can offer new approaches to a problem—but this is what is done with a dream when awake. Does Kächele mean that the attitude of the dreamer in the dream becomes more problem solving?

This leads us to the question of which attitude we should take as analysts towards a dream. Both Jimenez and Kächele take an open and creative attitude. Such a creative understanding of dreams is something specific and well described by Bion in his "PS-D, container-contained, selected fact" formula, in other words the tolerating of a not understanding, till a form finds the experience and gives sense to it. Jimenez's handling of Carmen's material is a fine example of it. This creative and intersubjective process adds something new to the manifest dream and is in this sense more than what Freud defined as the latent dream. The question remains, however, whether our task is to understand the content of the dream or to facilitate the dream function? A conquering Oedipus-like attitude versus a Sphinx attitude? And how far can the two be integrated?

Confronted with this question in my clinical practice, I rely on some thoughts of Wilfred Bion (Vermote, in press). Bion asked a patient: "Where were you last night?" Listening to dreams as coming from another country, from a different life that now and then surfaces as the mythical Alpheus. The analyst is at this gate, at this caesura as a kind of watcher (or midwife)—to make contact possible with the life-giving dream function. In other words, the dream may evoke new experiences that can have an influence on life, and vice versa that the dream life is in contact with life and all its unknown aspects. Bion states in a poetic way (I paraphrase) that if we have on the conscious side of the caesura the interpretation of dreams, then on the other and unconscious side we should have an interpretation of reality and its theories in dreams (Bion, 1991, p. 470). In this way of looking at them, dreams are more than just psychic transformations of experiences, thoughts, and feelings that have already happened (what Bion calls "transformation in knowledge"), they are also offering radically new and changing experiences ("ransformations in O") (Bion, 1970).

The text of Juan Pablo Jimenez shows such a radical influence of new experiences in the dream on the life of the patient and how the analyst helped to facilitate this. Jimenez states clearly that it was his impression that what the patient experiences in her analysis is a kind of first experience and this is how I understand the meaning of Bion's T(O).

But the opposite is also true: unexpected experiences reach and stimulate the dream function. They may produce a shift. The complex and creative interplay between analyst and patient treating the dream seems important. Jimenez is careful, but I can imagine that the sixty-nine interpretation was unexpected to the patient and must have resulted in a strong effect. We may also wonder what would have happened had Jimenez taken up the danger, illness, and death that are present in the dream (men in black, ravine, infected penis, fistulae).

In conclusion: what is the best attitude at the gate? Probably the most open attitude. Bion as well, for TK (or change through creative understanding and psychic processing) as much as for T(O) (or new and changing psychic experiences), comes to the same conclusion at the end of his last theoretical book, *Attention and Interpretation*:

> It may, therefore, seem surprising if, at this stage and in relatively few sentences, I describe what is perhaps the most important mechanism employed by the practising psycho-analyst. … Any attempt to cling to what he knows must be resisted for the sake of achieving a state of mind analogous to the paranoid–schizoid position. For this state I have coined the term "patience" …
>
> Patience should be retained without "irritable reaching after fact and reason" until a pattern "evolves". This state is the analogue to what Melanie Klein has called the depressive position. For this state I use the term "security" … I consider the experience of oscillation between "patience" and "security" to be an indication that valuable work is being achieved.
>
> (1970, pp. 123–124)

References

Bion, W. R. (1970). *Attention and Interpretation*. New York: Basic.
Bion, W. R. (1991). *A Memoir of the Future*. London: Karnac.
Green, A. (1999). *The Work of the Negative*. London: Free Association.

Grotstein, J. S. (1979). Who is the dreamer who dreams the dream and who is the dreamer who understands it—a psychoanalytic inquiry into the ultimate nature of being. *Contemporary Psychoanalysis, 15*: 110–169.

Leuzinger-Bohleber, M. (1987/1989). *Veränderung Kognitiver Prozesse in Psychoanalysen*. Ulm, Germany: PSZ.

Matte Blanco, I. (1988). *Thinking, Feeling and Being: Clinical Reflections on the Fundamental Antinomy of Human Beings*. London: Routledge.

Vermote, R. (in press). *Reading Bion: a Chronological Exploration of Bion's Writings*. Forthcoming publication.

PART III

CONCEPTUAL INTEGRATIONS

CHAPTER SEVEN

When theories touch: an attempted integration and reformulation of dream theory

Steven J. Ellman and Lissa Weinstein

Although Freud initially presented a complex model of dreaming, the emphasis of this model was on the wish. The wish, to paraphrase Freud, is the capital needed to fuel the dream, and Freud and those who followed him have focused heavily on the capital in the business of dreaming. Freud maintained that dreams are instigated by unconscious wishes. After making this assertion Freud (1900), in Chapter Seven of *The Interpretation of Dreams*, frequently reminds us of Socrates helping his listeners search for the meaning of the good and the beautiful. The sceptic might ask whether all dreams are instigated by a wish; what about anxiety dreams or dreams that feel horrific and typically are called nightmares? Freud answers these queries and his answers lead him to consider a realm of experience that up to that point in time had been largely unexplored, the earliest and deepest recesses of human experience. He defines an unconscious wish as a pleasure that has its source in early childhood. It is a pleasure that if activated shows the mind in conflict since what is pleasurable at one level (unconscious) will cause anxiety on another level (preconscious-conscious). This conflict is mediated by the censorship (which serves a defensive function) and these two levels of awareness are *primarily* governed by different modes of cognition (primary vs. secondary process).

Freud theorises about how different systems communicate and it is this communication that he labels as transference. It is via the dream that Freud gives theoretical definition to this concept that will gradually change the way he conceptualises the treatment situation. As a last point in this brief summary Freud (1901) attempts to show the similarities between dream formation, symptom formation, and, during the same time period, a variety of other phenomena (momentary forgetting, slips of tongue, etc.). In short, Chapter Seven is unparalleled in psychoanalytic thought in that Freud attempts the most general theory that has been put forth probably up to the present time. Despite this heroic attempt Freud will find various difficulties with his theoretical structure and certainly others will find even greater difficulty.

Related theoretical issues

When Freud wrote the dream book he was just beginning (or about to begin) to develop a drive theory. The first such theory that he formulated contrasted the drive or tendency towards survival of the self with survival of the species. There were a number of contrasting tendencies that emerged from this conceptualisation: ego (self) libido and object (other) libido were translated into issues that involved narcissism and object love. During the period that Freud utilised this drive theory he developed his most sophisticated (or at least most varied) points of fixation (fixation points not restricted to the Oedipal period). This phase (1906–1915) is what Ellman (2009) has called Freud's object-relations era.

Theoretical statement

We are presenting research that has been done in my laboratory from 1970- to the present. In this research we were trying to find the Holy Grail or perhaps more accurately we were trying to operationalise Freud's ideas about dreaming and drive or what we will call endogenous (internally) generated stimulation. Since dreaming is related to rapid eye movement (REM) sleep (at least the most vivid mentation that most people call dreams), it is not surprising that we, along with a variety of analysts, psychologists, and psychiatrists, were intrigued by the discovery of REM sleep. We will only mention three things about REM sleep;

1. The brain is extremely active during REM sleep (as active as in active waking) even though the organism (typically a mammal) is asleep (Ellman, 1992).
2. Dreaming is found in REM sleep. Or more accurately the most vivid sleep mentation is found in REM sleep. Various authors have called other stages mentation dreams, but we will limit the term dreams or dreaming to REM sleep mentation (Ellman & Weinstein, 1991).
3. If one deprives a mammal of REM sleep then there will be increased REM in subsequent sleep periods; this is called REM rebound (Ellman., Spielman, Luck, Steiner & Halperin, 1991).

Following Freud we have assumed that there is at least one (or two, counting the ascending reticular activating system, ARAS) neurophysiological system(s) that provide mammals endogenous stimulation. Freud saw the dream as a type of safety valve; we asked what could that mean in terms of modern psychobiology? The closest we could come to his ideas was to think about the REM sleep state as a type of regulator for what he called drive or cognitively, phantasy. Before we describe the regulation function of REM sleep we should spell out another assumption about REM mechanisms. REM in our view is a manifestation of what Kleitman (1963) called the basic rest activity cycle (BRAC). In Kleitman's view the 24-hour or circadian cycle is a series of alternating states of resting and activity. In our theory REM mechanisms fire periodically to create activity in mammals (and avian predators). This activity is a manifestation of drive or endogenous mechanisms[1] where thresholds for centres that are crucial to the animal's survival are regulated. Thus during this activity phase the animal is primed to perform crucial behaviours involved in the animal's or group's survival (food seeking, courting, nest building, etc.). REM sleep is part of BRAC and is an activity period during sleep. This activation allows for an unbroken period of sleep while also allowing for periodic activation of survival mechanisms in case the animal encounters an emergency (e.g., a predator). REM sleep also changes waking thresholds; if, for example, waking thresholds are high for drive behaviours (as in depression), there will tend to be less REM sleep or less discharge during sleep in an attempt to lower waking thresholds. In this way one can view REM sleep as performing a regulatory function or alternatively one can say that REM sleep is part of the basic rest activity cycle and is affected by waking thresholds and experiences. Implied in these statements is the idea that the same mechanisms that fire during REM sleep are also activated periodically during wakefulness (Ellman & Weinstein, 1991).

In attempting to operationalise Freud, we reasoned that if one had more drive (more discharge or activity) during the day (without introducing an external threat), then there would less of a need for REM sleep. Conversely if one had less REM sleep there would be more drive behaviour or lower thresholds for various drive behaviours during wakefulness. Dement had used a similar logic when he conducted his REM deprivation studies (1960). He assumed that if one eliminated REM sleep then there would be extreme psychological effects on his human subjects. He hypothesised that if REM sleep was eliminated there would be psychotic-like effects during the period of REM deprivation (REMD). We, however, thought that increased drive would not have the type of universal effect on humans that Dement had sought in his experiments. Instead we went to another aspect of Freud's theorising and noted that Freud was attempting to talk about the pleasure-unpleasure sequence in human experience. It was his view that pleasure and unpleasure were basic building blocks of human experience and so we attempted to find a physiological mechanism that corresponded to this Freudian concept.

To look at the physiological correlates of pleasure we studied positive reward systems in a variety of animals. These are sites that Olds first discovered (1956, 1962) when he found that if he delivered electrical stimulation to the hypothalamus, rats would learn a variety of tasks to obtain this stimulation. When the animal works to obtain this stimulation, this behaviour has been labelled intracranial self-stimulation (ICSS). Many areas in the mid-brain have been found to be ICSS or pleasure sites. Our laboratory (Ellman & Steiner, 1971) was the first (or one of the first) to elicit ICSS from the hind-brain or the pons (the area in the pons was the locus coereleus).

An aspect of pleasure pathways is that the determination of pleasure (reinforcement) is dependent on at least three factors: the intensity of the stimulation, the rate of delivery of the stimulation, and the extent that the animal is in control of the stimulation. Steiner et al. (1976)

have shown that stimulation of an ICSS site can produce escape and avoidance behaviour if the stimulation is made intense enough. Thus as intensity increases response rate increases up to a point, and then further increases in intensity lead to response rate decreases. When intensity is high enough stimulation to a positive site turns negative or aversive. One could show similar results varying the rate of stimulation. At some point when rate is increased enough, stimulation to positive sites turns negative. Interestingly, if one allows an animal ICSS at the same time each day, response rates will stabilise. If on one day, at the same time of day, rather than allowing the animal to respond the experimenter gives the animal the same intensity and rate of stimulation that the animal chose the day before, the animal will escape from this stimulation (Steiner et al., 1976). This is at least some evidence that the animal wants to regulate its own rate of stimulation even if the rate it receives was identical to the rate it chose the day before (at the same time of day). The assumption is that in humans the experience of being in control of the pleasure is as important a factor as it is in other mammals. The range of this experience can be huge, given both behavioural and cognitive responses as well as conscious and unconscious fantasies about control.

We posited a strong relationship between the dream and REM sleep and so we wondered if REM sleep might activate ICSS networks. In the strong form of our hypothesis we theorised that REM sleep is an ICSS network. In two related experiments we found that depriving rats of REM sleep was shown to lower their thresholds and raise their response rates for rewarding brain stimulation (ICSS). Conversely, allowing rats to self-stimulate while they were being deprived of this sleep form reduced the amount of REM rebound during recovery from deprivation (Steiner & Ellman, 1972). We concluded that there was a reciprocal relationship between REM and ICSS; if one eliminated REM then there would be more waking ICSS behaviour; if one allowed ICSS during wakefulness then there would be less REM sleep.

We ran a more stringent test in a subsequent experiment where we allowed subjects (Ss) as much ICSS as they desired (bi-lateral ICSS in the locus coereleus).[2] When animals were allowed ICSS they pressed for almost seventeen hours in a row (with time off for rest and NREM sleep but no REM sleep). Over a four-day period animals obtained a great deal of non-REM (NREM) sleep, virtually no REM sleep, and during the four-day recovery period there was no REM rebound. REM sleep was entirely replaced by ICSS from the pons (Spielman & Ellman, 2012). We concluded that REM sleep is an ICSS system. When REM mechanisms are activated ICSS pathways are activated. It is beyond the scope of the present discussion but in a large series of experiments we attempted to delineate these ICSS pathways. We will state three conclusions that we feel are supported by a reasonable amount of evidence:

A. We do not know the precise locus (or loci) of REM sleep.
B. We have demonstrated an ICSS pathway that includes pontine sites and courses through the mid-brain to the cortex. We have strong evidence that this pathway is activated during REM sleep (as shown by our studies and subsequent studies) (Bodnar, Ellman, Coons, Achermann & Steiner, 1979; Bodnar, Steiner, Frutus, Ippolito & Ellman, 1978; Ellman, Achermann, Bodnar, Jackler & Steiner, 1975; Ellman, Achermann, Farber, Mattiace & Steiner, 1974; Farber et al., 1976).
C. We have shown a reciprocal relationship between ICSS and REM sleep and from this we have concluded that they are the same neural system (Steiner & Ellman, 1972; Spielman & Ellman, 2011).

We have accumulated evidence for our theory that REM activates pleasure (ICSS) pathways or neural networks that are intimately tied to basic behavioural functioning. In the rat (to a pick a species with a good deal in common with humans) what we have called basic behaviours might include nest building, food seeking, courting behaviours, and most fundamentally, aggression. Whenever a mammal goes into REM sleep the ICSS or pleasure pathways are activated and in turn are a factor in regulating these behavioural areas. Memories associated with these areas are also stimulated. It is important to remember that in this theory pleasure centres include those areas responsible for aggressive behaviours. All centres where aggression can be elicited are also ICSS sites.

One might ask how this theory can be applied to primates or more specifically to humans. We are assuming that REM mechanisms function in humans as they do in other mammals. In humans frequently the activation of ICSS pathways triggers memory systems that involve conflict, and most typically the dream or the mentation present in REM sleep contains material about issues that are most relevant and/or threatening to the individual at any given point in time. This is not necessarily always true; one might dream about an unconflicted pleasurable situation but in our view for most adults (and most children) the most important situations in their lives involve some conflict. Under optimal circumstances the dream provides some way of resolving the conflict and if this is the case the dream is forgotten. At times intense pleasurable dreams will be remembered (usually by people who are good dream recallers) but this is unusual. Traumatic dreams are ones where the dreamer cannot envision a pain free resolution. The dreamer has a dream where he/she can only envision an outcome that would result in injury or death. Traumatic dreams are ones that are frequently repeated: unfortunately they express a threat of survival that the dreamer feels they cannot avoid. In the chapter authored by Weinstein and Ellman we cover some of the dream research from our laboratory.

We have emphasised the survival nature of dream mentation, but we should point out that, in optimal or good enough development, the first dream is hypothesised to be a memory of a satisfying event. The infant in this state envisions satisfaction of a need state that is important to its survival, and this memory is in turn consolidated. In good enough development the dream state is seen as adaptive rather than regressive. This theory leads to a revision of Freud's concepts of primary and secondary process. In the present theory if development is going well the first images of the infant are adaptive and self-enhancing, thus moving the infant to adaptive attachment behaviours. REM sleep is designed to facilitate a mutually gratifying interplay between infant and mother. However, even if Winnicott is correct in his view of absolute dependence, there will of necessity be conflict early on in the infant's life. No matter how dedicated the parent, optimal gratification will not always take place, and to some extent even the healthiest of infants will experience what Winnicott (1962) called "falling to pieces" or annihilation anxiety. Thus, registration of anxiety producing survival issues will enter the infant's dream world early in life. The issues that are brought up in REM sleep mentation are survival issues that usually (virtually always) involve an element of the body-self represented in the dream. Here by body-self we mean that the infant and developing child usually represents the self in terms of their bodily experiences or bodily functions. Are these survival issues, wishes?

From my perspective sometimes a motivating factor for a dream might be a wish that is seen by the dreamer as important for their well-being; however, a dream could just as easily be motivated by a fear or some anxiety that is not related to a wish (wishes in Freud's sense of the term are however always involved in the conflict). In this theoretical statement the adaptive and survival functions of the dream are the central postulates. It is important to recognise that because there was an attempt at an adaptive solution it is not necessarily the case that the solution continues to prove to be adaptive. It is perceived to be the best solution available to the dreamer at a certain point in their life. Given the repetitive nature of some conflicts the perceived adaptive solution typically comes from a period that is early in the dreamer's life and no longer is adaptive. This view is correlated with a view of mine that in the analytic situation interpretive efforts should include the adaptive aspect of the conflict.

Pleasure and object, not pleasure versus object

Let me stray to issues from my most recent book (Ellman, 2009). How do these views interplay with some psychoanalytic controversies? Fairbairn and Mitchell maintain that humans are object seeking as opposed to pleasure seeking. This in my mind is a false dichotomy; infants are both object and pleasure seeking. In ideal development these things are coordinated so that the main object or mother is also the main pleasure giver. If things are going well the mother also gradually receives a good deal of pleasure from the infant. This reciprocal interaction provides the infant the greatest probability of survival with a sense of security. Here what we mean by security is that the infant's sense of "going on being" is a secure feeling and minimally disturbed during development. This is then the primary thesis, that survival of the self is the main motivational issue; a feeling of security or trust is a key factor in this sense of survival. Obviously an infant can physically survive and still be severely disrupted or traumatised and so when we say survival of the self we are not talking only about physical survival; rather survival with a feeling of intactness and a sense of going on being that is not severely disrupted. In Winnicott's terms the child does often experience falling to pieces or annihilation anxiety (Hurvich, 2003).

Although one might say that the first modes of communication between infant and mother are through pleasure and unpleasure sequences, we would agree with Ellman's reading of Fairbairn and

Mitchell (Ellman, 2009), and Bowlby (1969, 1973, 1980), that the overall function of these modes of communication is to bind the mother–infant pair into a (libidinal) unit … In the present theory this is in order to ensure the survival of the infant. Here then we might say that for the health of the infant, both mother and infant have to eventually be object seeking. This is an aspect of early development that Freud barely mentions and when he does his most important statement is in a long footnote (Freud, 1911). However, if we look at the infant at birth, Fairbairns's dictum that humans are object seeking rather than pleasure seeking seems out of touch with an infant that is mostly sleeping, eating, and needing a variety of biological functions to be monitored. In a sense both object seeking and pleasure seeking seem out of touch with an infant that needs mostly to receive and be held. Although the infant is certainly more active mentally than one might have imagined in 1900, it is still primarily sleeping (ten to seventeen hours a day), eating, and needing to be changed and comforted (held). Winnicott's description of absolute dependence seems to me the most accurate description of the activities between the mother and infant. Winnicott is not merely describing the interaction but also picturing the internal state of the infant. He assumes these internal states need to be anticipated (object presenting) by the mother in such a manner that the infant experiences the environment as providing for it when a need arises or even slightly before a need arises. This is Winnicott's meaning of natural omnipotence; the sense of an infant that its experienced needs (no matter how inchoate the experience) are quickly gratified by the environment. In Winnicott's terms this is good enough mothering. Although we agree with Winnicott that the infant will be well taken care of with what he calls good enough mothering, we believe good enough mothering is hard to do.

Pleasure or object seeking, or a different vehicle

Let us return to a question that we seemingly had answered: is the infant object seeking, pleasure seeking, or both in its first few days of life? We have intimated that the dichotomy is a false one but we have also implied that perhaps neither theoretical postulate talks to the infant's primary needs. As James W. Prescott states (2001), what is crucial in mother–infant contact is "newborn/infant carrying [which] is another 'infra-human primate maternal universal' that has been largely lost to homo sapiens mothers. In [my] view, body movement (vestibular-cerebellar stimulation) is the external umbilical cord—the primary sensory stimulation in utero—that conveys continuing basic trust and security to the newborn/infant" (Prescott, 2001, p. 227). If Prescott is correct then the prime issue for a newborn infant is not pleasure or object seeking but a continuing sense of basic trust and security that makes the new environment more manageable and lessens the probability that birth and its immediate after-effects are traumatic. It seems that a prime way the mother makes contact with the infant is through comfort first of all. This is object seeking by the mother and undoubtedly pleasurable for the infant. If one wants this can be called object or pleasure seeking, but in my view it is primarily security building.

The good enough mother

In the previous summary the amount of REM sleep present in the newborn was not mentioned. Infants at birth may spend ten to twelve hours a day in REM sleep. To the extent that an infant is premature then to that extent the percentage of REM sleep increases. Therefore the mother must be able to recognise that the movements of the infant during REM sleep are not waking behaviours, and at times this is difficult to recognise particularly with infants with large pupils whose eyelids are not completely closed. The recognition of the infant's state is one aspect of good enough mothering.

For good enough (Winnicott's "good enough") mothering to occur the mother must be object seeking. How can we doubt that a mother is object seeking? While in Western societies we assume that the mother will be interested in her infant this is much less certain than most of us believe (Hrdy, 1999). As Winnicott (1962), Searles (1965), and others have pointed out the mother needs a good deal of support and gratification to provide what most infants need for mental and even physical health. The survival of the infant will be greatly increased if there is a good deal of maternal support. The main support for the mother is the environment that surrounds her (husband, mother, wise elder, etc.).

Less obviously, one of these sources may be the infant: if the infant is gradually becoming a pleasure giver to its carer(s) as well as a receiver of pleasure, the probability of its healthy survival is greatly increased.

Thus in the present picture if the infant does not make contact with its mother its survival is in jeopardy. Perhaps one should say that those infants that have a higher probability of surviving in health, find pleasure in object seeking. Clearly the highest probability for infants surviving combines infants and mothers that find pleasure in object seeking and in addition are supported by the environment around them.

The mother–infant dyad and REM sleep

In what follows we are, however, using some of our past experiments as a model for this theoretical exploration. To keep within the paradigm of our past experiments we are using the term stimulation instead of activity or behaviour, therefore there will be stilted sentences in what follows. These sentences will state that the mother stimulates the infant when in fact the mother is playing with, feeding, holding, or changing the infant. In any of these exchanges the mother to a certain extent stimulates the infant and this will be our focus. To begin this discussion we will picture an infant with a high level of endogenous stimulation. The hypothesis is that individuals differ in the amount of endogenous stimulation that they produce.[1] This stimulation is produced every seventy to ninety minutes in human beings (REM periodicity). Since we are imagining an infant with a large amount of endogenous stimulation, for this type of infant a small amount of external or exogenous stimulation will be mildly pleasurable and larger amounts or more intense stimulation will be unpleasurable. The summation of internal and external stimulation in this illustration pushes the infant into the negative or unpleasurable range of experience. Thus what other children experience as a normal amount of pleasurable stimulation may be experienced as unpleasurable for the high endogenous infant. This infant will be like the animal that receives too much stimulation, they will want to escape from the situation that is producing unpleasure or pain for them. Since the normal mother wants to bind with her infant it will be painful for her when her infant responds negatively to a range of her behaviours that she intends as behaviours to entertain or even soothe the infant. It will be the task of this mother to attenuate her responses and try to feel and accept what the infant is experiencing. If she can contain her disappointment and feel the infant's experience, the infant has a greater probability of binding with its mother. It is a difficult task for a mother to be able to feel her infant's painful experiences even though the mother perceives herself to be behaving in a "normal" manner. Of course there may be the ideal mother who does not take it as a narcissistic blow if the infant responds negatively to her seemingly moderate attempts at engagement. Most mothers will want the infant to respond positively to their ministrations and when this does not occur it requires a resilient mother to accept this and learn to titrate (learn to effectively modulate) the level of her activities with the infant. What happens if she feels that she is a failure or feels that there is something wrong with her infant? This may spur her either to provide more stimulation for the infant (to desperately try to attract the infant) or alternatively keep her distance from her child. It can easily be a narcissistic blow (not to mention a depressant) for a mother if a baby fails to respond to what LaPlanche (1997) has called the mother's seductions. This might happen actually or metaphorically. The task of dealing with a high endogenous stimulation infant may be quite difficult for a mother who for one reason or another wants to be active in producing responses in her infant. For a high endogenous infant the adaptive internal response may be to begin to develop false self responses. In other terms the infant learns to respond to a mother who is disappointed and wants the infant to enjoy her active stimulation. False self in this context means that the infant is forced to comply with external demands at a time when it requires effort and requires the infant to inhibit its normal responses. In this description of early development (birth to five weeks) the infant should not be overly concerned with external objects. The beginning of a false self development signals the infant's attempts at limiting its spontaneous actions (gestures). Other infants who are unable to falsely comply may turn away and fail to engage with their environment. A mother who is able to feel the infant's displeasure in active or intense stimulation and is able to modulate her responses may gradually be delightfully surprised by the infant's, or developing toddler's, spontaneous activity. The word toddler is put in here since it may take a period of time for the mother to be able to actively enjoy her child. This type of infant-toddler might then be able to seduce and intrigue its mother. If the mothering is facilitating, this may allow the infant to be in touch with its active internal life and eventually enjoy its sense of self. An infant with a mother who is negatively affected by the infant's sensitivity might lead the infant to try to silence or actively inhibit its internal stimulation or actively evacuate its mind in some manner. Certainly Klein's concept of projective identification is relevant in the way these infants may evacuate their minds.

What about an infant with low levels of endogenous stimulation? Here one sees a child that will be less likely to respond to normal amounts of exogenous stimulation. The exogenous stimulation may not be pleasurable or intense enough to entice the child. This mother may be disappointed because of the lack of response of the infant. The disappointment may be less intense than in the mismatched mother of the high endogenous infant since the low endogenous infant is not turning away or fretting as actively, it is simply not responding with enough pleasure. Again, the ideal mother feels that the baby either needs more stimulation to engage it, or at times the mother deals with her disappointment that the infant is not as reinforcing as she would wish. If the mother cannot contain her disappointment then she may either turn away herself or try to get the infant to act in a manner that is uncomfortable for the infant. She may try too continuously to produce a response in the infant. This type of mismatch also may produce a false self as may be the case with a number of mismatched mother–infant dyads.

Some other theoretical issues

We might ask whether it is useful to conceive of developmental issues in either innate or experiential terms. The way most theories are stated there is a universal tendency that is crucial and other "less important" influences are also included. That human beings are object seeking, not primarily pleasure seeking, is an example of such a statement. The Freudian view of the primacy of instinct is another example. In the present theoretical matrix the major influence differs depending on the individual and the stimulating environment the individual encounters. One infant may primarily be affected by experiential circumstances while another may be primarily affected by innate considerations. Even this statement is misleading since it is not truly an interactive statement. The high or low endogenous stimulation infant may not be affected by innate factors in some environments. A more precise formulation is to state that there is a higher probability for these infants to be affected by innate factors in some societies.

Our prevailing transferences may prevent us from looking at the mother–infant dyad in interactive terms. It is hard to see both sides of the interaction and not focus on the side that our bias moves us towards. That is why in viewing this type of situation statistical findings are best forgotten, and it is useful with dyads as well as individuals to be as without memory and desire as we can be.

An example—Melanie Klein (1975) emphasises the infant's frustration tolerance as important in understanding early development. She writes as if this is a characteristic inherent in the infant as opposed to one that is the result of interactions between mother and infant. In the high endogenous infant more of these infants will display lower frustration tolerance, given that they are more sensitive to a range of stimuli and often harder for mothers to consistently read. However, a mother who can read this type of infant may help develop an infant/child who eventually has greater than normal frustration tolerance. This type of child may experience the mother's mind and caring in a manner that leads to more gratitude than is usually the case. In addition, this type of infant may develop into a person who has access to a greater range of internal states. If one can access and control these states frustration tolerance may develop along wide and deep lines. Thus frustration tolerance, while important, should also be seen as almost always a product of environment-infant interaction. Moreover, high endogenous infants are more likely to look like Kleinian infants than infants in the mid-range of endogenous stimulation.

Winnicott's version of good enough mothering makes it seem as if good enough mothering is a normal state for mothers. While he acknowledges that the mother needs support, nevertheless he writes as if mothering is a state that a woman can easily transition into once the infant is born. Reading Hrdy's book (1999) about mothers, infants, and natural selection, one gets a view of mothering from a number of different perspectives. Hrdy (1999) relates how important it is for the infant to seduce the mother into caring since it is her thesis that motherhood is neither instinctive nor automatic. While puerperal insanity (a term Winnicott uses) may invade some mothers, Hrdy documents higher rates of infanticide and abandonment than would occur if all mothers developed this type of fever. Magurran (2000) in a review states that Hrdy, "goes so far as to suggest that the extraordinary plumpness of newborn humans, much fatter than other infant primates, is an attempt to convince their parents that they are worth rearing. Even an infant's smile becomes, in Hrdy's eyes, part of its strategy to seduce its mother." Even with this seductiveness many mothers have a hard time attaching to their infant: perhaps because some infants are not that seductive, more likely because some mothers are not ready or able to mother at some points in their lives. In terms of the interaction between mother and infant, Hrdy makes it clear that the seduction by the infant is an important part of most interactions. Winnicott, with all his sensitivity, is still writing largely from the baby's perspective. He accentuates the mother's tasks in providing an auxiliary ego for the infant but he has a hard time in remembering how the mother needs to be at least somewhat induced (seduced) to mother the baby. This seduction is particularly important given all that the mother has to provide during what Winnicott describes as the period of absolute dependence.

Summary

We have presented a model of endogenous stimulation that we have posited explains aspects of dreaming as well as aspects of early development. We have tried to present a truly interactive model where neither innate nor environmental factors are seen as supravalent but rather where there are important interactions given the infant's biological tendencies, its environment, and the social environment that surrounds the mother–infant pair. We have tried to untangle what we believe are unfortunate dichotomies in psychoanalytic theorising. We have also tried to untangle well worn phrases that have proved to be obstacles towards developing a more complete psychoanalytic theory.

Notes

1. For an analytic audience we will primarily use the term drive instead of endogenous stimulation.
2. Locus coereleus is an area in the pons that our laboratory discovered to be an ICSS site (Ellman & Steiner, 1971; Ellman, Achermann, Bodnar, Jackler & Steiner, 1975).

References

Bodnar, R., Ellman, S. J., Coons, E. E., Achermann, R. R. & Steiner, S. S. (1979). Differential locus coerulues and hypothalamic self-stimulation interactions. *Physiological Psychology*, 7: 269–277.

Bodnar, R., Steiner, S. S., Frutus, M., Ippolito, P. & Ellman, S. J. (1978). Hypothalamic self-stimulation differs as a function of anodal locus. *Physiological Psychology, 6*: 48–52.

Bowlby, J. (1969). *Attachment and Loss: Vol. 1. Attachment.* New York: Basic.

Bowlby, J. (1973). *Attachment and Loss: Vol. 2. Separation.* New York: Basic.

Bowlby, J. (1980). *Loss: Sadness and Depression.* London: Hogarth.

Dement, W. C. (1960). The effect of dream deprivation. *Science, 131*: 1705–1707.

Ellman, S. (1992). Psychoanalytic theory, dream formation and REM sleep. In: J. Barron, M. Eagle & D. Wolitsky (Eds.), *Interface of Psychoanalysis and Psychology* (pp. 357–374). Washington, DC: American Psychological Association.

Ellman, S. (2009). *When Theories Touch: A Historical and Theoretical Integration of Psychoanalytic Thought.* London: Karnac.

Ellman, S. & Weinstein, L. (1991). REM sleep and dream forma-tion: A theoretical integration. In: *The Mind in Sleep: Psychology and Psychophysiology.* New York: Wiley.

Ellman, S. J., Achermann, R. F., Bodnar, R. J., Jackler, F. & Steiner, S. S. (1975). Comparison of behaviors elicited by electrical brain stimulation in dorsal brain stem and hypothalamus of rats. *Journal of Comparative Physiological Psychology, 88*: 316–328.

Ellman, S. J., Achermann, R. F., Farber, J., Mattiace, L. & Steiner, S. S. (1974). Relationship between dorsal brain stem sleep sites and intracranial self-stimulation. *Physiology and Behavior, 2*(1): 31–34.

Ellman, S., Spielman, A., Luck, D., Steiner, S. & Halperin, R. (1991). REM deprivation: A review. In: S. Ellman & J. Antrobus (Eds.), *The Mind in Sleep: Psychology and Psychophysiology.* New York: Wiley.

Ellman, S. J. & Steiner, S. S. (1971). Relation between REM sleep and intracranial self-stimulation; a reciprocal activating system. *Brain Research, 19*(2): 290–296.

Farber, J., Ellman, S. J., Mattiace, L., Holtzman, A., Ippolito, P., Halperin, R. & Steiner, S. S. (1976). Differential effects of bilateral dorsal hindbrain lesions on hypothalamic self-stimulation in the rat. *Brain Research, 117*: 148–155.

Freud, S. (1900). *The Interpretation of Dreams. S. E., 4–5.* London: Hogarth.

Freud, S. (1911). Formulations on the two principles of mental functioning. *S. E., 12*: 213–226. London: Hogarth.

Freud, S. (1915). Instincts and their vicissitudes. *S. E., 14*: 109–140. London: Hogarth.

Hrdy, S. B. (1999). *A History of Mothers, Infants, and Natural Selection.* New York: Pantheon.

Hurvich, M. (2003). The place of annihilation anxieties in psycho- analytic theory. *Journal of the American Psychoanalytic Association, 51*: 579–616.

Klein, M. (1975). The development of a child. In: *Love, Guilt and Reparation, and Other Works, 1921–1945* (pp. 1–53). New York: Free Press.

Kleitman, N. (1963). *Sleep and Wakefulness* (2nd ed.). Chicago: University of Chicago Press.

Laplanche, J. (1997). The theory of seduction and the problem of the other. *International Journal of Psychoanalysis, 78*: 653–666.

Magurran, A. (2000). *New York Times* on the Web, 23 January, p. 20.

Olds, J. (1956). A preliminary mapping of electrical reinforcing effects in the brain. *Journal of Comparative and Physiological Psychology, 49*: 281–285.

Olds, J. (1962). Hypothalmic substrates of reward. *Physiological Reviews, 42*: 554–604.

Prescott, J. W. (2001). Along the evolutionary biological trail. A review and commentary on *Mother Nature: A History of Mothers, Infants, and Natural Selection* by Sarah Blaffer Hrdy. *Journal of Prenatal and Perinatal Psychology and Health, 15*(3): 225–232.

Searles, H. F. (1965). *Collected Papers on Schizophrenia and Related Subjects.* New York: International Universities Press.

Spielman, A. J. & Ellman, S. J. (2012). The effects of locus coeruleus ICSS on the sleep cycle in rates in preparation. Forthcoming publication.

Steiner, S. S., Achermann, R. F., Bodnar, R. J., Jackler, F., Healey, J. & Ellman, S. J. (1976). Alteration of escape from rewarding brain stimulation after d-amphetamine. *International Journal of Neuroscience, 2*: 273–278.

Steiner, S. S. & Ellman, S. J. (1972). Relation between REM sleep and intracranial self-stimulation. *Science, 172*: 1122–1124.

Winnicott, D. W. (1962). Ego integration in child development. In: *The Maturational Processes and the Facilitating Environment* (pp. 56–63). New York: International Universities Press.

"It's only a dream": physiological and developmental contributions to the feeling of reality

Lissa Weinstein and Steven J. Ellman

In his story, "The Night Face Up", Julio Cortazar describes a young man who finds himself in a hospital after a motorcycle accident. The protagonist's day, ordinary until he is surprised by a careless pedestrian, is transformed as he moves in and out of a dream while he lies in traction. In the dream, he is a Motecan Indian fleeing Aztec hunters trying to capture him for a mass sacrifice. Elements of the hospital are incorporated into the dream as he struggles against a rising fever: the surgeon's knife transformed into the priest's sharp stone, the odours of the operating room now interpreted as the smell of woods, swamp, and death. For most of the story, the protagonist is sure that he is the man injured in the hospital, but at the last minute, as he lies on an altar awaiting the cut of the priest's obsidian knife, "He knew that he was not going to wake up, that he was awake, that the marvelous dream had been the other, absurd as all dreams are—a dream in which he was going through the strange avenues of an astonishing city, with green and red lights that burned without fire or smoke ... In the infinite lie of the dream, they had also picked him up off the ground, someone had approached him also with a knife in his hand, approached him who was lying face up, face up with his eyes closed between the bonfires on the steps" (Cortazar, 1968).

Like Cortazar, Freud (1900) makes the question of the dream's reality central to his exploration as he introduces chapter VII of *The Interpretation of Dreams* with the "Father, don't you see I'm burning?" dream, a dream that in his own words "raises no problem of interpretation and the meaning of which is obvious, but which, as we can see, nevertheless retains the essential characteristics that differentiate dreams so strikingly from waking life and consequently call for explanation (p. 510)". The dream serves as his point of departure into an examination of the "structure of the apparatus of the mind" and "the play of forces operating in it" (p. 511), leaving behind the complex grammar and syntax of dreams to develop a more abstract model seeking to explain "... the most striking psychological characteristic of the process of dreaming: a thought, and as a rule a thought of something that is wished, is objectified in the dream, is represented as a scene, or as it seems to us, is experienced (p. 534)".

In this paper, we present the results of our own research on the vicissitudes of the reflective self representation in dreams, that is, the awareness of oneself as the thinker or dreamer, in order to flesh out (so to speak) the relationship between REM sleep physiology, endogenous stimulation, and conscious experience. In doing so, we will try to present evidence for a model of the development of self reflection that takes into account the bidirectional relationship of the physiological patterning of REM sleep and maternal sensitivity within the development of the attachment relationship, and touch briefly on the multiple forces that contribute to the nightmare in the context of the analytic situation, itself conceptualised as a variant of the dream (Ferro, 2002). Current theories of dreaming will be briefly reviewed in order to place our interest in self representation within the historical context of sleep research (see Nir & Tononi, 2010 for a more extensive review).

To return momentarily to Freud's quote, two questions are conflated: first, what is the nature of the internal stimulation that gives rise to this phenomenological experience of reality; how is it generated and modulated? And second, how does meaning come to be attached to these scenes that connects to the waking personality? Although Freud was careful to note that his model spoke only of psychical and not physical locality that could be tied to any "anatomical preparation", as Pribram and Gill (1976) and Schore (1997) among others observe, Freud's model in chapter VII can only be understood in conjunction with his then unpublished neurological treatise, "The Project for a

Scientific Psychology". Current sleep researchers continue to struggle with the same dichotomy that Freud's formulation alludes to, and in fact, the field has become increasingly bifurcated, much in the same way that controversies over the relevance of neurophysiology have divided the analytic world, with Green (Green & Stern, 2000) and more recently Blass and Carmelli (2007) arguing that the "objective" data of neurobiology have little to offer the clinical analytic process, which has its own methodology for the collection of information about the functioning of the mind.

On one hand, there is a burgeoning literature on the physiology, neuroanatomy, and neurobiology of sleep, "bottom up" theories that ignore the complex symbolic processes in dreams, and making a distinction between the formal properties of dreams (their hallucinatory perceptions, delusional beliefs, bizarre cognition, memory loss, and confabulation) and the meaning of any individual dream content. This is not to say that REM sleep physiology does not have a psychological function in some of these models, such as the consolidation of memory traces in long-term memory or the provision of a virtual reality model as the brain prepares for integrative functions such as learning (Hobson, 2009), but rather that these theorists deny that the particular content of a dream has any adaptive function. Surprisingly, the interrelationship between cognition and physiology in sleep has inspired researchers both in favour of psychoanalysis, for example Solms (1997), who uses evidence of NREM dreaming to support the relative independence of dreaming from any underlying state, and those opposed, for example Crick and Mitchison (1983) or Hobson (1998) and Hobson, Pace-Schott, and Stockgold (2000), for whom the dream is a by-product of the neurophysiological processes in the brain during REM sleep, an attempt at forebrain synthesis of the random limbic activation generated by REM.

Over the last decade neuroimaging of REM sleep has sought to provide an explanation of dream characteristics (Dang-Vu et al., 2010), offering a picture of regional cerebral activity during REM sleep—activation of the pons, the thalamus, temporo-occipital and limbic/paralimbic areas (including the amygdala), along with a relative quiescence of dorsolateral prefrontal and inferior parietal cortices. Thus amygdala activation is seen as consistent with the predominance anxiety and fear in reported dreams. Temporo-occipital activation is in keeping with the prevalence of visual stimuli, and prefrontal deactivation explains the cognitive impairments in dreams—the lack of temporal and spatial orientation, problems with working memory, and the acceptance of bizarre occurrences.

A variety of models have sought to explain the elusive relationship between the physiology of REM sleep and its accompanying mentation, all based on a premise that physiological phenomena could be directly translated into mental events either with a one-to-one correspondence (i.e., Roffwarg, Muzio & Dement, 1966) or that the intensity of psychological activation would be isomorphic with physiological activation at least to the operation of rank ordering, the premise behind Hobson's activation-synthesis hypothesis (Hobson & McCarley, 1977) as well as his later activation-input-modulation (AIM) model. None of these models included an assessment of individual differences in the way that activation was processed or cognised.

An increasingly separate literature, typified by the work of cognitivists, among them Domhoff (2002, 2005a, b), Foulkes (1985), Hall and Van de Castle (1966), and Hartmann (2008, 2010), strive to interpret the dream through the lens of its own symbolic language. They tend to stress the relative ordinariness of many dreams, seeing them as "top down" processes that begin in abstract thought and are processed back into imaginal, perceptual representations, and they explain the seeming bizarreness of dreams through the lens of waking linguistic processes such as metaphor, conceptual blending, and irony. Content analytic studies support the continuity between dreams and waking life, through the kind of interpenetration of themes and images seen in the Cortazar story as well as the same "everyday" problems expressed in both states (Foulkes, 1985), with emotions appropriate to their content (Foulkes, 1999), structured by the feelings and activities of the waking individual (Domhoff, 2002; Hall & Van de Castle, 1966) and manifesting considerable topic consistency over time (Bulkeley & Domhoff, 2010). REM sleep is not taken as a model for dreaming, as similar mentation to REM can be found at sleep onset or occasionally, during NREM sleep. In these models, dreaming is not seen to have any function; borrowing from ideas of Stephen Gould, Flanagan (2000) terms dreams "spandrels", likening them to the mosaic decorations that accompany the arches on fan vaulted ceilings, which in themselves have no structural purpose, but are by-products of another adaptive need and have simply been carried along. Thus, the meaning of the dream is not inherent in its original construction, but is made, like any other fantasy, when integrated with the waking life.

While it seems intuitively obvious that the work of the cognitivists, who share with Freud a "top down" approach to understanding the dream, would be closer to the analytic perspective, in fact this is not the case. The cognitivists emphasise that dreams, while they do express individual ways of abstracting knowledge from experience, do not refer to actual episodes in one's life, nor are they directly related to a memory of previously lived experience, as analysts would claim for the day residue. There is no distinction made between latent and manifest content, no examination of associated mentation, or any discussion of defence or condensation. A typical methodology involves word counts of characters, social interactions, emotions, settings, and descriptive modifiers, providing the advantage of good inter-rater reliability, but rarely touching on the complexity of the way dreams are understood in analysis, both as synthesis of past material and a reflection of current transferential concerns. Here, surprisingly, we find ourselves in agreement with Hobson (2005), who commented that while he did agree with Domhoff's conclusions about the personality of a dream journal's author, he "hardly needed to analyze his dreams to reach that conclusion [that the owner was shy, meticulous, and constricted]", but that he could have ascertained that from the dreamer's introduction to the journal. Instead, as Ellman (2009) has noted, the psychophysiological studies of dreams, at least potentially, provide a bridge between Freud's quantitative notions of drive and the effects of endogenous stimulation on mentation.

The suspension of reflective self representation in dreams

Our choice of which aspect of sleep mentation to study was influenced primarily by psychoanalytic contributions on the nature of dreaming. In addition to Freud (1900), both Rapaport (1951) and Schafer (1968) had focused on the diminished capacity to test reality in dreams, a state comparable in some regards to infancy, when the ability to distinguish what is internally generated from what is external is limited. The development of the ability to make this distinction is tied to the maturation of reflective awareness, the awareness of oneself as the thinker of a thought, which is one aspect, certainly a later stage in the development, of self/object differentiation. During waking, this awareness exists along a continuum—nearly absent in states of sexual pleasure or intense physical exertion and heightened in states of anxiety that generate painful self awareness; the reversible suspension of reflective self representation was thought to be an aspect of what lent intense transference states their mutative power. We reasoned that this awareness ebbs and flows during sleep as well, with the difference that during sleep, due to the relative isolation from external sensory input and motor inhibition, it would vary primarily with the intensity of endogenous stimulation.

REM sleep is a convergence of both tonic processes, that go on continuously throughout the REM period, such as an aroused EEG and suppressed muscle tone, and those that are episodic or phasic, such as eye movements, middle ear muscle contractions, and the hypersuppression of muscle tone. We had postulated that episodes of phasic activity provided the most intense endogenous stimulation. In confirmation of this hypothesis, recent functional magnetic resonance imaging (fMRI) evidence shows phasic and tonic REM periods to have different functional substrates (Wehrle et al., 2007), characterised by an almost complete lack of cortical responsivity to external auditory stimuli during REM phasic, but not REM tonic episodes, leading the authors to postulate a closed loop thalamocortical network including limbic and parahippocampal areas specifically active during phasic REM periods. Another way of stating our hypothesis was that phasic activity would decrease the presence of reflective awareness and increase the likelihood that the dream would be experienced as real and compelling. REM sleep, and particularly phasic episodes within REM sleep were seen as periods of high endogenous stimulation and hence a suspension of reflective awareness would be most likely during REM phasic episodes, less likely during REM tonic episodes, and least likely during NREM sleep.

However, while phasic and tonic processes can be dissociated, there was only equivocal evidence that the mentation from tonic and phasic episodes of REM sleep were qualitatively different. Previous studies had examined such variables as the presence of visual or auditory imagery, bizarreness, emotional quality, or recall. Pivik (1991), in summarising this data, suggested that attempting to match discrete physiological measures with specific aspects of mentation required an impossible degree of introspection from subjects and had reached a point of diminishing returns, but allowed there might still be a qualitative aspect of dream phenomenology which might be a correlate of phasic activity.

Our results, in two carefully controlled studies, provided evidence that the primary psychological correlate of phasic REM activity was the experience of the dream as real, and that as a consequence the dreamer reports mentation in a manner that communicates his or her immersion in the event (Weinstein, Schwartz & Ellman, 1988, 1991). The scales that we had developed to target immersion in the dream experience were more successful at making the discrimination between phasic and tonic activity, than previous scales which tapped into related, partly correlated aspects such as "dreamlikeness" and primary visual experience. In fact, our most sensitive scale involved no conscious reflection on the part of the subject. It did not discriminate REM from NREM sleep, but was the best discriminator of REM phasic versus REM tonic awakenings. Based purely on the spontaneous dream report in response to the question, "What was going through your mind before you were awakened?", the report was scored for the presence of absence of a grammatical form of self reflection, i.e., "I was dreaming that I was driving a car" versus a statement such as "I was driving." Thus, how a concept is measured and the amount of introspection the subject is asked to engage in may alter the results, such that asking the subject to reflect on their experience may lessen their reported experience of involvement (Kahan, 1994).

What we had not predicted was that there would be powerful individual differences. During baseline nights, subjects who tended to respond in a socially desirable manner on a waking self report personality measure, thus making themselves appear more "normal" to an observer, were the least likely to show a differentiation between phasic and tonic REM reports. During the time when we would expect subjects to be most immersed, they paradoxically reported that the dream did not feel at all real. Subjects who were least influenced by demand characteristics were more likely to show a differentiation between phasic and tonic REM reports.

A second study looked at responses to REM deprivation. On recovery nights following REM deprivation, an increase occurs in the absolute amount of phasic activity in REM sleep; hence one would expect subjects to report that they were very immersed in the dream at that time. However, those subjects who did not discriminate phasic from tonic episodes from REM sleep on baseline, had less absorbing mentation from REM phasic episodes during recovery nights. In other words, this subgroup of subjects paradoxically showed an increase in reflective awareness and invoked the disclaimer, "I was only observing; I knew it was just a dream."

For some, but not all subjects, higher levels of endogenous stimulation caused them to defensively (or perhaps adaptively, viewed from another angle) insist that the dream was simply a thought. Schaefer (1968) conceptualised the suspension of reflective awareness as one form of loss of self-object differentiation, which can be pleasurable or, depending on both context and the individual, as frightening. In so far as the dream expresses desires that the dreamer may find disturbing, experiencing the dream as real could be threatening, and the experience had to be warded off by those who were less tolerant of anxiety producing thoughts during waking. Looking at the level of endogenous stimulation in conjunction with defensive style allowed us to make predictions about an individual's dream experience, apart from any specifics of the dream's content.

Recent studies of the experience of the self in different sleep states are not directly comparable to ours, in part because self awareness is a multi-varied concept (reviewed in Kozmova & Wolman, 2006) and the measures used to evaluate self awareness tap into different aspects of that trait. McNamara, McLaren, and Durso (2007) attempted to characterise the representation of the self in REM and NREM dreams, but made no distinctions between phasic and tonic events within REM sleep, did not consider individual differences, and measured the self using self concept related dream content indexes such as bodily misfortunes, dreamer-involved success, and the nature of social interactions which were derived from the Hall/Van de Castle dream content scoring system. Further, they compared REM and NREM dream reports equated for length, lowering any probability of being able to find distinctions between the two sets of reports, as they essentially chose the least "REM-like" REM reports. They did, however, note that the dream self was significantly more often an aggressor in REM sleep as opposed to NREM sleep, a finding which would be in agreement with earlier findings by Pivik (1971) and Watson (1972), who noted that phasic arousals from REM sleep contained significantly more hostility. Occhionero, Natale, Esposito, Bosinelli, and Cicogna (2000) found significant differences between REM and Slow Wave Sleep in self representation, with self hallucinations more often reality-like during REM, and Fosse, Stickgold, and Hobson (2001), using a definition of hallucination similar to the suspension of reflective self representation, found a clear increase in this state from sleep onset through NREM sleep and reaching a peak in REM sleep.

Our results provided clear evidence of the effect of endogenous stimulation on mentation, but in addition, that other factors, such as defence, or the tolerance for an altered state of the self, also determined how the dream would ultimately be experienced and reported. In sum, we reasoned that the tolerance for various kinds of mentation was a function both of the level of endogenous stimulation, which we assumed to be a normally distributed trait among the population, and a person's developmental experiences, which altered the thresholds for what they might experience as pleasurable or unpleasurable.

Although the level of endogenous stimulation in REM sleep continued to have an effect in adulthood, we wondered what developmental experiences might influence the individual differences we found. One obvious candidate would be the attachment relationship, particularly given the large body of research tying attachment to the development of reflective function (Fonagy & Target, 2002).

REM sleep in infancy: endogenous contributions to the organisation of attachment behaviours and the development of the reflective self representation

Based on the selectively activated neuroanatomical structures and neurochemical processes during REM sleep, McNamara and his colleagues (McNamara, Andresen, Clark, Zborowski & Duffy, 2001; McNamara, Belsky & Fearon, 2003; McNamara, Dowdall & Auerbach, 2002; Zborowski & McNamara, 1998) reasoned that REM sleep is necessary to promote and maintain biological attachment processes and aids in the development of reproductive strategies. They noted a partial overlap between the anatomy of attachment and that of REM sleep, following Steklis and Kling's (1985) finding that the limbic system sites, particularly the amygdala, central to the regulation of homeostasis and emotional behaviours, as well as the anterior temporal cortex and the orbital frontal cortex, were critical for attachment, and limbic and cingulated frontal regions also evidenced the high activation during REM sleep. Furthermore, REM sleep was associated with the release of oxytocin, a hormone centrally implicated in attachment (Insel, 1997), with oxytocin peaks occurring at 4 o'clock in the morning when REM sleep starts to predominate over NREM sleep. Attachment (McNamara,

Dowdall & Auerbach, 2002) was actually thought to occur during sleep and nursing periods when the infant elicits nutritional and thermal resources from the mother, and when the entrainment of physiologic and behavioural rhythms through "heat transfer, touch, grooming, suckling in the infant, milk ejection in the mother ... active sleep/REM activation in the infant, arousal overlaps, hormonal rhythm overlaps, temperature cycle entrainment ..." can take place. Additionally, REM sleep was seen to activate behaviour such as cooing, crying, smiling, and sucking that would elicit caring from the mother.

The selective increase in paradoxical sleep after laboratory imprinting sessions (Solodkin, Cardona & Corsi-Cabrera, 1985), as well as the negative effect on sexual function in several mammalian species of early deprivation of REM sleep (Kraemer, 1992; Mirmiran et al., 1983; Kraemer, 1992), further supported the role of REM sleep in attachment. More recent research suggests a bidirectional influence with changes specific to REM sleep in response to stress of both male and female rats which underwent maternal separation (Tiba, Palma, Tufik & Suchecki, 2003; Tiba, Tufik & Suchecki, 2004, 2007), the hypothesised mechanism being that maternal separation induced a hyper-reactive hypothalamic-pituitary adrenal axis which led to a stress reduced impairment in sleep architecture.

Several studies document a relationship between sleep disorders in later childhood and insecure maternal attachment (see Benoit, Zeanah, Bucher & Minde, 1992 for a review of early studies). Later work by Anders (1994), Mahoney (2009), McNamara, Belsky, and Fearon (2003), and Scher (2008), found in a large sample study that insecure resistant attachments had a significantly greater number of night awakenings of longer durations than their insecure avoidant counterparts.

Zyborowski and McNamara (1998) spell out the causal relationships in their model as follows: a biological clock periodically activates REM processes that go on both in sleep and during the day (Kripke & Sonnenschein, 1978); REM then activates limbic and oxytocinergic brain systems that support attachment, which builds both through attunement of the biological rhythms of the two people in the dyad while sleeping and also through dreaming, which supports the internalisation of the mnemonic images of the object which guide waking search strategies. Through this developing entrainment, the mother can regulate the infant's biological processes, while dreaming contributes to the construction of an internal cognitive working model, an adaptive remembering of the complex of events and objects that have been soothing in the past.

This model is in some respects similar to the one we propose, stressing the entry into a symbiotic attachment as a necessary precursor to further individuation processes (Mahler, Pine & Bergmann, 1975), the midwife of which is the mother's synchronous attunement to her infant's communications. However, we were further interested in the mechanisms through which subjectivity and the reflective self developed, particularly in evidence for the endogenous contributions to this bidirectional adaptation, as our adult studies demonstrated that the capacity to retain reflective function varies both with physiological parameters and with individual differences. Let us say at the outset that the developmental studies which would offer definitive proof of the model we are presenting have yet to be undertaken, and the evidence is, at best, correlational, but we present it as it offers a rationale for a clinical stance and supports some of our research on repetition in the analytic situation and its relationship to ruptures in the transference.

Studies of sleep in infancy noted wide individual variations in the early development of the sleep cycle (Burnham, Goodlin-Jones, Gaylor & Anders, (2002)). In addition to the well documented higher percentage of REM sleep in infancy (mean Active Sleep (AS) per cent was 66.2 Standard Deviation of nine), there was considerable inter-individual variability from night to night and at each age when measured at monthly intervals during the first year of life. At one month AS ranged from a low of 41 per cent to 92.5 per cent. By twelve months the mean was 41 per cent with a range of 20 per cent (approximately the adult percentage) to a high of 68.5 per cent. Burnham and colleagues used videosomnography so the architecture and cohesion of REM sleep at the different ages could not be measured. However, earlier studies (Emde & Metcalf, 1968; Roffwarg, Muzio & Dement, 1966) noted the presence of undifferentiated REM states, segments of sleep which are poorly organised during periods when the infant is fussing, crying, drowsy, or sucking, as well as REM when sleeping. Neonatal REM thus showed an initial high variability of physiological patterning (Anders & Weinstein, 1972; Dittrichova, 1966; Emde & Walker, 1976; Hoppenbrouwers, Hodgman, Arakawa, Giedel & Sterman, 1988; Parmelee, Wenner, Akiyama, Schulz & Stern, 1967; Petre-Quadens, 1966), with poorly organised states with mixed features which tended towards stability over the first three months, particularly a marked increase in quiet sleep over the first three months, considered as an important correlate of maturation of forebrain inhibitory centres and a decrease in ambiguous sleep over the first year (Ficca, Fagioli & Salzarulo, 2000). This change is concomitant with the finding that at three months sleep begins with NREM instead of REM sleep. In these studies as well, there were significant individual differences in the decline of indeterminate sleep. Providing further evidence that REM was not a unified state in early infancy, Anders and Roffwarg (1973) found that it was impossible to selectively deprive infants of REM sleep. Roffwarg's thesis was that the high percentage of REM sleep in infancy provided an endogenous source of stimulation which could provide excitation to higher centres, in the absence of exogenous stimulation, and that REM would decrease as the infant became more able to process exogenous stimulation.

Clinical studies of later pathology predicted from neonatal sleep records (Monod, Dreyfus-Brisac, Eliet-Flescher, Pajot & Plassart, 1967) found that the absence of the normal concordance between physiological measures, reflected as an increased proportion of indeterminate sleep, was the most common pathological finding. While the prediction of minor sequelae from EEG records was overall poor, the absence of cyclical activity in EEG patterns and persistent absence of occipital activity were prognostically unfavourable. More recently, Sheldon (2007) and Scher (2008) have reiterated that the clear development of "states" can reflect the functional maturation of the nervous system, with lags in state development potentially evident through both structural and developmental repercussions. At three months, both relational (parental response times to infant awakening) and sleep variables (level of quiet sleep) significantly predicted an infant's ability to self soothe at twelve months (Burnham, Goodlin-Jones, Gaylor & Anders, 2002).

The role of the attachment relationship in patterning the infant's nascent neurobiological organisation has been well documented and shall not be reviewed here (see Fonagy, Gergely, Jurist & Target, 2002; Fonagy, Gergely & Target, 2007; Hofer, 2006; Weinstein, 2007). We would suggest that at certain critical periods in the development of the attachment relationship, physiologic dysregulation enters as an independent variable in the long journey to recognise and represent the contents of one's own mind. The seemingly critical time for the organisation of the REM sleep period at around three months is also a central juncture in terms of the attachment relationship. Fonagy and his colleagues (Fonagy, Gergely, Jurist & Target, 2002; Fonagy, Gergely & Target, 2007;

Fonagy & Luyten, 2009; Gergely & Unoka, 2008) proposed that the infant discovers and becomes able to make second order representations of its own primary procedural affect states through early mirroring transactions with the caregiver that are both contingent (that is, reflective of the child's actual emotional state) and/or marked (that is, slightly exaggerated or transposed to another modality of expression so that the mother shows understanding of the affect while indicating she is not expressing her own feelings). Watson (1994) noted that a maturational switch in normal infants took place at around three months, so that the preferred target in the infant's contingency detection module changed from a formerly preferred perfectly contingent self image to a preference for non-contingency, or more specifically, a high but imperfect contingency. This maturational shift marks the infant's developing ability to turn towards "the exploration and representation of the social world" (Fonagy, Gergely, Jurist & Target, 2002), and away from the endogenous stimulation which occurs as part of REM sleep and which was critical to the development of sensory systems (Graven, 2006). Any dysregulation in the innate contingency detection mechanism that registers both relative intensity and the temporal and spatial relations between the infant's efferent motor responses and the consequent events will hamper the child's ability to differentiate stimulus events that are the outcome of their own motor responses from those that come from others. This basic dysregulation may contribute to a preference for repetitive and perfectly contingent motor activity at a point when normally developing children turn to the less-than-perfect contingencies represented in the social world (Bahrick & Watson, 1985; Gergely & Cibra, 2009), a finding noted in autistic children.

Children with these irregularities might require more exact repetitions in order to establish the critical image of the object, and may find their ability to establish this image more easily impaired, particularly if overstimulated or frightened by the external environment (Gergely, 2001; Gergely & Watson, 1999). We would suggest that the delayed development of clear REM states would interfere with attentional mechanisms that would allow the infant to recognise the "marked" facial expressions that help them ultimately define its own individuality. In addition, the infant's disorganisation might make it more difficult for the caregiver to correctly "read" the infant's state in order to correctly mirror it back to them. While the coalescing of REM processes might only be a delay, it could have longer-lasting consequences in terms of the development of attachment, as Koback, Cassidy, Lyons-Ruth & Ziv (2006) (cited in Fonagy, Gergely & Target, 2007) suggest: changes in attachment organisation decrease over time as mismatches may become harder to correct.

The subtlety of the necessary adjustment was highlighted by a recent study of maternal affective communication in a low risk sample at four months and infant attachment disorganisation at one year (Miller, 2010). The study found the quality of anomalous maternal behaviour at four months that best distinguished organised from disorganised dyads at one year was that mothers of disorganised infants were more apt to become aggressive with their infants and more likely to respond inconsistently to infant distress. However, in the two and a half minute taped interaction, even the mothers of infants that were later classified as disorganised were described as "often pleasant ... with, at times, only brief moments of hostility, aggression or anomalous response to infant distress." Similarly, while these mothers were not judged as disrupted in their overall maternal affective communication, they displayed a marked difficulty tolerating their infant's distress or evidenced at least isolated markers of aggression or other egregious anomalous acts ... including not responding to their infant's neutral/positive cues. One way of explaining these initially puzzling findings is that it is possible that, momentarily, these infants were harder to read.

In sum, we see first that the development of the attachment relationship and its contribution of the reflective self is an interaction of physiological and intersubjective factors, in infancy as well as adulthood. Second, the level of endogenous stimulation will always affect the ability to distinguish self from other, and internal from external.

Conclusion

In this somewhat roundabout exploration, we seem to have travelled far from the dream, so let us return momentarily to the nightmare, most likely autobiographical in nature, that forms the basis of the Cortazar story. It should be obvious that we see the dream, at least partly as a representation of bodily states underlying its construction, and partly as influenced by processes of attachment which modify an individual's set points in their evaluation of affective experience, determining whether an experience is felt to be aversive or pleasurable, mediating anxiety and altering the necessity for the mobilization of defense throughout development. What then happens in the nightmare? If we see the function of REM sleep as supporting attachment, as "calling out" to the object in early development, then as representational structures develop, these processes will inform both the affective tone of the dream and the character/self interactions. Nielsen and Lara-Carrasco (2008) and Hartmann (1996, 1998), among others, have suggested an emotion regulation function for dreaming that is facilitated when an individual's affective concerns are contextualised within a dream by becoming attached to visual imagery which then incorporates new associations, making use of the more flexible memory systems active in REM sleep. Their explanation for nightmares includes a heightened activation of subjective and autonomic correlates of emotion under the control of the amygdala (a state variable), but also the contribution of a trait variable (affect distress) believed to be controlled by the anterior cingulate cortex and shaped by the emotional history of the individual. Thus the nightmare involves both heightened fear, and a failure of the object to regulate that fear. They suggest that this may be represented in the content of the dream in terms of increasingly malevolent character/self interactions. In the Cortazar story, the protagonist's objects are, at first, benevolent, offering something soothing to drink, but as his illness progresses, the nurses begin to make wisecracks, and the surgeon stands over him with something gleaming, and he can no longer reach the soothing bottle of water. Ultimately, the last hope of a frightened child, the mother's soothing statement "It's only a dream," is lost, and he can no longer pull himself out of the horrific experience.

Processes of attachment have been shaped by, and in turn regulate the ways in which endogenous stimulation is experienced, cognised, and symbolised. To return to our earlier summation of the current bifurcation of dream theory, the poles of physiology and meaning, it should be obvious that neither position can, by itself, express the complexity of the dream process. Perhaps this is why Freud gave up the Project, a realisation that while state could be predicted from neuronal firing, the wide variations in symbolic representation would never be tied with precision to physiology.

However, endogenous stimulation remains critical to our understanding of how the transference is experienced. The necessary "reality" of the transference is bound to the accrual of ungratified desires which light our vision of the transference object. Our central metaphors are likewise generated in the cauldron of the body, incorporating traces of the body's demands and rhythms, or what we have variously called drive or endogenous stimulation. Throughout development, experiences of our bodies are woven into ever more complex narratives shaped by the objects that populate our world. We can only attempt to ever more precisely articulate the interacting contributions of body, object, and history to the events in our real and fantasy lives and the dreams we report in the analytic situation.

References

Anders, T. F. (1994). Infant sleep, nighttime relationships, and attachment. *Psychiatry, 57*(1): 11–21.

Anders, T. F. & Roffwarg, H. (1973). The effects of selective interruption and deprivation of sleep in the human newborn. *Developmental Psychobiology, 6*: 77–89.

Anders, T. F. & Weinstein, P. (1972). Sleep and its disorders in infants and children. *Pediatrics, 50*: 312–324.

Bahrick, L. R. & Watson, J. S. (1985). Detection of intermodal proprioceptive-visual contingency as a potential basis of self-perception in infancy. *Developmental Psychology, 21*: 963–973.

Benoit, D., Zeanah, C., Bucher, C. & Minde, K. (1992). Sleep disorders in early childhood: Association with insecure maternal attachment. *Journal of the American Academy of Child and Adolescent Psychiatry, 31*: 86–93.

Blass, R. B. & Carmelli, A. (2007). The case against neuropsychoanalysis: On fallacies underlying psychoanalysis' latest scientific trend and its negative impact on psychoanalytic discourse. *International Journal of Psychoanalysis, 88*: 19–40.

Bulkeley, K. & Domhoff, W. G. (2010). Detecting meaning in dream reports: An extension of a word search approach. *Dreaming, 20*(2): 77–95.

Burnham, M. M., Goodlin-Jones, B. L., Gaylor, E. E. & Anders, T. F. (2002). Nighttime sleep-wake patterns and self soothing from birth to one year of age: a longitudinal intervention study. *Journal of Child Psychology and Psychiatry, 43*: 713–725.

Cortazar, J. (1968). The night face up. *The New Yorker*, April 22, p. 49.

Crick,, C. & Mitchison, G. (1983). The function of dream sleep. *Nature, 304*: 111–114.

Dang-Vu, T., Schabus, M., Desseilles, M., Sterpenich, V., Bonjean, M. & Maquet, P. (2010). Functional neuroimaging insights into the physiology of human sleep. *Sleep: Journal of Sleep and Sleep Disorders Research, 33*(12): 1589–1603.

Dittrichova, J. (1966). Development of sleep in infancy. *Journal of Applied Physiology*, 21: 1243–1246.

Domhoff, G. W. (2002). *The Scientific Study of Dreams: Neural Networks, Cognitive Development, and Content Analysis*. Washington, DC: American Psychological Association.

Domhoff, G. W. (2005a). The content of dreams. Methodologic and theoretical implications. In: M. H. Kryger, T. Roth & W. C. Dement (Eds.), *Principles and Practice of Sleep Medicine (4th ed.)* (pp. 522–534). Philadelphia, PA: Saunders.

Domhoff, G. W. (2005b). Refocusing the neurocognitive approach to dreams: A critique of the Hobson versus Solms debate. *Dreaming*, 15: 3–20.

Ellman, S. J. (2009). *When Theories Touch: a Historical and Theoretical Integration of Psychoanalytic Thought*. London: Karnac.

Ellman, S. J. & Weinstein, L. (1991). REM sleep and dream formation: A theoretical integration. In: *The Mind in Sleep: Psychology and Psychophysiology*. New York: Wiley.

Emde, R. N. & Metcalf, D. R. (1968). Behavioral and EEG correlates of undifferentiated eye movement states in infancy. *Psychophysiology*, 5: 227.

Emde, R. N. & Walker, S. (1976). Longitudinal study of infant sleep: Results of 14 subjects studied at monthly intervals. *Psychophysiology*, 13: 456–461.

Ferro, A. (2002). Some implications of Bion's thought: The waking dream and narrative derivatives. *International Journal of Psychoanalysis*, 83: 597–607.

Ficca, G., Fagioli, I. & Salzarulo, P. (2000). Sleep organization in the first year of life: Developmental trends in the quiet sleep-paradoxical sleep cycle. *Journal of Sleep Research, 9*: 1–4.

Flanagan, O. (2000). *Dreaming Souls: Sleep, Dreams and the Evolution of the Conscious Mind*. New York: Oxford University Press.

Fonagy, P. & Luyten, P. (2009). A developmental, mentalization based approach to the understanding and treatment of borderline personality disorder. *Development and Psychopathology*, 21: 1355–1381.

Fonagy, P. & Target, M. (2002). Early intervention and the development of self regulation. *Psychoanalytic Inquiry, 22*: 307–335.

Fonagy, P., Gergely, G. & Target, M. (2007). The parent infant dyad and the construction of the subjective self. *Journal of Child Psychology and Psychiatry, 48*: 288–328.

Fonagy, P., Gergely, G., Jurist, E. & Target, M. (2002). *Affect Regulation, Mentalization and the Development of Self*. New York: Other.

Fosse, R., Stickgold, R. & Hobson, J. A. (2001). Brain-mind states: Reciprocal variation in thoughts and hallucinations. *Psychological Science, 12*: 30–36.

Foulkes, D. (1985). *Dreaming: A Cognitive-Psychological Analysis.* Hillsdale, NJ: Lawrence Erlbaum.

Foulkes, D. (1999). *Children's Dreaming and the Development of Consciousness.* Cambridge, MA: Harvard University Press.

Freud, S. (1900). *The Interpretation of Dreams. S. E., 4–5.* London: Hogarth.

Gergely, G. (2001). "Nearly, but clearly not, like me": Contingency preference in normal children versus children with autism. *Bulletin of the Menninger Clinic, 65*(3): 411–426.

Gergely, G. & Cibra, G. (2009). Does the mirror neuron system and its impairment explain human imitation and autism? In: J. A. Pineda (Ed.), *The Mirror Neuron Systems: The Role of Mirroring Processes in Social Cognition.* Totowa, NJ: Humana.

Gergely, G. & Unoka, S. (2008). Attachment and mentalization in humans: The development of the affective self. In: E. Jurist, A. Slade & S. Bergner (Eds.), *Mind to Mind: Infant Research, Neuroscience and Psychoanalysis.* New York: Other.

Gergely, G. & Watson, J. (1999). Early social-emotional development: Contingency perception and the social biofeedback model. In: P. Rochat (Ed.), *Early Social Cognition: Understanding Others in the First Months of Life* (pp. 101–137). Hillsdale, NJ: Lawrence Erlbaum.

Graven, S. (2006). Sleep and brain development. *Clinical Perinatology, 33*: 693–706.

Green, A. & Stern, D. (2000). *Clinical and Observational Psychoanalytic Research: Roots of Controversy.* London: Karnac.

Hall, C. S. & Van de Castle, R. L. (1966). *The Content Analysis of Dreams.* New York: Appleton-Century–Crofts.

Hartmann, E. (1996). Outline for a theory on the nature and functions of dreaming. *Dreaming, 6*: 147–170.

Hartmann, E. (1998). *Dreams and Nightmares: The New Theory on the Origin and Meaning of Dreams.* New York: Plenum.

Hartmann, E. (2008). The central image makes "big" dreams big: The central image as the emotional heart of the dream. *Dreaming, 18*: 44–57.

Hartmann, E. (2010). The dream always makes new connections: The dream is a creation, not a replay. *Sleep Medicine Clinics, 5*(2): 1–6.

Hobson, J. A. (1998). The new neuropsychology of sleep: Implications for psychoanalysis. *Neuropsychoanalysis, 1*: 157–183.

Hobson, J. A. (2005). In bed with Marc Solms? What a nightmare! A reply to Domhoff (2005). *Dreaming, 15*(1): 21–29.

Hobson, J. A. (2009). REM sleep and dreaming: Towards a theory of protoconsciousness. *Nature Reviews Neuroscience, 10*: 803–813.

Hobson, J. A. & McCarley, R. (1977). The brain as a dream-state generator. *American Journal of Psychiatry, 134*: 1335–1348.

Hobson, J. A., Pace-Schott, E. F. & Stockgold, R. (2000). Dreaming and the brain. Toward a cognitive neuroscience of conscious states. *Behavioral and Brain Sciences, 23*: 739–842.

Hofer, M. (2006). Psychobiological roots of early attachment. *Current Directions in Psychological Science, 15*(2): 84–88.

Hoppenbrouwers, T., Hodgman, J., Arakawa, K., Giedel, S. A. & Sterman, M. B. (1988). Sleep and waking state in infancy: normative studies. *Sleep, 11*: 387–401.

Insel, T. (1997). A neurobiological basis of social attachment. *American Journal of Psychiatry, 154*: 726–735.

Kahan, T. (1994). Measuring dream self reflectiveness: A comparison of two approaches. *Dreaming, 4*: 177–193.

Koback, R., Cassidy, J., Lyons-Ruth, K. & Ziv, Y. (2006). Attachment, stress and psychopathology: A developmental pathways model. In: D. Cicchetti & D. J. Cohen (Eds.), *Development and Psychopathology (2nd edition), Vol 1. Theory and Method* (pp. 334–369). New York: Wiley.

Kozmova, M. & Wolman, R. (2006). Self-awareness in dreaming. *Dreaming, 13*: 196–214.

Kraemer, G. (1992). A psychobiological theory of attachment. *Behavioral and Brain Sciences, 15*: 493–541.

Kripke, D. F. & Sonnenschein, D. (1978). A biologic rhythm in waking fantasy. In: K. S. Polpe & J. L. Singer (Eds.), *The Stream of Consciousness: Scientific Investigations into the Flow of Human Experiences* (pp. 321–332). New York: Plenum.

Mahler, M., Pine, F. & Bergmann, A. (1975). *The Psychological Birth of the Human Infant: Symbiosis and Individuation.* New York: Basic Books.

Mahoney, S. (2009). Attachment styles, sleep quality and emotional regulation in severely emotionally disturbed youth: A psychobiological perspective. *Dissertation Abstracts Online.*

McNamara, P., Andresen, J., Clark, J., Zborowski, M. & Duffy, D. (2001). Impact of attachment styles on dream recall and dream content: A test of the attachment hypothesis of REM sleep. *Journal of Sleep Research, 10*: 117–127.

McNamara, P., Dowdall, J. & Auerbach, S. (2002). REM sleep, early experience and the development of reproductive strategies. *Human Nature, 13*(4): 405–435.

McNamara, P., Belsky, J. & Fearon, P. (2003). Infant sleep disorders and attachment: Sleep problems in infants with insecure-resistant versus insecure-avoidant attachments to mother. *Sleep and Hypnosis, 5*(1): 17–26.

McNamara, P., McLaren, D. & Durso, K. (2007). Representation of the self in REM and NREM dreams. *Dreaming, 17*: 113–126.

Miller, L. (2010). Personal communication.

Mirmiran, M. (1995). The function of fetal/neonatal Rapid Eye Movement sleep. *Behavioral Brain Research, 69*: 13–22.

Mirmiran, M. & Someren, E. V. (1993). The importance of REM sleep for brain maturation. *Journal of Sleep Research, 2*: 188–192.

Mirmiran, M. J., Scholtens, N. E., van de Poll, H. G., Uylings, S., van der Gugten, J. & Boer, G. J. (1983). Effects of experimental suppression of active REM sleep during early development upon adult brain and behavior in the rat. *Behavioral Brain Research, 69*: 13–22.

Monod, N., Dreyfus-Brisac, C., Eliet-Flescher, J., Pajot, N. & Plassart, E. (1967). Disturbances in the organization of sleep in the human newborn. *Electroencephalography and Clinical Neurophysiology, 23*(3): 285.

Nielsen, T. & Lara-Carrasco, J. (2007). Nightmares, dreaming and emotion regulation: A review. In: D. Barrett & P. McNamara (Eds.), *The New Science of Dreaming: Volume 2. Content, Recall, and Personality Correlates.* Westport, CT: Praeger.

Nir, Y. & Tononi, G. (2010). Dreaming and the brain: from phenomenology to neurophysiology. *Trends in Cognitive Science, 14*(2): 88–100.

Occhionero, M., Natale, V., Esposito, M. J., Bosinelli, M. & Cicogna, P. (2000). The self representation in REM and SWS sleep reports. *Journal of Sleep Research, 9*(s1): 142.

Parmelee, A. & Stern, R. (1972). Development of states in infants. In: E. Clemente, D. Purpura & E. Mayer (Eds.), *Sleep and the Maturing Nervous System.* New York: Academic.

Parmelee, A., Wenner, W., Akiyama, Y., Schultz, M. & Stern, E. (1967). Sleep states in premature infants. *Developmental Medicine and Child Neurology, 9*: 70–77.

Petra-Quadens, O. (1966). Ontogenesis of paradoxical sleep in the newborn. *Journal of Neurological Science, 4*(1): 153–157.

Pivik, R. T. (1971). Mental activity and phasic events during sleep. (Doctoral dissertation, Stanford University. University microfilms No. 71–19746.)

Pivik, R. T. (1991). Tonic states and phasic events in relation to sleep mentation. In: *The Mind in Sleep: Psychology and Psychophysiology.* New York: Wiley.

Pribram, K. & Gill, M. (1976). *Freud's Project Reassessed.* New York: Basic.

Rapaport, D. (1951). States of consciousness: A psychopathological and psychodynamic view. In: M. Gill (Ed.), *The Collected Papers of David Rapaport.* New York: Basic, 1967.

Roffwarg, H., Muzio, J. & Dement, W. C. (1966). The ontogenetic development of the human sleep-dream cycle. *Science, 152*: 604–619.

Schafer, R. (1968). *Aspects of Internalization.* New York: International Universities Press.

Scher, M. (2008). Ontogeny of EEG-sleep from neonatal through infancy periods. *Sleep Medicine, 9*: 625–636.

Schore, A. (1997). A century after Freud's project: Is a rapprochement between psychoanalysis and neurobiology at hand? *Journal of the American Psychoanalytic Association, 45*: 807–840.

Sheldon, S. (2007). Ontogeny in pediatric sleep medicine: A rapidly moving target. *Sleep Medicine, 9*: 597.

Solms, M. (1997). *The Neuropsychology of Dreams: A Clinico-anatomical Study.* Hillsdale, NJ: Lawrence Erlbaum.

Solodkin, M., Cardona, A. & Corsi-Cabrera, M. (1985). Paradoxical sleep augmentation after imprinting in the domestic chick. *Physiology & Behavior, 35*(3): 343–348.

Steklis, H. & Kling, A. (1985). Neurobiology of affiliative behavior in nonhuman primates. In: M. Reite & T. Field (Eds.), *The Psychobiology of Attachment and Separation* (pp. 93–134). New York: Academic.

Tiba, P. A., Tufik, S. & Suchecki, D. (2004). Effects of maternal separation on baseline sleep and cold stress-induced sleep rebound in adult Wistar rats. *Sleep, 27*: 1146–1153.

Tiba, P. A., Tufik, S. & Suchecki. D. (2007). Long lasting alteration in

Tiba, P. A., Palma, S., Tufik, S. & Suchecki, D. (2003). Effects of early handling on basal and stress-induced sleep parameters in rats. *Brain Research, 975*: 158–166.

REM sleep of female rats submitted to long maternal separation. *Physiology and Behavior, 93*(3): 444–452.

Watson, J. S. (1994). Detection of self: The perfect algorithm. In: S. Parker, R. Mitchell & M. Boccia (Eds.), *Self-Awareness in Animals and Humans: Developmental Perspectives.* New York: Cambridge University Press.

Watson, R. K. (1972). Mental correlates of periorbital potentials during REM sleep. (Unpublished doctoral dissertation, University of Chicago.)

Wehrle, R., Kauffman, C., Wetter, T. C., Holsboer, F., Pollmacher, T. & Czisch, M. (2007). Functional microstates within human REM sleep: evidence from fMRI of a thalamocortical network specific for phasic REM periods. *European Journal of Neuroscience, 25*(3): 863–871.

Weinstein, L. (2007). Can sexuality ever reach beyond the pleasure principle? In: D. Diamond, S. Blatt & J. Lichtenberg (Eds.), *Attachment and Sexuality.* New York: Analytic.

Weinstein, L., Schwartz, D. & Ellman, S. (1988). The development of scales to measure the experience of self-participation in sleep. *Sleep, 11*: 437–447.

Weinstein, L., Schwartz, D. & Ellman, S. (1991). Sleep mentation as affected by REM deprivation: A new look. In: *The Mind in Sleep: Psychology and Psychophysiology.* New York: Wiley.

Zborowski, M. & McNamara, P. (1998). The attachment hypothesis of REM sleep. *Psychoanalytic Psychology, 15*: 115–140.

CHAPTER NINE

Discussion of Steven J. Ellman's and Lissa Weinstein's chapters

Peter Fonagy

I am pleased to discuss two superb chapters. Fortunately for me as discussant, both chapters were closely linked in terms of intellectual stance and theoretical framework. They reflect an attempt at integration at a number of levels: (1) the integration of psychoanalytic theory and experimental science; (2) the integration of object relations and drive theories; and (3) the integration of clinical work with complex high level theoretical accounts. Again, fortunately for this discussant, the integration succeeds at all these levels.

At the core of both chapters is the notion of *endogenous stimulation* which is truly a new "drive" theory. Although the theory is not equivalent to any of Freud's views of drives, it explores a number of theoretical oppositions or paradoxes which psychoanalytic theoreticians have learned to embrace over the years. For example, as we shall see, accepting the notion of endogenous stimulations we can no longer debate whether people are pleasure or object seeking. In some ways this is reminiscent of the resolution of the contradictions surrounding the particle and wave theories of light. Understanding the physical, bodily experience that appears to underpin the experience of dreams helps us unpack many complex psychoanalytic ideas.

Chapter Seven

Steven Ellman started this chapter with one of the most eloquent and concise statements of Freud's Chapter Seven in *The Interpretation of Dreams* that I have ever read. I feel like repeating it for the sheer aesthetic pleasure but in the interest of focusing on Steve's original thinking I shall move on. The pithiness of his presentation is a hallmark of his intellectual work over the years. Papers in *Science* and *Nature* are remarkably short. But to get there is, of course, the result of a long and arduous process of work.

So, REM is a marker of endogenous stimulation for which the analogue is ICSS, intracranial self-stimulation, a field of research where Steve's work was absolutely groundbreaking. While rodents doing lever-presses to receive these stimuli is obviously not the biological equivalent of the wish-fulfilment theory of dreams, but the link is far more than metaphoric. In a brilliant demonstration, Dr Ellman and his team showed that REM deprivation made the experience of intracranial self-stimulation more intense, more rewarding for the animal as if they were "hungry" for this kind of stimulation.

Further, a sort of orgy of ICSS, being allowed as much stimulation as they wanted, satiated the animals to the point that even an extensive period of sleep (and therefore REM) deprivation did not cause a REM sleep rebound. Dream sleep then probably involves the activation of ICSS pathways. In other words, REM probably activates pleasure or reward pathways. This is of course more than just offering support for Freud's intuition. It is framing REM sleep as a prototypical experience of generating an internal experience of physical pleasure, not just in sex (in the broadest term) but also aggression (and even destructiveness).

Now, the subsequent chapter linked the pleasure system underpinning REM to Thomas Insel's model of the neural underpinnings of mother–infant and infant–mother attachment. Her contribution covered a considerable amount of evidence pointing to dreaming as, in part at least, an activation of the experience of absolute dependence on the primary object. But developmental time moves on, and the infant dream becomes a vehicle for adaptation to the "good enough" parent who (as Winnicott taught us) cannot and should not deliver optimal gratification. The neurophysiological link between earliest attachment and the dream explains many of its core characteristics including the predominance of bodily experience and sexuality and aggression.

Steven Ellman suggests that "issues that are brought up in REM sleep mentation are survival issues that usually involve an element of the body-self represented in the dream". Human dreams are developmentally early (albeit possibly "time-expired") adaptive solutions to conflicts invariably generated by wishes. This is a profound reformulation of the conflict theory of dreams. The origin of the dream state in the physical dependence of the human newborn means that the struggles depicted in dreams will be, at least in structural terms, life-death issues. They will pertain to the infant's struggles for its own self and its attempt to conquer, in the sense of winning the heart of, the woman he loves.

This immediately catapults us to individual differences. Both low and high levels of endogenous stimulation are maladaptive. Moderate levels represent healthy adaptation. For the infant with high levels of endogenous stimulation a small amount of external stimulation will be pleasurable, excessive stimulation from the mother will cause distress and trigger avoidance. This mirrors the behaviour of animals for whom excessive intracranial stimulation has evidently aversive effects and who, given the choice, would wish to take control over intracranial stimulation, just like humans might.

Human maternal sensitivity is then, according to Ellman, in part a mother being aware of the cyclic nature of her infant's endogenous simulation and conversely his need for exogenous stimulation in order to avoid distress and the need to generate a false pleasing self. For a high endogenous infant the adaptive internal response, as Steve described, may be to respond to the mother who is disappointed at her ministrations not having the desirable effects, by falsely complying with the mother's demands. This has evident clinical implications as to the timing of psychoanalytic interventions, mindful of the basic rest activity cycle (or as it manifests in the clinical setting).

From the Weinstein and Ellman sleep studies we know that the pattern of needing to present a pleasing (false) self, in the sleep laboratory, reflects an underlying need to adopt an artificially distancing defensive stance towards the participant's most immersing dream experiences. The developmental story might trace this back to a situation where the false self develops because the mother's disappointment with herself as mother is experienced as "impinging", leading to an adult experience of endogenous stimulation that is exceptionally intense. And probably because these intense experiences are indeed excessively real, the participant with a tendency to false self denies the reality of the dream in phasic REM.

The theory of endogenous stimulation reveals the dichotomy of pleasure and object seeking to collapse when viewed from the perspective of the newborn who seeks "a continuing sense of basic trust and security that makes the new environment more manageable". The "social orientation of the infant", commonly cited by developmentalists as evidence for the object seeking view of infancy, is seen by both Ellman and Weinstein as the infant's evolutionarily enhanced attempt to ensure maternal care in a state of absolute dependency. This has, as Steve emphasised, considerable benefits for the long-term healthy physical as well as psychological development of the individual.

Steve reminded us of Sarah Hrdy's views of mothering but she also provides dramatic illustrations of the need for human "allo parenting" (allo parenting is the need for more than one adult to be present to ensure "good enough parenting" can take place). Infanticide by mothers only occurs when mothers are unsupported—when the sensible strategy from the point of view of her own survival is to look after herself, kill the child, and have a go later at passing on her genetic material. From an evolutionary standpoint the mother can become "object seeking" (seeking her object the baby) only to the extent that she can afford not to have to seek resources for herself, but this may not take place unless there is a support system for her also present.

But this, in turn, following Steve's thinking, determines the extent to which the infant is object conscious (chooses to be aware of and seek his objects). I find this an illuminating explanation for attachment strategies. When the infant is unaware of another being responding sensitively (contingently) to his actions, he knows he will be forced to look after himself and increases his "threshold" for exogenous stimulus and prioritises endogenous stimulation. Attachment theorists would recognise this as an insecure attachment strategy. It is maintained because when the infant fails to respond, the mother disengages further to limit her disappointment and hurt, pushing the infant back further upon his strategy of self-sufficiency.

It is in relation to individual differences then, that the theory of endogenous stimulation is particularly helpful. A highly original and intriguing implication of their model is a view on the availability of the infant to external stimulation. Infants vary in the probability to which they will be affected by genetic and environmental influences, depending on social context. Infants with high endogenous stimulation may not be so affected by environmental influences as infants who are less extreme in this dimension. Their constitutional traits, unmoderated by their psychosocial environment, will influence who they become. They are not necessarily more clinically vulnerable as a consequence but their problems will be less closely linked to personal history.

This is interesting to link to recent findings concerning the short allele of the 5-HTT serotonin transporter gene. This genotype has been shown to mark individuals who are more "sensitive" to their environments. Sensitive mothering may make these individuals more likely to be securely attached, while those with the alternative polymorphism (the long allele, more efficient transcription) are uninfluenced by the mother's sensitivity in their attachment security. Regardless of the validity of this particular molecular genetic model, the general idea of variation in openness to experience is an important and intriguing challenge to psychoanalytic models. It is also something we do not normally consider.

Yet it is perfectly possible that some of the different psychoanalytic models of development may be rooted in these genetic differences between infants. They may all be accurate descriptions of genetically very different individuals. The high endogenous infants are more like Kleinian infants than infants in the mid-range of endogenous stimulation. Good enough mothering must be looked at from the perspective of evolutionary time and current social contexts, not just the perspective of the baby. I will return to Steven Ellman's contribution but let me briefly consider Lissa Weinstein's work in the next chapter.

Chapter Eight

Lissa Weinstein wonderfully complements Steven Ellman's magisterial overview of the interplay of infant mental function and the mechanisms of dreaming. Lissa's focus was on the emergence of the reflective self from the "dreaming relationship" between infant and mother. She drew attention to the crucial distinction between tonic processes occurring throughout REM (e.g., aroused EEG) and phasic processes (e.g., eye movements). Ellman and Weinstein postulated that phasic REM activity contributed most to endogenous stimulation and was the most potent when it came to decreasing the presence of reflective awareness.

Phasic REM dreams are thus expected to be particularly compelling (e.g., "real"). Using an exceptionally elegant measure, they showed that dream reports where the dream report was *not* phrased using the language of intentionality ("I was driving" vs. "I dreamt *that* I was driving") were most likely to be associated with having been woken from phasic REM activity. By implication then, phasic REM switches off intentionality, as Daniel Dennett (2001) has described this—it reflects a state of consciousness beyond (or prior to) the reflective part of the self.

This was so in most participants, but not all. It was "'paradoxical" in those volunteers who had what seem like "false self structures". Such structures may be markers for a predisposition for endogenous stimulation. These individuals may have had histories of having to present a false placatory presence to a disappointed caregiver who had not been able to reach them because they were too endogenously stimulated, perhaps within infantile phasic REM states. They then currently find their dream (that inevitably reflects conflict) more threatening because they actually feel it to be too real. So they respond with an exaggerated and inappropriate act of reflectiveness.

More generally, Lissa Weinstein presented the view that tolerance for one's own thoughts and feelings (a manifestation of the reflective self) was related to endogenous stimulation and experience with the mother, which might alter the threshold of what is experienced as pleasurable. The more balanced an individual's status with respect to endogenous stimulation, the more robust the reflective disposition might be expected. This could be linked to tendencies, we have reported, for those with histories of secure attachment, to find a reflective stance to be more accessible following the early years.

It is in this context that Lissa advanced the view that the biological function of REM sleep could be to promote and maintain attachment processes. Evidence for this, as we saw, comes not only from the temporal association of entering REM dominated sleep and the peaking of oxytocin at 4am, but the association of sleep disorders with insecure attachment across individuals. Perhaps the procedural learning often linked to REM sleep could represent the internalisation of the relationship pattern (working model) between mother and infant. After all, the development of internal working models represents a kind of procedural learning process (although it is not often thought about that way).

This may be related to how REM sleep dominates early infancy, just as the formation of attachment bond dominates the mother–infant relationships. This has been shown, as we have learned, in sleep studies of infants, which could be interesting to carry out in relation to monitoring the quality of the mother–infant relationship. Also striking, from a developmental standpoint, is the temporal coincidence of the reorganisation of sleep architecture at three months, and the infant's move from a preference for one hundred per cent contingent stimuli (its own body) to highly but never perfectly contingent ones, as John Watson observed. It may be relevant to mention that the attachment neuropeptide, oxytocin, is also a kind of viagra for mentalisation—intranasal oxytocin enhances reflective capacities even in men!

The move then to creating second order representations of internal states, the reflective self, is perhaps rooted in turning towards social contingencies from the overwhelming domination of endogenous stimulation of phasic REM that was critical to developing the sensory systems. The delayed development of REM would interfere with this switch from internal to external (the infant aiming to find himself within the reflective mind of the observer). The model adds to the hypotheses advanced by Gergely, Watson, and colleagues by linking the physiological to the intersubjective factors. Endogenous stimulation, the internal activation of bodily states, has the potential to eliminate the differentiation of self from other and internal from external.

Taken together, Ellman and Weinstein succeed where psychoanalysts before them have often failed. They bring together the object relations (attachment) model with the model of the drives. They do so by modifying both approaches. Their theory of drives places the emphasis of drives on pleasure and uses the metaphor of brain stimulation. Their object relations theory is focused on the role of reflective self function, the psychological capacity for self-other differentiation rather than on the memories of specific instances of relating. By freeing both frameworks from the non-essentials, freeing them from what we called the over-specification of theories, the integration is smooth, compelling, and advances our collective theoretical constructions.

Their model is parsimonious and comprehensive of many aspects of the models they aim to replace, or perhaps more appropriately thought of as models they aim to develop and advance. They show

how individual relationships shape but in turn are shaped by the ways in which endogenous stimulation is experienced, cognised, and symbolised. This category of work is almost unique in psychoanalysis. To finish, I would like to highlight the ways in which the Ellman programme of work in my view has "beacon status" in psychoanalytic theory building (to be emulated):

1. It evolves a model of mind from basic laboratory research
2. It makes minimal assumptions about the nature of the mind
3. The theoretical exploration continues to drive a programme of empirical enquiry, generating findings which further enrich the theory building enterprise
4. The clinical applicability of the model thus created remains one of the criteria for the testing of its postulates
5. There is remarkable scholarship offered as part of the model with careful referencing of related empirical and theoretical work
6. Most important, there is genuine creativity in the theory building and empirical research
7. And related to this, Ellman's work is *collaborative*. And let me end on a final serious note about our profession. While collaboration may not be sufficient to achieve distinction, it is essential for doing so. In modern science none of us can do it alone. The average number of authors of a medical paper in 1955 was 1.5. This rose to 3.0 by 1985 and 5.0 by 2010. During the same period in the *International Journal of Psychoanalysis* the average number of authors per paper figure increased "dramatically" from 1.0 to 1.1. Science is collaborative and needs us to work together to make progress.

For all these reasons and many besides, *"When Theories Touch"* is a work of great scholarship and an even greater integrative intellectual achievement for which future generations of psychoanalytic researchers, empirical and clinical, will be grateful and which they will admire for many years to come.

Reference

Dennett, D. (2001). Are we explaining consciousness yet? *Cognition, 79*(1–2): 221–237.

PART IV

CLINICAL AND EXTRACLINICAL
RESEARCH IN ONGOING PROJECTS
AND DREAMS IN MODERN LITERATURE

Changes in dreams of chronic depressed patients: the Frankfurt fMRI/EEG study (FRED)

Tamara Fischmann, Michael Russ, Tobias Baehr, Aglaja Stirn, and Marianne Leuzinger-Bohleber

Introductory remarks

In this chapter we are summarising changes in dreams in a patient investigated in the on-going FRED study. With this single case we would like to illustrate our attempt to combine clinical and extraclinical (experimental) research in the large on-going LAC depression study.[1] Marianne Leuzinger-Bohleber has reported the changes of dreams as one indicator for therapeutic changes from a clinical perspective in Chapter Five. The same patient, part of a sub-sample of the 380 chronic depressed patients[2] recruited in the LAC depression study, was willing to spend the necessary two nights in the sleep laboratory of the Sigmund-Freud-Institut because investigating his severe sleeping disturbances was of clinical importance. His severe sleeping problem, shared with many of the patients, is one of his most burdening symptoms and indeed the EEG data elicited showed pathological sleep patterns such that he had to be referred to a medical expert for sleep disturbances, who prescribed him the necessary medications to improve his sleeping behaviour. We are thus investigating several patients of the LAC study also by EEG and fMRI and will publish additional single case studies as well as the results of the group comparisons between the changes in dreams of these patients and a non-clinical control group.

As a result of this "therapeutic intervention" in the sleep laboratory we were able to compare his dreams obtained there with those reported in psychoanalysis, giving us the unique opportunity to compare changes in dreams obtained "naturalistically" in psychoanalytic treatment with those dreams collected in the frame of an experimental sleep laboratory[3]. Analysis of both methods was done blind, i.e., the clinical analysis of the dreams was done independently from the analysis of the laboratory dreams, where both the analyst and the experimental dream rater were unaware of the other's evaluation.

In this chapter we can only give a short overview of a model of the generation of dreams developed by Moser and von Zeppelin (1996)[4]. This is the theoretical background for our hypotheses looking at changes of dreams in depressed patients, applying a coding system for investigating the manifest dream content based on this model (see 1). In a second part of this chapter we briefly summarise some arguments for investigating psychoanalytic changes also by neurophysiological measures, and our attempt to develop the experimental design of the FRED study (2). We then focus on the description of the single case study contrasting the experimental findings of the changes in dreams from the sleep laboratory with those reported in psychoanalysis (3 and 4).

1   Dream and depression

Dreaming is described in contemporary dream research as a thought process, engaging our inner system to process information (Dewan, 1970). Inner (cognitive) models are constantly being modified in coordination with what is perceived. In contrast to a dreaming state the reactions to our environment are immediate while we are awake, thus enabling information to be consolidated into memory with one constraint, namely that consolidation processes are not always possible due to capacity restrictions of the system. Consolidation processes do continue, though, during sleep, in an "offline" modus, thus enabling integration to long-term memory (Esser, Hill & Tononi, 2007; Louie & Wilson, 2001; Vyazovskiy et al., 2011).

According to Moser and von Zeppelin (1996)[5], psychoanalysts and dream researchers at the same time, so-called "dream complexes"—activated by current events, process the entirety of information from unsolved conflicts and traumatic situations while dreaming. The dream searches solutions or rather best possible adaptations for these dream complexes. A dream, which is usually pictorial, consists of at least one situation produced by a "dream organiser". Dream organisation may be considered—according to Moser—as a bundle of affective-cognitive procedures, generating a micro-world—the dream—and controlling its course of action. Within this system the "dream complex" may be considered as a template facilitating dream organisation.

Thus it may be assumed that a "dream complex" originates from one or more complexes stored in long-term memory, rooted in conflictive and/or traumatising experiences, which found their condensates in *introjects*. They are closely related to triggering stimuli from the outside world, which are structurally similar to stored situations of the complex. The searched-for solution of the complex is governed by the need for security and wish for involvement, i.e., the *security principle* and the *involvement principle* which govern dream organisation.

Wishes within these complexes are links between self and object models and RIGs (i.e., representation interaction generalised), which are accompanied by convictions and a hope for wish fulfilment. Conflictive complexes are areas of bundled wishes, RIGs, and self and object models with a repetitive character, thus creating areas of unbound affective information. Affects within such an area are interconnected by

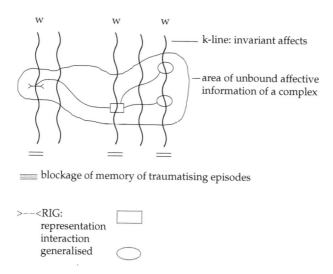

Figure 1. Memory model of conflictive complexes according to Moser and von Zeppelin (1996).

k-lines, which are blocked and thus not localised. In order to solve these conflictive complexes it is necessary to retrieve this affective information into a relational reality to make them come alive (Fig. 1). This is being attempted in dreams whose function it is to search for a solution of the complex. This search for a solution within a dream is governed by the above-mentioned need for security and wish for involvement, i.e., the *security principle* and the *involvement principle*. The following illustration may serve as an elucidation of this model.

2   When psychoanalysis engages in a fruitful relationship with neuroscience: some theoretical considerations, the design of the FRED study and first observations

FRED (Frankfurt fMRI/EEG Depression Study)[6] is an example of a fruitful combination of two domains—psychoanalysis and neurosciences. This very ambitious project currently conducted at the Sigmund Freud Institute (SFI) and BIC (Brain Imaging Centre) in cooperation with the MPIH Frankfurt (Max Planck Institute for brain research)[7], is looking to investigate changes of brain functions in chronic depressed patients after long-term therapies, aiming to find multimodal neurobiological changes in the course of psychotherapies.

When looking at depression from a brain physiological angle, some interesting findings have been put forth: for instance, that depression is related to a neurotransmitter disorder, or a frontal lobe dysfunction (Belmaker & Agam, 2008; Caspi et al., 2003; Risch et al., 2009). Northoff and Hayes (2011) have convincingly put forth that the so-called "reward system" is disturbed in depression and that there is evidence that deep brain stimulation can improve severe depression.

But despite all these findings no distinct brain physiological marker for depression has been found so far. From this it seemed plausible to pose the research question of whether changes in the course of therapy have brain physiological correlates, which we are currently investigating in FRED.

Generally speaking, psychotherapists—especially psychoanalysts—work with what can be remembered and with recurring—usually dysfunctional—behaviours and experiences. We assume that this has some precipitations within the brain in some way or the other, like synapse configuration, priming, axonal budding, and more, giving ground to the hypotheses of FRED that (1) psychotherapy is a process of change in encoding conditions of memory, and (2) elements of memories can be depicted in fMRI by a recognition experiment of memories related to an underlying conflict. This constitutes the neuro-psychoanalytic aspect of the FRED study, of which some preliminary results will be given in the following material. Another aspect of change relevant for our study is that of clinical change found in dreams in the course of psychotherapy. The analysis of dreams with the specific method of Moser and von Zeppelin (1996)—as will be outlined—enables us to compare empirically elicited findings with clinically reported ones from the therapist. Results of this will be given in parts 3 and 4 of this chapter.

To investigate our hypotheses we recruited chronically depressed patients, with whom we conducted in a first diagnostic phase for one an operationalised psychodynamic diagnostics (OPD) interview concentrating on axis II (relational) and a dream interview (see Table 1 below). From these two interviews the stimuli for the fMRI scanning are created individually for each patient[8]. For one, dream words are taken from a significant dream elicited in the dream interview and for the other confrontational sentences taken from the OPD interview are formulated. Brain activation patterns resulting from these stimuli in the fMRI serve as dependent variables (DV, see Table 2). Measurements are taken at three different time points revealing changes in activation patterns occurring in the course of therapy.

Thus far we have recruited ten chronically depressed patients (from PA group; cf. Table 2), of which we have obtained so far seventeen dreams (T1 + T2).

Assuming that a dream is a linguistically coded memory it—being a significant one—will contain some conflict-laden material. It will have

Table 1. Time schedule and measurement points within FRED.

Diagnosis	• OPD • Dream	
EEG	• Sleep-efficiency • REM-Dream	
fMRI	• OPD > Traffic-stimulus • Dream-words > neutral words	
T1	T2	T3

Table 2. FRED design—one-factorial design with repeated measurement and control-group. PA: Psychoanalytic treatment group; CBT: cognitive-behavioural treatment group.

	Factor A: Type of therapy		
	Patient	Patient	Control
DV	PA	CBT	—
Sleep efficiency	a_1	a_2	a_3
REM dream	b_1	b_2	b_3
Dream words	c_1	c_2	c_3
Interaction conflict	d_1	d_2	d_3

portentously emotional qualities, which will be related to the primary dream process, and dream words will have a different quality from words taken from an "all-purpose story".

We assume that in the fMRI those dream words when recognised will reactivate dream-specific encoding conditions in specific brain areas. This memory recognition task with dream words is the dream experiment part of FRED.

In fact, results of our dream experiments revealed that patients confronted with dream words in contrast to so-called neutral words (taken from an all-purpose story) showed differential activation of the precuneus, the ventro-lateral pre-frontal cortex (VLPF), and the anterior cingulate gyrus, among others. These three brain areas are known to be involved in self processing operations (experience of self agency), generation of basic causal explanations, and regulating emotions (see also below), where the ACC is also known for its conflict monitoring feature.

In the course of therapy we could show that the recognition or rather re-sounding of initially significant dream content at the beginning of therapy activated specifically the precuneus and the left parietal lobe, which did not substantiate after one year of therapy. The disappearance of these areas—which are involved in attention processes but are also significant to emotional processing by the self—at T2 allude to the supposition that possibly the dream content has lost its special importance and is experienced now in the same manner as the neutral story (cf. Fig. 2).

As for the OPD part of FRED, it consists of three conditions in the fMRI scanner, which are repeated six times each. In condition 1 four subjectively confrontational (conflict-oriented) statements extracted

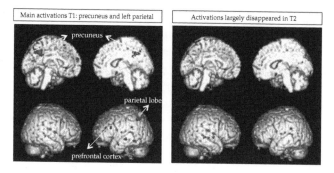

Figure 2. T1 and T2 comparison of dream word recognition in a single case.

Table 3. The three conditions of stimulus presentation in the fMRI. Condition 1 exemplified here is individually composed for each patient/ subject, whereas Conditions 2 and 3 are the same for all patients/subjects.

	Condition 1	Condition 2	Condition 3
1.	Most of the time I had to control myself and to manage by myself	A traffic participant is acting wrong	Think of a safe place
2.	Now I feel very lonesome and need someone to take care of me	You are annoyed with him	Relax
3.	I can bear closeness only badly and	You react	Get your head free
4.	Don't think that anyone is really interested in me	He reacts inappropriately	Don't think about anything

from the previously conducted OPD interview (relational axis II) are presented consecutively in the fMRI scanner on a screen. In condition 2 subjects see four statements of an all-purpose situation presented in the same manner, and finally condition 3 is composed of four relaxation statements (cf. Table 3).

Analysis of the fMRI brain scans contrasting the different conditions (dysfunctional sentences > traffic + relaxation) revealed specific activation patterns again in the precuneus, and above that of the posterior and anterior cingulate gyrus, medial prefrontal cortex (MFC), occipital cortex and the left hippocampus for condition 1 (dysfunctional sentences). The occipital cortex and precuneus are important brain structures for primary visual processes (occipital c.) and visual-spatial imagery (precuneus). But besides this the precuneus is also known to be an important brain area for episodic memory retrieval and self-processing operations, i.e., for first person perspective taking and experience of agency. The cingulate gyrus being an important part of the limbic system helps regulate emotions and pain and constitutes an important feature of memory just like the hippocampus, which is aligned for memory formation, specifically long-term memory (episodical biographic). The MFC is postulated to serve as an online detector of information processing conflict (Botvinick, Cohen & Carter, 2004) but also has a regulative control function of affective signals (Critchley, 2003; Matsumoto, Suzuki & Tanaka, 2003; Posner & DiGirolamo, 1998; Roelofs, van Turennout & Coles, 2006; Stuphorn & Schall, 2006).

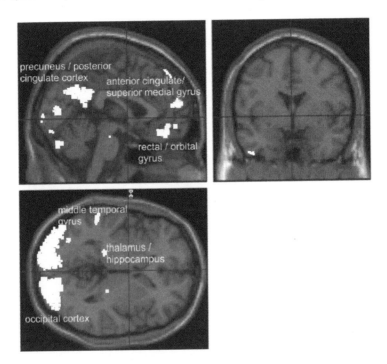

Figure 3. fMRI scans contrasting dysfunctional sentences (condition 1) > traffic (condition 2) + relaxation (condition 3). Second level analysis p < 0.05, FDR corrected; N = 13.

In a single case study we could also show that MFC activation could no longer be detected after one year of psychotherapy, suggesting that the conflict impact has diminished in the course of therapy.

In summary, data from both domains—neurobiology and psychoanalysis—strongly suggest that emotionally meaningful life experiences are encoded in memory by sensory percepts that were registered during the life experience that they encoded. These encoded memories will recur in dreams, as both dreams and memory tap the same brain areas. Therefore dreams can no longer be considered as randomly generated, not conveying any meaning.

Within the FRED study, dreams were not only studied from a neurophysiological perspective but also from a psychoanalytical standpoint, by analysing the manifest dream using a specific method—namely the Moser method. This method has its basis in the analysis of dreams under problem solving aspects, which strongly relies on affect regulation, since the success or failure to resolve a conflictive complex, assumed to be underlying the dream, will, ultimately, be determined by it. Analysis is done by scrutinising the manifest dreams for certain aspects, among others: elements positioned within the dream world, observable interactions taking place between self and others or the absence of them and interruption of dream scenes, which allude to affective overflow making such interruptions necessary. The following describes the dream coding system of Moser and von Zeppelin as it was used here.

The dream coding system of Moser and von Zeppelin

The dream coding method of Moser and von Zeppelin (1996) is an evaluating system used to analyse the dream material based on their model of cognitive-affect regulation, using formal criteria to investigate manifest dream content and its changing structures.

According to Moser and von Zeppelin the regulating processes of dream organisation are based on:

Positioning elements into the dream world
Monitoring the dream activity
A working memory containing (affective feedback) information of each dream situation and its consequences, and
Regulating procedures responsible for changes.

Formal criteria and structures of a dream are: the number of situations contained in a dream, the type of places and social settings named in a dream (descriptions, attributes), objects occurring (descriptions, attributes), placement, movement, interactions of objects as well as the question of whether the dreamer himself was involved in interactions, or if he remains spectator, and finally the ending and beginning of a situation (how, when).

The dream coding system aims at making these structural aspects of dreaming transparent in order to better understand the affect regulation processes taking place.

Two principles of affect regulation are assumed: (1) the security principle and (2) the involvement principle. The former becomes transparent through "positioning" and the latter through "interactions". These two principles are moderated via trajectories (movement traces) leading from a positioning to an interaction or out of an interaction back to a position. Common to both principles is their ruling by negative and positive affects, i.e., anxiety is the motor for an enlargement of security, also regulating involvement by, for instance, breaking off interactions and generating a new situation. Likewise hope is active in the security as well as in the involvement principle. It is assumed that problem-solving can only take place and be tested in interaction; therefore the dream tends towards interaction.

To facilitate transparency of the coding three columns are being used: (1) the positioning field (PF), (2) the field of trajectories, and (3) the interaction field (IAF). The positioning field contains all objects or rather cognitive elements (CE) as well as their attributes and their position. In the field of trajectories all movements of objects and CEs are coded and interactions are coded in the interaction field column specifying changes to the self, reaction relations, and response relations of the objects while specifying whether they are happening to the dreamer himself or to others or are only observed by the dreamer.

It is assumed that the more elements used in the dream scene (mirrored in different subjects and objects summarised in the positioning field), the more possibilities are available for the dreamer to regulate his affects and contents processed in the dream. If the dream remains in the positioning field, security aspects dominate, indicating that the dreamer is hesitant to get involved in interactions. Codes appearing in the second column, i.e., field of trajectories, signify what has been named by the authors "loco time motion" (LTM) and indicate preparations for interaction that will follow. These interactions can be summarised as changes that develop during evolvement of a dream scene without interrupting the scene. Finally, all types of interactions are summarised in the third column, the IAF: codes in this column signify the ability of the dreamer to get involved with others, even if the interaction might fail or end in a destructive way.

A fourth element normally ignored by dream researchers is the so-called "interrupt". It comprises all kinds of abrupt endings or interruptions of the dream situation, but also cognitive processes (CP) like commenting on a dream situation in an emotional or cognitive way may to some extent create a distance and interrupt the dream experience.

The following clinical case with analyses of a series of four dreams elicited in the laboratory in the first two years of therapy of the patient highlights how clinical and experimental data together give an exciting insight into changes occurring in the course of treatment.

3   Clinical case: analysis of a dream series in the course of therapy

Biography and trauma history

Marianne Leuzinger-Bohleber describes the clinical and biographical background of this patient extensively in chapter 5 of this book. She illustrates how the manifest dreams as well as the dream work changed during psychoanalysis from her clinical perspective and also reports on the transformation of the inner (traumatic) object world. In this chapter we would like to contrast her clinical views with a more systematic investigation of the changes in the manifest dreams.

Just a short summary of the clinical material here:

The patient explained in the assessment interviews that he had been suffering from severe depression for the last twenty-five years, and that he is coming to our Institute because after the last depressive breakdown he had submitted an application for retirement pension. The doctor who assessed his application concluded that he did not require a pension, but an "intelligent psychoanalysis", initially a response Mr W found highly insulting. He felt that he had not been taken seriously, especially his substantial physical symptoms: the unbearable pains covering his entire body, his acute eating disorders, as well as his acute suicidal tendencies. Furthermore, the patient suffered from severe sleep disorders. Often he is unable to sleep at all. As a rule, he wakes up after one and a half hours, or after three hours at the most. He feels physically exhausted and is barely able to concentrate his mind on anything.

Mr W had already undergone several unsuccessful attempts at therapy, including behavioural therapy, Gestalt therapy, "body therapy", as well as several in-patient treatments in psychiatric and psychosomatic clinics. He is among that group of patients for the most part apparently unable to respond to psychotropic drugs, and whose relapses occur at ever-shorter intervals and with increasing intensity. After many consultations with various psychiatrists and neurologists, he then discovered that only Lyrica[9] helped him to more or less deal with his states of physical stress and anxiety attacks.

The patient is an only child. One of the known details about his early history is that he was a "cry-baby". When he was four years old Mr W's mother fell seriously ill. Mr W was admitted to a convalescent home for children, evidently founded on authoritarian, inhumane educational principles reminiscent of National Socialist ethos. Just how traumatic an experience this stay in a home was is something that became transparent during psychoanalysis. Mr W's first childhood memories revolve around the following event: he recalls how his father took him by the hand and led him out of the home. He also recalls how a girl had been forced to eat her own vomit.

Mr W experienced two further separations from his ill mother, but these incidents had proved less traumatic since he had been taken in by relatives.

In spite of the dissociative states following the traumatic separations and his social isolation, Mr W was a good pupil, who went on to complete his first apprenticeship training and later his university studies. During adolescence, he had a psychosomatic breakdown, which the parents diagnosed as a "crisis in growing up". At the age of fifteen years, he met his first girlfriend. His condition improved. At the age of twenty-two he separated from his first girlfriend because he fell in love with another woman. Although the separation ran in his favour, he reacted very severely to it. He also initiated the separation from his second girlfriend, though suffered for weeks due to the separation. After entering another relationship he was dramatically overcome by a nervous breakdown during a party held by his new girlfriend: he had to be taken to hospital due to hyperventilation (panic attacks).

As already mentioned, Mr W had undergone several psychotherapies. Although all his therapies alleviated him, "none of them cured him". His depressions became worse and worse and became chronic.

Dream series elicited in the dream laboratory

In the following a total of four dreams—two from the end of the first year of therapy and two elicited one year later—will be analysed for changes in the course of therapy using the Moser method.

Dream 1—end of first year of treatment

> I am standing on a bridge over a dam. Right and left are steep slopes—mountains (S1). There is a landslide. I see the slope and an entire house approaching me very fast, rapidly sliding, rushing towards me (S2). I think to myself that I will not be able to escape it (/C.P./). I am running (S3) and am amazed at how fast I can run (/C.P./). I succeed in saving myself from the rapidly descending house (S3). I am in safety at the edge of this bridge (S4).

In order to analyse this dream with the Moser method each and every element of a situation is given a code in the respective column of either the positioning field (PF), the field of trajectories (LTM), or the interaction field (IAF):

Sit.	PF	LTM	IAF
S1	SP PLACE (dam) CEU_1 (bridge) CEU_2 (mountains) ATTR (steep)		
S2	SP PLACE (slope) CEU_3 (house)	LTM CEU_2 1 ATTR	
/C.P./			
S3	SP CEU_3 ATTR (rapidly sliding)		IR.C
/C.P./			
S4	SP CEU_1		IR.S

From here the dream may be analysed as follows: the first situation of this dream (S1) is coined by the security principle—many cognitive elements are simply being placed. But it also hosts a multitude of involvement potential as many attributes are being named for the elements placed. In the second situation (S2), a first attempt is made to deal with this potential—albeit rather limited (LTM)—but again increasing potentiality by adding another attribute (ATTR). As a result the affectivity seems to increase to such an extent that the dream scene has to be interrupted by a comment (/C.P./). In S3 the dreamer finally succeeds in invoking a *"successful"* interaction between the threatening cognitive element (CEU$_3$ (house)) and himself (SP). Initially this leads to another interruption: the dreamer is surprised by his capabilities, and finally in S4 a cathartic self-changing interaction is conjured up: he is in safety.

In summary, the patient describes a threatening situation, which is initially determined by the security principle. The relatively sophisticated description of the first scene bears potential, which the dreamer makes full use of in order to regulate the threatening affects. The wish to "bring himself to safety" is fulfilled in this dream.

Dream 2—end of first year of treatment

> There are more people in the room. I wear this cap. You three are here and somebody else, who will come up right after me. He has a lot of pretensions. It is morning and I wake up. I wear this cap and am linked up to all those cables (S1). It is lively around me and you and the others are walking around and talking to each other. I pick up on you whispering and being annoyed at someone or making fun of him. The one that you are annoyed at is in the room as well, and he is supposed to get the cap on after me (S2). I remember that I have seen him already once in front of the door of my analyst (S3). He is here in the room and constantly poses pretensions. Everything should be the way he wants it. You are annoyed that you have to fulfil these wishes (S4). I think to myself: "Just take it easy" (/C.P./).

Obviously this is a "laboratory dream". The patient uses the research situation as an opportunity to regulate his anxieties to be "too pretentious". He projects this into an object processor (OP) and by this he himself becomes an observer. Thus he successfully distances himself, which gives him the possibility to comprehend the events in more detail.

The coded version of this dream:

Sit.	PF	LTM	IAF
S1	SOC SET (laboratory) SP ATTR (wired) CEU_1 (cap) OP_1 (G) (researcher) OP_2 (patient) ATTR (pretentious)		
S2	SP OP_3 (researcher) 1 ATTR AFF OP_1 (G) 1 ATTR AFF OP_2 CEU_1 IMPLW	LTM OP_1 (G)	
S3	SP OP_2 OP_4 (analyst) IMPLW		
S4	SP OP_2 1 ATTR PLACE (room) OP_1 (G) 1 ATTR AFF CEU_2 (wishes)		IR.D ((IR.C res $OP_2 \rightarrow OP_1$ (G))) ATTR AFF OP_1 (G)

/C.P./

In the first situation (S1) there is a lot of potential to regulate affects—albeit still governed by the security principle. It includes a social setting (SOC SET), variable attributes (ATTR), and a lot of processors inviting action. By placing another patient (OP_2) into the dream scene the dreamer (subject processor SP) gets the opportunity to take an observational stance, which leads in S2 to a movement (trajectory LTM) of the OP_1 group of researchers.

It remains unclear whether S3 may be considered to be a dream scene at all or whether it should be considered to be an interruption containing a cognitive process (/C.P./). No matter what, it is regulated by the security principle. The potential existent in S2 (LTM) cannot be exploited in S3. In S4 finally this is successful in that an interaction takes place just to disembogue in another interruption. The affectivity of the situation increases to such an extent that it has to be interrupted: the dreamer cautions the object processor (OP_2) or rather himself "to take it easy".

Dream 3—second year of treatment

A Formula 1 race with Michael Schumacher (S1). Directly after the race he flies to Germany, in order to inaugurate a bridge (S2). Totally bonkers (/C.P./). He is in Germany and inaugurates the bridge (S3). He speaks with a few people sitting at a table. I am sitting at the next table and observe him and the others in debate (S4). How do I come up with something like this (/C.P./)?

The coded dream:

Sit.	PF	LTM	IAF
S1	SOC SET (Formula 1 race) SP OP_1 (Schumacher)		
S2	SOC SET (Formula 1 race) SP OP_1 CEU_1 (bridge)	LTM OP_1	
/C.P./			
S3	SP OP_1 CEU_1 PLACE (Germany) POS REL		IR.C $OP_1 \rightarrow CEU_1$
S4	SP OP_1 OP_2 (G) CEU_2 (table) 2 POS REL		IR.D ((IR.C. resp OP_1 OP_2 (G)))
/C.P./			

Here again the dreamer takes an observational stance. In contrast to the previous dream he succeeds in creating a connecting interaction between two CEs, which is not interrupted but seamlessly leads into a displacement relation. Although this may still be considered to be a distancing manoeuvre from an affective event, it is not as marked as in the previous dream. The involvement principle is more distinct here than it had been previously. The interruption at the end of the dream is not a rebuke as before, but rather expresses astonishment at what occupies his mind and a (conscious) approximation to the underlying complex may be assumed.

Dream 4—second year of treatment

> I am on the way with my little son. Other children and adults are with us. A boy is there too, who has something against my son. It is summer. It is warm. We are walking along the river banks (S1). We want to buy a wagon or trailer (S2). The children are of different ages. One boy is already eleven or twelve years old. This boy is on edge, because the other children and also my son are so young and they cannot do what he wants them to do, because they are too small for this (S3). Then my mother appears. She sews a button back onto my shirt (S4). I don't know how this fits in (/C.P./). I say: "Just leave this stupid button alone." This unnerves me (S5). I am there to oversee everything. A woman is there too. She is the mother of that boy (S1).

This dream begins with a sophisticated placing of cognitive elements (CE) and a movement relation (LTM). The dream is regulated by the involvement principle from the beginning, which alludes to an advanced therapeutic effect. In all successive situations more interactions appear: connecting as well as self-changing relations of subjects and objects. The self-processor (SP) himself is involved and does not have to retreat into an observing position any more (no IR.D)—he faces his affects increasingly. After S4 triggers an interruption, the dreamer (SP) interactively "fends this off" via a verbal relation (V.R.).

Thus we might assume that the dreamer (SP) progressively deals with the affects underlying the dream complex in an interactive manner and is able to depict them in dream scenes. The affects are no longer

The coded version of this dream:

Sit.	PF	LTM	IAF
S1	SP OP1 (son) OP2 (G) (children) OP3 (older boy) OP4 (mother of the older boy) PLACE (river bank) ATTR	LTM	
S2	SP OP1 (son) OP2 (G) (children) OP3 (older boy) OP4 (mother of the older boy) PLACE (river bank) ATTR CEU1 (wagon)		IR.C int (we want to buy a wagon)
S3	SP OP1 (son) OP2 (G) (children) OP3 (older boy) ATTR (age) ATTR AFF (unnerved)		IR.S OP3
S4	SP OP5 (patient's mother) CEU2 (button) CEU3 (shirt)		IR.C OP5 → CEU
/C.P./			
S5	SP OP5 (patient's mother)		V.R.

isolated—which implies that previously isolated affects of the dream complex can now be integrated.

To illustrate the changes occurring from a more experimental perspective the following graph might seem to be helpful:

There is a clearly recognisable increase in potentials (PF) from T1 to T2, which can be exploited for interaction (IAF). The finding of an enhanced ability to get involved can be seen here from just having looked at the manifest dream.

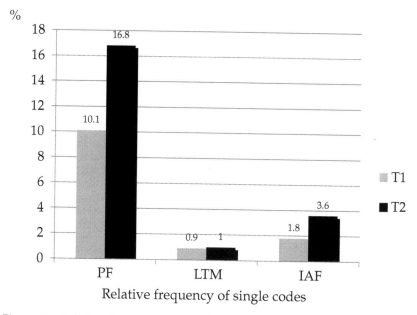

Figure 4. Relative frequency of single codes relativised by the average number of words.

Concluding remarks

In summary, it can be said that via the analysis of the manifest content of Mr W's laboratory dream series, by applying a specific empirically validated method (Doell-Hentschker, 2008), we gained insights into his clinical improvement. His laboratory dreams from the end of his first year in therapy were still abundant with anxieties and yearning for security making him hesitant to get involved with others. Nevertheless he already showed in these dreams potentials of what we might consider to be the result of the ongoing therapy, i.e., signs of involvement abilities, in that he could make use of others by projecting his fears into them and *testing* if he could bear the rising anxieties involved in the actions he projected onto them while he still remained in a distant observer position. In the end his fears of getting involved dominated, as he could not yet exploit these potentials.

In the second year of analysis his dreams reveal his enhanced abilities to get involved (dream 4 is largely dominated by the involvement principle from the beginning) and are abundant with interactions with others portraying his increased ability to face his affects. Rising affectivity is now met albeit still with an *interruption* but followed by a dream scene of a different quality: he fends off his rising anxiety via a more *aggressive* response (V.R. S5 in dream 4) alluding to a progressive approach to the underlying (unconscious) conflict-laden dream complex. Affects are no longer isolated but more and more integrated into existing memory networks.

Let us now compare these *experimental* findings with those reported clinically (see Chapter Five) for their consistency. In the clinical analysis given by M. Leuzinger-Bohleber she applies an analysis of changes in manifest dreams stemming from a former study (Leuzinger-Bohleber, 1987, 1989, p. 324) where she compared manifest dreams in the first and last 100 sessions of five psychoanalyses. This technique is largely based on Moser's memory and affect regulation models, and gave rise to the subsequently developed dream generation model and its coding technique used here in the analysis of the laboratory dreams.

Comparing the clinical dreams from the beginning of psychoanalysis with those of the third year of analysis, she observed changes in the pattern of the relationships, where *the dream subject shows better relationships with others* (e.g., the helping couple in the last dream reported). In the first dreams the dream subject mostly has been alone: no one helped him and smoothed his anxieties, panics, and despair. *The range of actions of the dream subject are increased and the emotional spectrum is enlarged* (in the dreams at the beginning of psychoanalysis we find only panic—in the third year of analysis we also observe surprise, joy, satisfaction, humour, although still anxieties and pain).

There is also a noted change in the dream atmosphere, with the *variety of affects as well as its intensities increased and manifest anxiety being less frequent. The dreamer's increased capability to perceive different and even contradictory emotions* become more and more visible. New feelings of anger and rage but also positive affections, tenderness, and sexual attractions appear towards the second year of treatment. The dream subject is no longer a (distant) observer but plays an active part and is involved in intensive emotional interaction with others.

Furthermore, Leuzinger-Bohleber distinguished from the manifest dreams *clearer problem-solving strategies* (more successful than non-successful problem-solving) and a *broader range of different problem-solving strategies*. The dream subject is no longer as inundated as in a traumatic situation in which he experiences extreme helplessness and lack of power. In his dreams he encounters objects willing to help and support him. This seems a very important indicator that the inner object world of the severely traumatised patient has changed (see last dream in the case report, Chapter Five).

The consistencies of the clinical and extraclinical analyses are remarkable, which is from a scientific perspective of utmost relevance. But to be sure the clinical case study still provides greater psychodynamic relevant clinical and structural information, as the extraclinical analysis suffices with the content of the manifest dreams and has no further biographical data at hand with which results could be enhanced. The consistency in the finding on the other hand consolidates the reliability of the clinical case analysis, which substantiates the method of clinical case studies.

To combine clinical and extraclinical research remains a great challenge, particularly in psychoanalytical psychotherapy research. As discussed by M. Leuzinger-Bohleber in the "Preliminary remarks" of her extensive case report (Chapter Five), it is still a strength of clinical research in psychoanalysis to communicate the unique and complex insights gained in intensive psychoanalyses by narratives because many a "truth can only be told and not be measured". At the same time, psychoanalysis, as all "contemporary psychotherapies", is obliged to show the short-term and long-term effects of its treatments to the psychoanalytical as well as to the non-psychoanalytical community. The latter one often requires us to consider the criteria of the so-called evidence based medicine in such effectiveness studies (see the political context of the LAC depression study, www.sigmund-freud-institut.de). An alternative, innovative approach to "prove" therapeutic changes in an "objective way" is to investigate patients during their psychoanalyses by instruments like the EEG and the fMRI (if the patients are willing to undergo these procedures). Mr W, due to his own interest in curing his severe sleeping problems, was willing to be investigated by EEG in the sleep laboratory of the Sigmund-Freud-Institut, because he was convinced that these data would help him look for help from medical experts in sleeping problems parallel to his psychoanalysis. Mr W. agreed to report his dreams and to collaborate in the LAC depression study. Therefore we had the unique possibility of comparing his laboratory dreams with his dreams as told in his psychoanalytic sessions.

We hope to have illustrated the differences between a clinical use of dreams as one indicator for changes in the inner (traumatic) object world in psychoanalyses, and the systematic, "scientific" investigation of laboratory dreams by the so-called "Moser method". The case report (Chapter Five) focused on the importance of the psychoanalytic context of the dreams, the observation of transference and countertransference reactions, the associations of the patient and the analysand, etc. necessary to unravel the unconscious meaning of the dream. One great advantage of the psychoanalytical clinical "research" on dreams continues to be the understanding of the meaning of a dream in cooperation with the dreamer—the patient. His association, and conscious and unconscious reactions to a dream interpretation still are the criteria to evaluate the "truth" of the interpretation (see, e.g., Leuzinger-Bohleber, 1987, 1989, 2008). To make a long story short: the transformation of the unconscious world (like dreams)—and as products of it the maladaptive emotions, cognitions, and behaviours ("symptoms") of the patient—still remains the final psychoanalytical criterion for a therapeutic "success" based on "true insights" of the patient in his unconscious functioning.

On the other hand this kind of "truth" often remains fuzzy and subjective, at least in the eyes of the non-psychoanalytical, scientific community. Therefore we have seized the unique possibility to analyse changes in the manifest dreams—gathered in a controlled, laboratory situation—by a theory-driven, precise systematic coding system: the Moser method. These analyses have a high reliability—and inter-subjectivity—and thus may convince independent observers or even critics.

Notes

1. In the ongoing large LAC depression study we are comparing the short-term and long-term effects of long-term psychoanalytic and cognitive-behavioural psychotherapies. Until now we have recruited around 380 chronic depressed patients in different research centres: Frankfurt a. M., Mainz, Berlin, and Hamburg (participating research team and methods: see www.sigmund-freud-institut.de).

2. We are studying this subsample of the LAC study in the so-called FRED Study in cooperation wiith the Max Planck Institute for Brain Research (director, Wolf Singer) and the Psychiatric University Clinic Frankfurt (Aglaja Stirn). The FRED Study is, in parts, a replications study of the Hanse-Neuropsychoanalysis Study (Bucheim et al., 2010).

We thank all the colleagues of the Hanse-Neuropsychoanalysis Study for this opportunity and their generous cooperation (for details see www.sigmund-freud-institut.de and Fischmann et al., 2010).

3. We thank Prof. Volk and his team from his sleep laboratory in Hofheim for the productive cooperation.

4. We are grateful to Ulrich Moser for his continuous support and his corrections of our codings of the manifest dreams presented in this paper.

5. Ulrich Moser and Ilka von Zeppelin are fully trained psychoanalysts engaged in interdisciplinary research for decades. Ulrich Moser was professor of clinical psychology at the University of Zurich. Already in the 1960s and '70s he was involved in modelling parts of psychoanalytic theories. By means of computer simulation he tested the logical and terminological consistency of psychoanalytic theories of defence and the generation of dreams. Based on this basic research on dreams he developed his own model of the generation of dreaming as well as a coding system for investigating the manifest dreams. In this chapter as well as in the chapter by Varvin, Fischmann, Jovic, Rosenbaum, and Hau the dream model and the coding system by Moser and v. Zeppelin are applied.

6. We are grateful to the HOPE FOR DEPRESSION FOUNDATION (New York) and the Research Advisory Board of the International Psychoanalytical Association for the financial support.

7. We are grateful to the BIC and MPIH (W. Singer, A. Stirn, M. Russ) and the Hanse-Neuropsychoanalysis Study (A. Buchheim, et al., 2010) and LAC Depression Study for supporting us in an outstanding way.

8. Here we follow the OPD paradigm as described in Kessler et al. (2010). We would like to explicitly thank M. Cierpka and M. Stasch for eliciting and formulating the relevant stimulus sentences from the OPD interviews.

9. Lyrica (generic name: pregabalin) is an anticonvulsant drug used for neurotic pain, also effective for generalised anxiety disorder (since 2007 approved for this use in the European Union).

References

Belmaker, R. H. & Agam, G. (2008). Major depressive disorder. *New England Journal of Medicine, 358*: 55–68.

Botvinick, M. M., Cohen, J. D. & Carter, C. S. (2004). Conflict monitoring and anterior cingulate cortex: an update. *Trends in Cognitive Sciences, 8*(12): 539–546.

Buchheim, A., Kächele, H., Cierpka, M., Münter, T. F., Kessler, H., Wiswede, D., Taubner, S., Bruns, G. & Roth, G. (2010). Psychoanalyse and Neurowissenschaften. Neurobiologische Veränderungsprozesse bei psychoanalytischen Behanldungen von depressiven Patienten. In: M. Leuzinger-Bohleber, K. Röckerath, L. V. Strauss (Eds.), *Depression und Neuroplastizität* (pp. 152–162). Frankfurt, Germany: Brandes & Apsel.

Caspi, A., Sugden, K., Moffitt, T. E., Taylor, A., Craig, I. W., Harrington, H., McClay, J., Mill, J., Martin, J., Braithwaite, A. & Poulton, R. (2003). Influence of life stress on depression: Moderation by a polymorphism in the 5-HTT gene. *Science, 301*(5631): 386–389.

Critchley, H. (2003). Emotion and its disorders. *British Medical Bulletin, 65*: 35–47.

Dewan, E. M. (1970). The programming (P) hypothesis for REM sleep. In: E. Hartmann (Ed.), *Sleep and Dreaming* (pp. 295–307). Boston: Little, Brown.

Doell-Hentschker, S. (2008). Die Veränderungen von Träumen in psychoanalytischen Behandlungen. Affekttheorie, Affektregulierung und Traumkodierung. Frankfurt, Germany: Brandes & Apsel.

Esser, S. K., Hill, S. L. & Tononi, G. (2007). Sleep homeostasis and cortical synchronization: I. Modeling the effects of synaptic strength on sleep slow waves. *Sleep, 30*(12): 1617–1630.

Fischmann, T., Russ, M., Baehr, T., Stirn, A., Singer, W. & Leuzinger-Bohleber, M. (2010). Frankfurter-fMRI/EEG-Depressionsstudie (FRED). Veränderungen der Gehirnfunktion bei chronisch Depressiven nach psychoanalytischen und kognitiv-behavioralen Langzeitbehandlungen. Werkstattbericht aus einer laufenden Studie. In: M. Leuzinger-Bohleber, K. Röckerath & L. V. Strauss (HgEds.), Depression und Neuroplastizität. *Psychoanalytische Klinik und Forschung* (pp. 162–185). Frankfurt, Germany a. M. Brandes & Apsel.

Kessler, H., Taubner, S., Buchheim, A., Münte, T. F., Stasch, M., Kächele, H., Roth, G., Heinecke, A., Erhard, P., Cierpka, M. & Wiswede, D. (2010). Individual and problem-related stimuli activate limbic structures in depression: an fMRI study. *PLoS ONE, 6*(1): e15712. doi:10.1371/journal.pone.0015712.

Leuzinger-Bohleber, M. (1987). Veränderung kognitiver Prozesse in Psychoanalysen, Band I: eine hypothesengenerierende Einzelfallstudie. Ulm, Germany: PSZ.

Leuzinger-Bohleber, M. (1989). Veränderung kognitiver Prozesse in Psychoanalysen, Band II. Fünf aggregierte Einzelfallstudien. Ulm, Germany: PSZ.

Leuzinger-Bohleber, M. (2008). Vorwort. In: S. Doell-Hentschker, *Die Veränderungen von Träumen in psychoanalytischen Behandlungen. Affekttheorie, Affektregulierung und Traumkodierung* (pp. 7–10). Frankfurt, Germany: Brandes & Apsel.

Louie, K. & Wilson, M. (2001). Temporally structured replay of awake hippocampal ensemble activity during rapid eye movement sleep. *Neuron, 29*: 145–156.

Matsumoto, K., Suzuki, W. & Tanaka, K. (2003). Neural correlates of goal-based motor selection in the prefrontal cortex. Science, *301*: 229–232.

Moser, U. & v. Zeppelin, I. (1996). *Der geträumte Traum.* Stuttgart, Germany: Kohlhammer.

Northoff, G. & Hayes, D. J. (2011). Is our self nothing but reward? *Biological Psychiatry, 69*: 1019–1025.

Posner, M. I. & DiGirolamo, G. J. (1998). Executive attention: Conflict, target detection, and cognitive control. In: R. Parasuraman (Ed.). *The Attentive Brain* (pp. 401–423). Cambridge, MA: MIT Press.

Risch, N., Herrell, R., Lehner, T., Liang, K., Eaves, L., Hoh, J., Griem, A., Kovacs, M., Ott, J. & Merikangas, K. R. (2009). Interaction between the serotonin transporter gene (5-HTTLPR), stressful life events, and risk of depression: A meta-analysis. *JAMA: The Journal of the American Medical Association, 301*(23): 2462–2471.

Roelofs, A., van Turennout, M., Coles, M. G. H. (2006). Anterior cingulate cortex activity can be independent of response conflict in Stroop-like tasks. *Proceedings of the National Academy of Sciences, 103*: 13884–13889.

Stuphorn, V. & Schall, J. D. (2006). Executive control of countermanding saccades by the supplementary eye field. *Nature Neuroscience, 9*(7): 925–931.

Vyazovskiy, V. V., Olcese, U., Hanlon, E. C., Nir, Y., Cirelli, C. & Tononi, G. (2011). Local sleep in awake rats. *Nature, 472*: 443–447.

CHAPTER ELEVEN

Traumatic dreams: symbolisation gone astray

Sverre Varvin, Tamara Fischmann, Vladimir Jovic,
Bent Rosenbaum, and Stephan Hau

Introduction

An underlying claim in the research to be presented in this chapter is that formal laboratory based dream research may inspire clinical work with dreams in psychoanalysis and psychoanalytic psychotherapy and possibly change theory. A dream dreamt in a laboratory setting and a dream dreamt during a psychoanalytic process do not, however, necessarily express the same underlying process. The last will to a large extent be determined by the specific and actual transference-countertransference situation, in contrast to a laboratory setting where transference reactions are usually not accounted for or may be seen as a disturbance. In our research it became apparent, however, that those volunteering to participate in laboratory dream research did have expectations and transferences that were displayed in relation to the setting and the interviewers. A wish for security was obvious in many cases but many had also "unfinished business" that in one way or another appeared as themes in dreams and associations to the dream. This was especially visible in individuals with chronic post-traumatic states who often struggled with long-standing guilt and problems with aggression.

The knowledge gained from the research presented here strives to give insight into significant mental processes that are affected by traumatisation and thus contribute to psychoanalytic trauma theory and to a better understanding of how therapy works. Furthermore, the two different methods applied for the analysis of traumatic dreams deepen the understanding of affect-regulating processes, deducible from manifest dream content (Moser method) for one, and the dreams' transferential and object-relational facets contained in one- and two-person relations in dream telling (psychoanalytic enunciation analysis) for the other.

The traumatised mind

The traumatised mind is characterised by disintegrating, dissociative, and potentially rupturing processes that can be released or provoked by stimuli that bear resemblance (mostly in a metonymic way: *pars pro toto*, resemblance by part) to aspects of the reminiscences of traumatising events.

Because the integrating functions of the mind are impaired, perceptions of these stimuli activate primordial schemes of danger (Varvin & Rosenbaum, 2003; Rosenbaum & Varvin, 2007) and often set off cascades of fear reactions with concomitant neurophysiological patterns of reactions related to the sympathetic nervous system and the hypothalamic-pituitary-adrenal axis. One can observe in traumatised individuals difficulties in organising perceptions of both inner and outer stimuli, of relating perceptions to other perceptions and to earlier perceptions in a functioning memory, and, as a result, difficulties in organising experience as a whole, taking different aspects of the situation into consideration. Trauma does not only (or primarily) refer to memory traces from the past (explicit memory) but more importantly to the ongoing problems in regulating negative emotion, a dysfunction that reflects disturbances in symbolising capacity. The symbolising capacity is at the basis of the above-mentioned capacities (integrative function, mentalising capacity, and so forth) and we hold that post-traumatic disturbances basically are a disturbance of this function.

Dreaming and nightmares: the traumatic dream

Dreaming may serve an integrative and adaptive function in which actual problems are connected with previous significant situations and earlier unresolved problems. Clinical experience has shown that even if traumatic dreams relate to, and often appear as, earlier traumatic experiences, they comprise day residues that have provoked similar feelings and mental experiences as the original traumatic event, for example feelings of shame and humiliation, experiences that the traumatised often has due to deficiencies in mental functions (Lansky & Bley, 1995). The ubiquitous, but often ignored, presence of guilt in trauma survivors is also central.

The study of dreaming, it being a central part of the mind's work with unmetabolised, trauma related elements (Bion, 1977; Hartmann, 1984), may thus give a privileged insight into the workings of the mind (Freud, 1900) where the traumatised individual tries in his/her dreams to deal with day residues that are experienced in terms of earlier traumatic experiences and nightmares signifying aborted or failed attempts (Fischmann, 2007) of this. But also the clinical work with dreams—and nightmares—of traumatised patients has been shown to be of importance in aiding the traumatised mind to restore its symbolic function (Adams-Silvan & Silvan, 1990; Hartmann, 1984; Pöstenyi, 1996).

In the dream generating model of Moser and v. Zeppelin (1996) (used in this project), conflictive complexes are differentiated from traumatic complexes. The former revive negative affects together with attempted wish-fulfilment (wish-fulfilment is possible, albeit under restricted conditions), the latter contain episodes in which affective events cannot be integrated into a cognitive structure (traumatic dreams).

In the psychoanalytic enunciation model (the second model used in this research), dreaming is seen as an attempt to achieve containment and integration of unorganised imaginary elements in a symbolic mode of functioning (Rosenbaum & Varvin, 2007). The model describes thus the possible movement from unorganised non-symbolic dream material to more integrated symbolic dream scenes.

In our research we hypothesise that dreaming by traumatised individuals indeed is an attempt to organise experience and turn passivity into activity and that this process can be observed in the person's attempt to organise the traumatising experience in a dream narrative (Fosshage, 1997; Hartmann, 1999). Dreaming will, according to this line of thinking, be a kind of laboratory for studying some basic functions of the mind and the symbolising process *in statu nascendi*, as well as the effects that trauma has on relational capacities.

Post-traumatic states are, among others, characterised by intrusive phenomena within which dreams recalling the original traumatising experiences are frequent. However, what happens during the night for many traumatised individuals may have different qualities and may even be a distinct phenomenon, on a phenomenological level, a structural level, a dynamic level, and even a neurophysiological level, which makes—as we know from clinical experience as well—the distinction of dreams from nightmares, nightmares from hallucinations, hallucinations from vivid imagery, etc. difficult. In addition, it can be difficult to distinguish so-called night terrors, anxiety attacks while asleep with no mental content, from nightmares (Fischmann, 2007). It is therefore of both scientific and clinical interest to study the dream processes of traumatised persons in depth, which will be elaborated in the following with those traumatised in the Balkan war.

Post-traumatic dreams and symbolisation: context, method, and description of the sample

In the last decade of the twentieth century there were almost continuous wars throughout the western Balkans in the territory of what has come to be known as "ex-Yugoslavia".

Characteristic of these wars was the involvement of huge masses of people and coverage of large multi-ethnic territories. There were diverse ranges of combat activities (frontline to street fighting), but more than anything else it was a violence targeted against civilians, i.e., persecutions, killings, concentration camps, ethnic cleansing, and mass murders (Srebrenica not being the only case). Victims and participants of this conflict became subjects of our study.

At the International Aid Network Centre for Rehabilitation of Torture Victims (CRTV) in Belgrade (www.ian.org.rs), help is being provided to thousands of those who were imprisoned and tortured during the war and also to those from eastern Bosnia (including Srebrenica). Torture survivors proved to be difficult to work with. It is the torture itself that is inconceivable, as it entails the most monstrous acts of violence against other people without any "understandable" reason. It was only years after the war, when the staff at IAN encountered violence in institutions as well (prisons, psychiatric hospitals, and social institutions) that patterns were recognised which were similar both in war- and in peace-time, namely: dehumanisation of others, torture and pain as a vehicle to humiliation. The latter was governed by a powerful unconscious drive stemming from Oedipal anxieties, where castration fears turn into humiliation and feminisation of other men (one observation was that sexual acts were very much present during torture). At this level only "mild" forms of physical abuse (slapping, hitting, spitting, etc.) become transparent followed by humiliating rituals. It is only when "body barriers" (or "skin barriers") are breached that more severe forms of torture occur: cutting, burning, electrocuting of the skin, inserting objects in body openings, etc. It still needs to be understood better as to how these acts produce long-lasting damaging effects to personality. One line of thinking suggests that traumatic situations, annihilation anxieties, and the unbinding of the death instinct, as well as notions of the relation between symbolisation, integration, and interpersonal space, are dimensions worth considering. Our research aims at understanding dehumanisation, how it develops during war, and how such mechanisms are related to an increase of violence in post-conflict societies.

Subjects investigated for this purpose were all men, exposed to war-related stressors, divided into two groups: those with current PTSD (experimental group, N = 25) and those without PTSD (referential

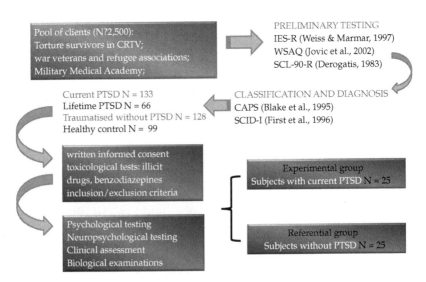

Figure 1. Recruitment, selection, and assessment procedure.

group, N = 25). Both groups were matched by age and education. They were recruited from a larger group of subjects participating in a "Psychobiology of PTSD" study and assessed by various psychological and neuropsychological instruments, and different biological, endocrinological, and genetic variables where elicited as well. They spent two consecutive nights in the sleep laboratory and were interviewed there in the mornings by two Serbian psychoanalysts. The interviews comprised also narratives of their dreams, which were recorded and translated into English. Polysomnographic recordings (i.e., comprehensive recording of the biophysiological changes occurring during sleep—like electroencephalography (EEG), eye movements (EOG), muscle activity (EMG), and heart rhythm (ECG), as well as respiratory functions) were elicited for the experimental but not for the referential group.

Subjects were also matched by the level and type of the traumatising events they survived, in order to control for traumatisation. The instrument used for this matching procedure, i.e., the war stressors assessment questionnaire—WSAQ (Jovic, Opacic, Knezevic, Tenjovic & Lecic-Tosevski, 2002)—a self-reporting instrument—consists of sixty-nine items describing eight different clusters of war-related stressors: active combat, witnessing of death or wounding, loss of organisational/military structure, war-related deprivation, injury, life

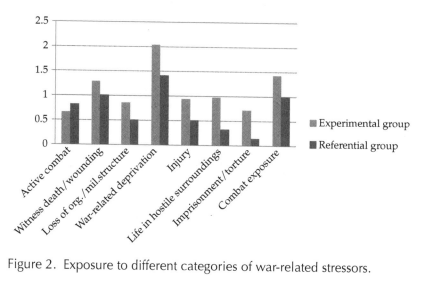

Figure 2. Exposure to different categories of war-related stressors.

in hostile surroundings, imprisonment/torture, and combat exposure. Matching of the subjects of both groups was performed by adding up the total number of positive items on the WSAQ, yielding an average number of positive items for the experimental group of 35.91 and of 25.25 for the referential group, which was not satisfactory. Nevertheless, subjects from both groups reported a significant number of different stressors (cf. Fig. 2), where the subjects from the experimental group had more positive items on clusters which may be summarised as "passive"—as they cover experiences in which the subject is only a witness, or a victim—and subjects of the referential group exhibited more positive items in the cluster of "active combat". This alludes to the notion that active role in combat can be a protective factor for development of PTSD, or that a passive role (and helplessness connected with it) could have a specifically traumatising effect.

Both groups consisted largely of refugees settling in Serbia after the war, most of them being unemployed or working in the grey economy, forgotten by everybody in a country that itself is impoverished and drowned in corruption and organised crime. Most of them were ill, suffering not only from psychological disturbances, but also from various psychosomatic disorders. Although the phenomenon of "lack of words for emotions" similar to what is seen in psychosomatic disorders was observable, the evidence from our research points to a distinctive quality in affect regulation of the traumatised.

The protocol of the sleep laboratory called for morning interviews after just a short acquaintance of the subjects and interviewers the previous evening largely "blinding" the interviewers and having them listen to narratives of dreams without knowing anything about the subjects, which gave them a quite unusual feeling of "walking in a dark room without any orientation" (personal note of interviewer). This procedure enlightened the aspect as to why so much research about war trauma is concerned with statistics (numbers), biological variables, and ideas about the damaged brain—as it is so much easier for the researcher not to deal with emotions, not to deal with horrible stories of human suffering as were revealed in the interviews conducted in our research. Narratives of subjects are abundant with horrible stories, like being witness of another man killing a woman who was holding a child, or of collected pieces of the friend's body, and yet another of how a torturer brought his ten-year-old son to beat the victim.

These narratives do have a traumatising effect upon listeners, as was recognised a long time ago (McCann & Pearlman, 1990). Another frequent observation was that when untrained and unprepared people (like secretaries who transcribed the material) were listening to these stories, they themselves reported anxieties and nightmares. This is a most vivid example of the effect of "undigested introjects", or "beta elements", demonstrating that it is extremely difficult to take in, digest, and contain feelings that these narratives evoke. This is frequently observed in a clinical setting and makes the work with trauma survivors so difficult.

The experimental situation in itself might have included the risk of re-traumatisation. By focusing on nightmares and their contents, a situation of heightened alertness within the subjects was created while simultaneously triggering anxiety that the subjects had somehow been able to control up until that point. The experimental situation in itself thus contained a risk for regressive processes and psychopathological symptoms. One example comprising transferential elements may demonstrate this point: the interviews were perceived by some as interrogations, as a part of an investigation or judicial procedure, and elements from the interview situation could appear in dreams dreamt in the laboratory. Ambivalence towards the interviewer could be observed in that the interview was marked by openness and collaboration (that sometimes was astonishing) while simultaneously causing withdrawal and persecutory anxieties.

It seems that in this perspective it could be understood that post-traumatic affect-regulation mostly comprised defence against destructive impulses in relation to others—from internal as well as from external reality. That is probably the reason why guilt plays such a significant role in the dynamics of post-traumatic states. Our protocols are abundant with themes related to guilt: scenes of friends being killed or dying, suicide of friends, young men being electrocuted, civilians being killed, bodies of teenagers found in the house which was previously shot at, and so forth. While it is easy to imagine the guilt in soldiers, it is rather difficult to understand it in torture survivors and victims in general. This guilt cannot be understood without taking into account unconscious dynamics: and that is probably why it is excluded from official criteria for diagnosis.

Post-traumatic dreams and symbolisation. The dream dreamt—a method of dream analysis by Ulrich Moser and Ilka von Zeppelin

In the dream generating model of Moser and von Zeppelin (1996), dreaming is assumed to reveal inner possibilities and constraints as well as individual patterns of both (Moser, v. Zeppelin & Schneider, 1991). Information integration and processing are considered to be actions of cognition as well as of affect-laden thought, moderating the dream, giving it its concrete composition. A dream is usually instigated by day residues (experiences, thoughts, wishes, affects), which stimulate a so-called focal conflict. The dream hence tries to find a solution for the thus activated conflict, which will provide the needed safety while accounting for the wished-for involvement—i.e., relationship to others. This stimulated focal conflict is embedded in a dream complex, which can express itself in various different focal conflicts. The notion of a dream complex is closely related to a memory model, where affects, self- and object-representations as well as representations of interactions that have been generalised (RIGs, cf. Stern, 1985) are interlaced in networks. Traumatic experiences form rigid areas within this otherwise flexible network, with not integrated free-floating affects searching for a solution for these traumatic experiences; they are activated in the same form over and over again and are often related to a failure of affect-regulation, causing fearful awakening.

Interrupting a dream scene is one of the most effective means to stop affective overflow when the affects cannot be integrated or become too intensive. Concrete affects and relationships, which may be experienced as verbalised in dreams once the person is capable of language, are considered to be distancing the dreamer from affects and provide him with more control as well as creating a distance between the dreamer and the actual dream event by transforming him into a spectator commenting on his dream.

The dream coding system of Moser and von Zeppelin—as it was used here—is described in detail in Chapter Ten of this volume.

Analysis of a dream

The following dream from the experimental group was analysed by using the Moser method. Hereby the dream is put into sequences of different scenes and transformed into the present tense in order to emphasise the coherent scenes experienced while dreaming.

Table 1. Dream from the experimental group.

S1	They torture me, burn my skin,
–	Don't know [cognitive process]
S1	With hot iron, in different ways.
–	Then I have a lot; all those things [cognitive process]
S2	They capture me, kill me,
–	I don't know [cognitive process]
S3	(They) shoot at me, I see blood.

The coding of this dream reveals the following structure:

Table 2. Coded version of the dream from the experimental group.

Situation	Positioning field	LTM	Interaction field
S1 /C.P./	OP_1 (they) SP		IR.C kin int[1]
S2 /C.P./	OP_1 (they) SP		IR.C kin int
S3 /C.P./	OP_1 (they) SP		IR.C kin int DISS IR.S

The structure of this dream is marked by two interruptions. The C.P. (cognitive process) marking the interruption serves the function to prevent charging the dream with affects. The dreamer remains passive, revealing a helpless self. He fails in creating connections for affects. All the objects remain anonymous, "they" are neither concrete as persons nor can one find interactions or mutual involvement in the dream. On the contrary, the threatening element of the underlying dream complex is not transformed but appears undisguised. There is no social setting, which would provide many possibilities for involvement; the positioning field is not circumscribed (indicating a total threat, not focused on a specific or circumscribed situation). The only way to handle the underlying affectivity (threat) is to interrupt (C.P.). Even though the dreamer makes three attempts, the situation deteriorates and ends in destruction. No solution can be found for how to integrate and manage the affects connected to the dream complex and thus how to interact, and the security principle cannot develop in an adequate way. In other words: simple interruptions with continuation of the same process again, without transformations. The dreamer has no perspective of a possible solution but can only observe his own disintegration.

Let us now contrast this dream from the experimental group with a dream of a subject in the referential group:

Table 3. Dream from the referential group.

S1	It is a kind of graduation, as if I am in a graduation ceremony, as it is a general staff, a general staff of an academy,
–	just like it was when I graduated a long time ago, and now it's like a graduation ceremony,
S1	there are all sorts of people there, a lot of my friends from the academy, then there are some friends from the war, then everything is there, some people from the negotiations I took part in,
–	it was when I was still; while there were some negotiations, I presided over a negotiation delegation, between those warring parties, I was leading one of the negotiation committees, through the mediation of the [agency], who organised our meetings with the [name] party. One party was represented by
S1	so that there is also that [name] who's in the Hague now,
–	he represented, he was; he represented the [name] party in one of those talks, and I represented our party in [toponym],[2] down there.
S1	Then, there are many of those generals,
–	who were later promoted here in;
S2	and then this general [name] appears,
–	I remember him, in the dream, now what I;
S2	there are many invalids as well, who are, who are often turning to me for help, so, it is a colourful company, but it is strange, we first have been all like in a cocktail,
S3	and then everybody disappears only to come back, one by one, to take their diplomas that need to be signed in something like an office, like,

(Continued)

Table 3. (*Continued*).

S4	after which they start collecting money for a festivity, for—for a barbecue, and so on, meaning, that's it, essentially, all that goes on without speeches, without—there is a lot of congratulations.
S3	It is something like this, two armchairs, on one side the man who hands in diplomas, on the other side me.
S4	Well, all are delighted, some of them are solemn, it is not a bad treatment, it is quite a nice relationship, a lot of congratulations, not only to me, but to everybody, so it is, well, a merry ambiance, strangely,
–	I rarely dream of such a merry [laughs] event.

Again the coded version of the present tensed and sequenced dream of a subject from the referential group:

Table 4. Coded version of the dream from the referential group.

Scene	Positioning field	LTM	Interaction field
S1	SP		
	SOC SET		
	OP_1 (G) (friends from academy)		
	OP_2 (G) (friends from war)		
	OP_3 (G) (people from negotiation)		
	OP_4 (toponym)		
	OP_5 (G) (generals)		
/C.P./			
S2	SP		
	SOC SET		
	OP_1 (G) (friends from academy)		
	OP_2 (G) (friends from war)		
	OP_3 (G) (people from negotiation)		
	OP_4 (toponym)		
	OP_5 (G) (generals)		
	OP_6 (name)		
	OP_7 (G) (invalids)		

(*Continued*)

Table 4. (*Continued*).

/C.P./		
S3	SP	IR.C FAIL
	SOC SET	IR.C
	OP_1 (G) (friends from academy)	
	OP_2 (G) (friends from war)	
	OP_3 (G) (people from negotiation)	
	OP_4 (toponym)	
	OP_5 (G) (generals)	
	OP_6 (name)	
	OP_7 (G) (invalids)	
	CEU_1 (armchair)	
	CEU_2 (office)	
	POS REL	
S4	SP	IR.C res
	SOC SET	ATTR AFF
	OP_1 (G) (friends from academy)	
	OP_2 (G) (friends from war)	
	OP_3 (G) (people from negotiation)	
	OP_4 (toponym)	
	OP_5 (G) (generals)	
	OP_6 (name)	
	OP_7 (G) (invalids)	
/C.P./		

It is immediately obvious that this dream is much more complex, comprising many situations. The first two sequences or situations (S1 and S2) are governed by the security principle. The dreamer does not dare to get involved in interactions. What is even worse, the first involvement fails and the objects disappear. However, in contrast to the dream examples from the experimental group, a rich positioning fields allows different options for finding solutions. In the end the involvement is rewarded. In S4 a resonance interaction takes place with positive affectivity. Thus the underlying dream complex seems to have found its resolution: there is a "merry ambiance" between the subject (SP) and the objects (OPs) involved. One might draw the conclusion that the dreamer wishes to find and finally finds an amiable way of how to interact with former friends and/or enemies.

In summary the dream from the experimental group revealed the following: interruptions occurred often, failure of connecting affects, no interactions or mutual involvement, threatening elements of the underlying dream complex appear undisguised, deterioration and destruction were frequent.

In contrast, the dream from the referential group is predominantly governed by the involvement principle; the dream ends with a success of involvement regulation. There is less security regulation necessary and more degrees of freedom in the attempt to solve problems of the dream complex.

Post-traumatic dreams and symbolisation: an empirical investigation by means of the psychoanalytic enunciation analysis

Definition

The psychoanalytic enunciation analysis (PEA) has its roots in psychoanalysis, semiotics, and pragmatics. It has been applied to the fields of psychiatry, psychotherapy, and psychoanalysis (Rosenbaum & Varvin, 2007)—especially concerning the mental conditions of psychosis, trauma, and suicide. In the investigation of dreams, the PEA can be defined as a method that combines the phenomenology of the dream with a psychoanalytically informed analysis of the structure and dynamics of the utterances of the dream telling.

Methodology

The main aim of PEA in our investigation is to evaluate the levels of symbolisation of the manifest dream, and to evaluate the internal subject-other relations (internal object relations) implicitly present in the dream telling.

The method of PEA implies: 1) division of the manifest dream text into enunciation "units"; 2) analysis of the structure of enunciation for each of these "units"; 3) analysis of each "unit" for its manifest and latent content (especially the latent content as emotional content); and 4) evaluation of the transferential relationship implied in the dream as a whole.

Digression on the structure of the enunciation

Benveniste (1970) defined enunciation as the *mise-en-scène* of language through the individual speech-act. That definition implies that the person, the subject who is speaking, is also at the same time embedded in and structured by the speech he is emitting. That characteristic goes equally for the dream-teller: by telling a personal dream the subject reveals its personal-bound characteristics to another subject who listens and to whom the thought of the speech is directed (regardless of the content of the message).

In its simple structure the enunciation is defined as "*I* (first person) say/tell/inform/ask/command/promise *you* (second person) that *this and this* (third person) is *the case* or *reference*".

This model of the simple enunciation implies the following elements: utterances always have traces of an implicit relationship between the first and second person of the dialogue; spatial and temporal references in the utterance are pointing both to what is happening in the outside world and to other elements in the internal world; thoughts are formulated either in a coherent or incoherent way (including dream thoughts); experiences of the bodily relations in the concrete interactions are linked with the verbal-based symbolic representations in the act of speech; single utterances must always be seen in the larger context of the narrative(s).

The term "model of the simple enunciation" signifies that the full or extended model of enunciation is more complex. We shall not describe the extended model here in detail; it suffices to underline that "behind" or "underneath" any utterance there are tacit internal enunciation structures working and they thus give depth to the utterance and define its final structure. When one person in telling his dream says "I do not know what I am saying" then he in reality says "[I say to you that] I do not know what I am saying". In the "[I say to you that]" lies an

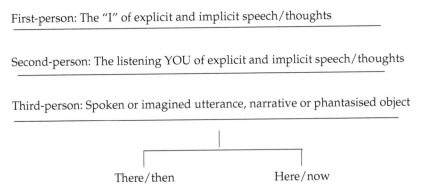

First-person: The "I" of explicit and implicit speech/thoughts

Second-person: The listening YOU of explicit and implicit speech/thoughts

Third-person: Spoken or imagined utterance, narrative or phantasised object

There/then   Here/now

Figure 3. Model of simple enunciation.

internal object relational structure which implies at least two modes of intersubjective dimensions: a *mirroring-imaginary mode* and a *symbolic mode*. In normal conversation these two modes are always present in the dialogue between two persons speaking to each other. But these modes do not necessarily demand a concrete dialogue between two persons present in the room. The two modes are working even in the situation where the person is alone and only engaged in his own fantasies. A person who in his mind has an imagistic scenario—including himself and others in a fantasised communication with him—or a scenario in which he is alone in his interaction with the world (perceiving or sensing the world, moving around, etc.), is also submitted to the enunciation structure. In taking this theoretical stance, the psychoanalytic enunciation analysis diverges from Benveniste's concept of enunciation (as defined above).

The *mirroring-imaginary mode* concerns the subject's immediate experiential reaction to and/or interaction with the world in its spatially conceived scenarios. When the person recounts that "There were two men in the room, and one of them stood in the corner there where darkness hid his face and the other was lying down on the floor that was covered with blood", then the utterance refers to a spatially ordered scenario which the listener can imagine without further verbal reflections as if he himself was present and spatially located in the room. The speaking person creates a mirror in which he himself and the other can mirror both his state of mind and the situation referred to.

If the speaker continues, saying: "They tortured me again and again and wanted me to confess plans that I did not know of. I tried to imagine how I could convince them that I was innocent", then the utterance takes another quality using concepts that are not spatial but rather get their value and meaning through a temporal process in which abstract, symbolic, value-based context-dependent words/concepts come into play. The listener can only understand—imagine, "figure out", "see"—what the message is about by means of the symbolic order (Lacan, 1977), which implies not only understanding the abstract content of the message but also understanding that not everything of what the speaking person wants to convey can be understood. This part of the enunciation structure is called the *symbolic mode*. It is developed through the person's life experiences: it is both situation-dependent and situation-independent, and in the concrete conversation/dream telling it sometimes appears just as immediate and premeditated as the fantasies of the imaginary mode; at other times it is more formed by reflective thoughts and thinking.

In the PEA both the *mirroring-imaginary mode* and the *symbolic mode* can be understood by psychoanalytic concepts. One dimension of the mirroring-imaginary mode has characteristics like the projective identification understood as communication (Bion, 1967; Ogden, 1994). It may consist of an outburst that has the character of no reflections, without an understanding of the content of the outburst, without a wish or capacity to relate to it, marked by confusion that has to be projected into the internal and/or external functioning other as an all-embracing container. Or it may show itself as an attempt to order the room by projecting his perceptions and movements into the other's mind. In opposition to the "ordering" of the imaginary mode, the symbolic mode has more qualities of introjective identification in which values, attitudes, meaningful and common sense words are taken in and brought into perspective as far as possible.

Both modes are necessary dimensions in an integrated symbolic representation of a dream, and in the normal telling of a dream the two modes are linked automatically. Unconscious and preconscious thoughts, images, and emotions are automatically integrated in the dream telling as a whole. As we shall see later, the dream of the severely traumatised person appears with an enunciation structure in which the linking of the mirroring-imaginary mode and the symbolic mode is often disconnected or unstable; that happens especially when the traumatic moments reappear in the retelling of the dream and when the dream has nightmare characteristics.

When it comes to the empirical investigation of the two modes then the notation of the linking/integration of the two modes will either be written as (+) or (–), dependent on whether such integration is either present or absent.

Further methodological remarks

In addition to the standard enunciation analysis as applied in conversational analysis, PEA investigates the content of the dream and the emotionality emerging in its telling. The emotionality of the relating of the dream is affected by: 1) present and past experiences, emotions, and conflicts; 2) the relationship between dream-telling subject and listening subject (the actual or imagined analyst); and 3) traces of unconscious material.

The emotion that concerns us most is the annihilation anxiety which has consistently been investigated by Hurvich (2003).

This concept is divided into different dimensions: fear of being overwhelmed and unable to cope; fear of merging, being devoured and entrapped; fear of disintegration of the self and of identity; fear of humiliation and mortification; fear of emptiness and of disappearing; fear of impingement, penetration, or mutilation; fear of abandonment and need for support; and apprehension over survival, persecution, catastrophe.

Assessing levels of symbolisation

Even though symbolisation has many meanings in the psychoanalytic literature we shall use it here as qualitatively different modes of making language expressions meaningful for another. This may range from meaning-destroyed or meaning-devoid expressions through emotional, imagistic, and primordial mind-state expressions (Robbins, 2011) and further to a thoughtful thinking mode. The latter may be expressed when the person recounts a dream in an understandable fashion so that the listener can follow and "see" the scenarios and the sequences, which may be described with nuances, integrating thoughts, and emotionality. We have chosen to evaluate four dimensions of symbolisation and "score" them on a Likert scale from 1–5.

1. Differentiation of descriptions of dreams (1–5),
2. Interactions and intersubjective relations (1–5),
3. The presence of emotions (1–5),
4. Relation to interviewer (predominance of symbolisation vs. collapse or instability of symbolisation).

Re 1: In evaluating this variable we listen to and assess: details and nuances of the presentation of perceived phenomena—locations, persons, scenarios; qualities of what is seen and what is heard; coherence of the description.

Re 2: This variable is assessed by the following criteria: the telling of intentions and actions involving self and/or other; the modes and nuances of the exchange between self and other.

Re 3: This variable is assessed by the general impression of whether emotions are available or absent in the dream.

Re 4: Here we evaluate whether the utterances are predominantly based in the symbolic mode of speech or in the imaginary mode. Also, we assess whether the two modes shall be considered integrated or dis-integrated. The notation of this is (+) for integration and (−) for dis-integration.

Analysis of two dreams with the psychoanalytic enunciation method

The first dream is presented by a person who has been through traumatic situations in war and who has afterwards been plagued by PTSD symptoms (the mark of "S" refers to the subdivisions of the utterances):

Dream from experimental group, part 2.

S1	After the "Oluja" I was in prison, I had horrific dreams,
S2	for example I dream that they torture me, burn my skin.
S3	What do I know,
S4	With hot iron, in different ways.
S5	Then I had at that time a lot …
S6	all those things that they capture me, kill me.
S7	What do I know,
S8	shoot at me, I see blood.

The table below summarises our findings of PEA, including the understanding of the manifest and latent level of the dream but excluding the transferential assumptions.

Table 5. Summaries of PEA.

Sequence/PEA	Manifest level	Latent level
S1 D3;+;D2	My experience of a horrifying event is linked to a horrifying dream	I am filled with feelings of horror. Annihilation anxiety
S2 D2;+;D3	I am imprisoned and brought to pain	Feelings of being mutilated and penetrated. Inability to defend myself

(Continued)

Table 5. (*Continued*).

S3 D1;+	I am not sure of the implication of or of the fact of what I am saying	Feelings of confusion and shaken identity; apprehension of catastrophe
S4 D2;+	Torturing instruments on my body	Instrumental, impersonal threat: mutilation, penetration
S5 D2;+	I have many other feelings/visions/memories of torture that I cannot mention	Wish to escape and fear of being trapped and of bodily mutilation
S6 D1;+	They kill me	Annihilation anxiety. Anxiety of not getting support for survival
S7 D1;+	I am not sure about what they exactly are doing	Confusion, no representation
S8 D1;+	Somebody is shooting, blood is coming	Catastrophic feelings of death, life running out

The global assessment of the dream

The following level of symbolic functioning could be asserted: degree of differentiation = 2; degree of interactions = 2; emotions expressed = 2.

As to the emotions, the dreamer was overwhelmed by annihilation anxiety, but able to convey his confused emotions.

We estimated that the dream was characterised by a dominance of bodily anchored symbol representation, i.e., mostly not-symbolised signifiers and signifiers in the imaginary mode.

As to the transferential assumptions, we found that the dream telling started with a belief in the interviewer as a "good object" listener. Soon the good object turned into someone who becomes a maybe reliable, maybe unreliable receiver of anxiety, fear of body mutilation and fear of death.

The referential group dream.

S9	Then, there were many of those generals, who were later promoted here in;
S10	and then this general (...) appears, I remember him, in the dream, now what I;

(*Continued*)

S11	there were many invalids as well, who are, who are often turning to me for help, so, it was a colourful company,
S12	but it was strange, we first had been all like in a cocktail, and then everybody disappeared only to come back, one by one, to take their diplomas that needed to be signed in something like an office, like,
S13	after which they started collecting money for a festivity, for—for a barbecue, and so on,
S14	meaning, that's it, essentially,
S15	all that went on without speeches, without—there was a lot of congratulations,
S16	That's what I dreamed of last night, nothing bad, so that's how it was, a dream that was quite OK.

The findings of the PEA for this dream are shown in the following table.

Table 6. Findings of the PEA for dream from referential group.

Sequence/PEA	Manifest level of dream	Latent level of dream
S9 D4;+;D2	Many generals promotion	Wondering about their promotion. Suspiciousness. Corruption?
S10 D4;+:D2	One special general	Uncertainty and insecure feeling
S11 D5;+;D2	Many people, invalidated by war. Colourful. i.e., differentiated/many-sided. I was a helper	Fear of mutilation, distancing himself from horror. Denial. Defensive self-appraisal
S12 D5;+;D2	Strange occurrence: cocktail party gathering followed by disappearance followed by reappearance getting their honour one-by-one	Feelings of separation, losing contact. Trying to find meaning. Underlying anxiety?
S13 D4;+;D2	Festivity, collective effort	Manic joyful feelings, mixed with uneasy surprise

(Continued)

Table 6. (*Continued*).

S14 D4;+;D2	I told the essential things	Closing the information down
S15 D4;+;D2	No formal speeches but congratulations	Surprise, deviation from standard: no voice, only gestures
S16 D4;+;D2	Finding oneself at ease with what happened	Pressure for convincing and comforting oneself

The global assessment of the dream

The following level of symbolic functioning could be asserted:

- Degree of differentiation   3
- Degree of interactions with others   4
- Emotions represented or expressed   3

As to the transferential relation:

The dreamer tried to develop a positive scenario to the analyst. He managed almost to create an atmosphere with positive connotations, good feelings and events, and a friendly relation to the interviewer. In the end he did not succeed: people appear separated, no speech is available to explain the situation, and a scenario with manic defence is created.

Summary

The psychoanalytic enunciation analysis enables the researcher to demonstrate the existence and function of both the imaginary mode and the symbolic mode in the dream and in the telling of it to the analyst/ researcher. Both levels of symbolisation and the quality of the relation between them inform us about the internal and external relationship between the individual who has had the dream and the listener. From analysis of these two dreams a picture comparable with results from the Moser/von Zeppelin method emerges: the referential group dream is characterised by higher level of symbolic and relational quality than the dream of the experimental group even though the trauma related latent material is obvious and even though it is not a "successful" dream in terms of integration of past and present and affect regulation. The dream of the individual from the referential group depicts thus higher security (less security regulation is necessary), more freedom to solve problems, and more involvement (good feelings, positive relations).

Concluding section: clinical significance of empirical results

From what has been demonstrated here, we would like to direct the focus to some aspects that seem to be of special significance in the treatment of patients who have suffered extreme traumatisation.

The analysis of dreams performed showed that post-traumatic states and especially post-traumatic dreams represent more or less failed attempts at restoring meaning in the internal world, meaning in relation to others and, maybe most of all, failed attempts to regain a sense of security and safety. A threatening catastrophe is looming everywhere for the traumatised, both from inside and, projected or not, from outside. The traumatised experiences a host of anxieties and fears including fear of loss of object love, fear of loss of the internal good object, and castration anxiety. What seems to be at the root of this psychic helplessness characteristic for traumatisation (Freud, 1926), may be well depicted by the concept of annihilation anxiety, which seems to be related to symbolising/desymbolising processes and feelings of guilt.

Freud distinguished traumatic neuroses from other neuroses in terms of the nature of the conflict in the ego (Freud, 1919). In ordinary neuroses the "enemy" is the libido, which threatens the ego from within. "In traumatic and war neuroses, the human ego is defending itself from a danger which threatens it from without or which is embodied by a shape assumed by the ego itself" (Freud, 1919, p. 210). Fixation at the moment of the traumatic experience is the basis of a traumatic neurosis, and such patients regularly repeat the traumatic situation in their dreams (Freud, 1916).

From here one may well assume that symptoms of traumatic neuroses (Freud, 1919) represent a regression to a more primitive mode of functioning: "The painful situation which overwhelmed the ego is constantly being repeated in fantasy, thought and dream, as an attempt of the ego to master belatedly the overwhelming influx of stimuli it had failed to handle in the traumatic moment" (Greenson, 1945, p. 194). Furthermore, according to van der Kolk (1996), traumatic memories usually come back as emotional and sensory states without the capacity to represent them verbally. He attributes this failure of processing information on a symbolic level to the core of PTSD, as it is this essential ability that is needed to properly categorise and integrate traumatic experience with other experience.

Laub (2005) impressively described the overwhelming experience that hampers the process of construction when attempting to account for traumatic experiences. He states that in order to process information, i.e., to make it our own, we employ the process of symbolisation in order to perceive, grasp, or participate in reality.

For this, symbols are needed that will allow us to communicate not only with the outside world, but also to communicate with our self— i.e., with an empathic object in the internal world—in order to create meaning. According to Freud the process of symbolisation is characterised by an internal psychic event, i.e., a thing representation, becoming linked to another psychic event, i.e., a psychological word representation, and that this linking of thing and word representations creates a symbol. In other words, Freud saw the formation of the symbol as occurring in the context of an internal communicative process, or as Laub puts it: "One comes to know one's story only by telling it to oneself," and "Reality can be grasped only in a condition of affective attunement with oneself" (Laub, 2005, p. 315). In extreme traumatic situations these internal and external dialogic relationships are being subject to deadly assault, in that the empathically, in tune, and responsive other threatens to disappear both in the internal world and also in the external world. This, so it seems, characterises the core aim of a traumatising assault, which ultimately aims to abolish the "good object" that enables and safeguards the communicative process of symbolisation.

Traumatic dreams are characterised among others by their repetitiveness. As Varvin (2003) has put it, trauma is the result of the loss of internal protection related to the internal other—primarily the loss of basic trust and mastery, which is experienced as loss of the protective and empathic other, who in other circumstances gives meaning to thoughts and actions. In such traumatic conditions, the process of symbolisation is distorted to the extent that thoughts cannot be given a temporally meaningful place in the emotional autobiographical narrative. As a result the traumatised feels dehumanised, frequently accompanied by feelings of shame. In order to regain a humanised state, repetition compulsion comes into play, forcing the traumatised to relive the traumatising experience repeatedly in the attempt to find symbols and protosymbols for opposing forces experienced within, to avoid a catastrophic fusion of the two antagonistic forces and (re-)gain the ability to distinguish the good from the bad and ultimately avoid psychic death. From clinical experience it is well known that extreme traumatisation may produce defects or deficits in this ability to symbolise and think or reflect.

Dreaming may be considered as a central part of the mind's work with unmetabolised, trauma-related elements (Bion, 1977; Hartmann, 1984). The study of dreams may thus give a privileged insight into the working of the mind (Freud, 1900). Working with dreams and especially nightmares of traumatised patients has proved to be of great importance in aiding the traumatised mind to restore its symbolic function (Hartmann, 1984; Adams-Silvan & Silvan, 1990; Pöstenyi, 1996). Furthermore, traumatic dreams seem to be dominated by claustrum-like internal object-relation patterns where speech or narratives will be more of an imaginary kind and lacking symbolising capacities.

When treating traumatised patients the quality of the experienced trauma seems to be relevant for the yielded convalescence in psychotherapy. Torture survivors—the most difficult group of patients to treat—exhibit some specifics worth mentioning here, as the torture itself contains such monstrous acts that make them inconceivable not only to the victim but also to the listener of accounts given by the victim, as described earlier. There does not seem to be a possibility of making sense of acts performed by the perpetrator, thus inhibiting the capacity to symbolise these acts in a comprehensible manner. But it is exactly this capacity that will enable the victim to grasp his feelings, emotions, and reactions. It is the dehumanisation that both victims and perpetrators encounter and the humiliation forced onto the victim that limit the capacity to symbolise, i.e., to put into words what has happened and make sense of it.

This can be considered to be a self-defence (Torsti, 2000; Gaddini, 1984), a refusal to integrate, motivated by integration anxiety. In a state of non-integration, anxiety threatens from two directions of time: the past catastrophic experience of loss of the total self and the threat of future integration—a threat because it assumes remembering and thus arouses the fear of renewed anxiety due to loss of self. This "annihilation anxiety" is motivated by the wish to avoid the catastrophic experience and it prevents both integration and the symbolisation process.

Considering the dream process as a special kind of thought process that excludes the typical reality perception of waking thought will be helpful in understanding the traumatised mind. In this dream-thought process interactions may take place. In contrast to a waking state, subjects and objects in the dream scenario may easily change dimension impossible to everyday life.

By looking at the dreams of the traumatised through the focal point of the Moser method, disturbances of affect-regulation become apparent. Those disturbances reflect the dreamer's inability to get involved with others in the dream scenario due to anxieties, especially annihilation anxiety, evoked by such involvement. In the Moser analysis we say that the security principle (avoid anxiety) overrules the involvement principle in these dreams. Here the extreme helplessness of the patient becomes evident. From this point of view a wish is fulfilled, namely the wish to regain a feeling of internal security (by avoiding anxiety provoking situations in the dream scenario).

Within the theoretical framework of Moser's dream-generating model (1996), the dreamer's capacity to get involved is an indicator of his ability to find a solution for an activated conflict, which in the context of trauma is embedded in a rigid traumatic complex. In our study we hypothesised that traumatised dreamers would exhibit a great lack of involvement capacity. This we have demonstrated in the dream from the experimental group. The capacity to get involved—although initially accessible—is consequently disrupted by the dreamer's distancing manoeuvres that are activated in order to avoid upcoming overwhelming emotions of life and death. In contrast, dreams of the referential group exhibit a higher level of integration, where the involvement principle predominates and security regulation seems less necessary. This is seen as potentially helping the dreamer towards a resolution of the underlying traumatic complex. This process implies binding free-floating, anxiety laden and incomprehensible emotions to generalised memories of experiences that did make sense earlier in one's own past.

When researching dreams one must be aware of the fact that a dream dreamt in a laboratory setting is distinct from one dreamt during a psychoanalytic process. Mainly it is the context that differs, as a dream dreamt in a psychoanalytic process will be determined to a large extent by the specific transference situation, which will be quite different from the transferential aspects of dreams dreamt in a laboratory, where the setting will elicit special expectations regarding the research.

Nevertheless, changes in transference patterns may be detected by the PEA method, indicating the extent to which the analyst or the interviewer in a laboratory is used as an all-embracing container for anxieties, sadness, or fragmented self-experience. "Soon the listener of the dream becomes a receiver of anxiety, fear of body mutilation, fear of death" (Rosenbaum & Varvin, 2007). The dream of the person from the experimental group exhibited bodily anchored symbol presentations, which are mostly not-symbolised signifiers portraying thus the overwhelming annihilation anxiety. In contrast to this, the dream of the person from the referential group portrayed the dreamer's ability to develop a positive scenario managing to almost create an atmosphere with positive connotations. But even here—this person,who did not suffer from PTSD—did not succeed in his integrating endeavours in the end, and was forced to create a scenario of manic defence.

Thus, PEA, by analysing the form and content of the imaginary mode, i.e., the mode in which a person presents himself in a monadic and dyadic way, enables a closer analysis of the pain-evacuating, projective, claustrum-like internal object-relation patterns that dominated his dream world and his inner world. PEA thus reflects the influence that trauma has on our psyche: there was a dominance of the imaginary mode and absence of the symbolic mode of speech. That is, the absence of an other-oriented mode, signifying a mentalising, self-reflective, inter- or trans-subjective internal object-relation pattern.

We do not expect the clinical working analyst to apply these methods to dreams, but we hope to have encouraged analysts to listen to narratives and dreams in a modified way. From a clinical perspective the findings presented here call for the analyst to pay more attention to what degree the dreamer gets involved in his dreams and how this involvement is realised. On the one hand the dreamer may withdraw, for example by interrupting interactions in a scene to fend off unbearable emotions; on the other hand one may see development of interactions which may imply strengthening of the symbolic mode of functioning.

In summary it can be stated that traumatic dreams are not different from other dreams in that they in fact are dreams containing—like all dreams—thought processes in a dream state with all the mechanisms of dreams at work in a more or less successful search for alleviation of the incomprehensible dehumanising forces at work at the time of the traumatising experience.

Notes

1. Interactional relation of kinesthetic intentional quality, that is: moving with an intention.
2. Name of location.

References

Adams-Silvan, A. & Silvan, M. (1990). A dream is the fulfillment of a wish: Traumatic dream, repetition compulsion, and the pleasure principle. *International Journal of Psychoanalysis, 71*: 513–522.

Benveniste, E. (1970). L'appareil formel de l'enonciation. *Langages, 17*: 1218.

Bion, W. R. (1967). *Second Thoughts. Selected Papers on Psychoanalysis.* London: Karnac.

Bion, W. R. (1977). *Seven Servants.* New York: Aronson.

Blake, D. D., Weathers, F. W., Nagy, L. M., Kaloupek, D. G., Gusman, F. D., Charney, D. S. & Keane, T. M. (1995). The development of a clinician-administered PTSD scale. *Journal of Traumatic Stress, 8*(1): 75–90.

Derogatis, L. R. (1983). *SCL-90-R. Administration, Scoring, and Procedural Manual.* Baltimore, MD: Clinical Psychometric Research.

First, M. B., Spitzer, R. L., Gibbon, M. & Williams, J. (1996). *Structured Clinical Interview for DSM-IV Axis I Disorders—Patient Edition (SCID-I/P, Version 2.0).* New York: Biometrics Research Department, New York State Psychiatric Institute.

Fischmann, T. (2007). Einsturz bei Nacht: Verarbeitung traumatischer Erlebnisse im Traum. In: H. Raulff & M. Dorrmann (Eds.), *Schlaf und Traum* (pp. 51–58). Cologne, Germany: Böhlau.

Fosshage, J. L. (1997). The organizing functions of dream mentation. *Contemporary Psychoanalysis, 33*: 429–458.

Freud, S. (1900). The Interpretation of dreams. *S. E. 4* : ix–627.

Freud, S. (1917). Introductory lectures to psychoanalysis (part III). *S. E. 16*: 241–463.

Freud, S. (1919). Introduction to psychoanalysis and the war neurosis. *S. E. 17*: 205–216.

Freud, S. (1926). Inhibitions, symptoms and anxiety. *S. E. 20*: 75–176.

Gaddini, E. (1984). The presymbolic activity of the infant mind. In: A. Limentani (Ed.), *A Psychoanalytic Theory of Infantile Experience* (pp. 164–177). London: Tavistock/Routledge, 1992.

Greenson, R. R. (1945). Practical approaches to the war neuroses. *Bulletin of the Menninger Clinic*, 9: 192–205.

Hartmann, E. (1984). *The Nightmare. The Psychology and Biology of Dreams.* New York: Basic.

Hartmann, E. (1999). Träumen kontextualisiert Emotionen. Eine neue Theorie über das Wesen und die Funktionen des Träumens. In: H. Bareuther, K. Brede, M. Ebert-Saleh, K. Grünberg & S. Hau (Eds.), *Traum, Affekt und Selbst* (pp. 115–157). (Psychoanalytische Beiträge aus dem Sigmund-Freud-Institut, 1.) Tübingen, Germany: Edition Diskord.

Hurvich, M. (2003). The place of annihilation anxieties in psychoanalytic theory. *Journal of the American Psychoanalytic Association*, 51: 579–616.

Jovic, V., Opacic, G., Knezevic, G., Tenjovic, L. & Lecic-Tosevski, D. (2002). War stressors assessment questionnaire—psychometric evaluation. *Psihijatrija Danas*, 35: 51–75.

Lacan, J. (1977). *Écrits.* Harmondsworth, UK: Penguin.

Lansky, M. & Bley, C. R. (1995). *Post Traumatic Night Mares. Psychodynamic Explorations.* Hillsdale, NJ: Analytic.

Laub, D. (2005). Traumatic shutdown of narrative and symbolization: A death instinct derivative? *Contemporary Psychoanalysis*, 41(2): 307–326.

McCann, I. L. & Pearlman, L. A. (1990). Vicarious traumatization: A framework for understanding the psychological effects of working with victims. *Journal of Traumatic Stress*, 3: 131–149.

Moser, U. & von Zeppelin, I. (1996). *Der geträumte Traum.* Stuttgart, Germany: Kohlhammer.

Moser, U., von Zeppelin, I. & Schneider, W. (1991). The regulation of cognitive-affective processes. A new psychoanalytic model. In: U. Moser & I. v. Zeppelin (Eds.), *Cognitive-Affective Processes* (pp. 87–134). Heidelberg, Germany: Springer.

Ogden, T. H. (1994). The analytic third: Working with intersubjective clinical facts. *International Journal of Psychoanalysis*, 75: 3–19.

Pöstenyi, A. (1996). Hitom lustprincipen. Dröm, trauma, dödsdrift. (Beyond the pleasure principle. Dream, trauma, death drive.) *Divan*: 4–16.

Robbins, M. (2011). *The Primordial Mind in Health and Illness.* London: Routledge.

Rosenbaum, B. & Varvin, S. (2007). The influence of extreme traumatisation on body, mind and social relations. *International Journal of Psychoanalysis*, 88: 1527–1542.

Stern, D. (1985). *The Interpersonal World of the Infant.* London: Karnac.

Torsti, M. (2000). At the sources of the symbolization process: The psycho-analyst as an observer of early trauma. *Psychoanalytic Study of the Child*, 55: 275–297.

van der Kolk, B. A. (1996). Trauma and memory. In: B. A. Van der Kolk, A. C. McFarlaine & L. Weisëth (Eds.), *Traumatic Stress* (pp. 279–302). New York: Guilford.

Varvin, S. (2003). *Mental Survival Strategies after Extreme Traumatisation.* Copenhagen, Denmark: Multivers.

Varvin, S. & Rosenbaum, B. (2003). Extreme traumatisation: Strategies for mental survival. *International Forum of Psychoanalysis*, 12: 5–16.

Weiss, D. & Marmar, C. (1997). The impact of event scale—revised. In: J. Wilson & T. Keane, (Eds.). *Assessing Psychological Trauma and PTSD* (pp. 399–411). New York: Guilford Press.

CHAPTER TWELVE

Communicative functions of dream telling

Hanspeter Mathys

Introduction

Why do people share their dreams? What motivates patients in therapy to communicate their dreams to their therapists and analysts? What expectations are connected with telling dreams?

In psychoanalysis we assume that the analyst is the expert in the interpretation of dreams; analysands tell the analyst their dreams to learn something about themselves (Boothe, 2006). In the favourable case, analysands are able to examine and analyse their dream contents, and in the even more favourable case there is appropriation and reconciliation with portions of their personality that are alien to them and not very welcome. Bartels (1979) emphasises that the motivation to communicate dreams lies in the irritating experience of the mysterious, the enigmatic: we know what we dreamed, but we do not know why and what for (see Freud, 1916/1917, p. 94). It is this *break* between dream and waking life that provokes the wish for an explanation, for interpretation (Bartels, 1979, p. 102, freely translated here). This was the starting point for the single case study of the dream dialogue between "Amalie X" and her analyst presented in the following.[1]

Strange disinterest in her own dreams

I assumed that the analysand, Amalie X, and her analyst would to some extent be interested in and make an effort to understand the contents of the dreams that Amalie X told. However, I found that this was not necessarily the case with the analysand. She seemed strangely uninterested in the content of her dreams, or better said, in joint examination of the meaning of her dreams. The question thus arose: why did this patient share ninety-five dreams in her analysis, if she did not at all want to know what they meant?

This phenomenon is not unknown in psychoanalysis. There is risk involved when we share our dreams. Just how much we are disclosing is not at all foreseeable at the point in time when we communicate the manifest dream. It is only through the course of in-depth conversation on the dream and in (joint) thinking about the hidden meaning of the latent content that the challenge that is hidden in the dream becomes gradually revealed. Dream narratives thus involve a great deal of lack of control. This is why persons sharing dreams have such mixed feelings. For one, dreamers want to share the enigmatic experience with someone, in the hope that the expert can say what the dreams mean. For another, dreamers do not want to share the dream at all, because things can come to light that they do not want to know anything about. If the latter feeling dominates, we call this resistance.

However, in the sessions that I examined, the resistance interpretation did not always fit. Instead, I found that this patient often communicated her dreams in a very particular way—namely, she shared her dreams in a way that the telling of the dream had a very definite function in the course of the conversation. In psychoanalytic dream research, this way of looking at things has come to be called the "communicative function of dream telling".

The communicative function of dream telling

Kanzer (1955) originally used the phrase, "the communicative function of the dream". Starting out from a comment by Ferenczi (1913), Kanzer (1955) began to develop a perspective according to which the person chosen by the dreamer to listen to a dream was "preferably the actual subject of the dream" (p. 260). According to Kanzer, "The urge to communicate, therefore, arising out of the dream may be seen as a continuation of a tendency within the dreamer to establish contact with reality, as represented by the day's residue" (p. 260). A good ten years later, Bergmann (1966) developed this idea further, among other things by placing it in a historical/cultural context. Especially interesting for the psychoanalytic situation is Bergmann's explanation of how communication of a dream comes about at all. Bergmann saw the telling of dreams as arising out of the simultaneous mobilisation of two antagonistic driving forces: a desire to communicate, and resistance to communicating. The wish to communicate puts the dream on the agenda, so to speak; resistance makes the dream incomprehensible. The telling of dreams thus has a function of lightening a person's load, for by sharing the dream, conflict-laden feelings can be expressed that cannot otherwise be communicated. This assessment was taken up by John Klauber, who also studied the meaning of the telling of dreams in psychoanalysis. Klauber (1969) presented further ideas on this in the form of eight metapsychological assertions defining dream telling as a clinical phenomenon, which can be read as the instinct theory foundation of Kanzer's and Bergmann's ideas:

> The partial breaking through of a repressed wish in a dream produces in the dreamer the urge to share the dream, since drive impulses that are no longer under complete control by the ego must seek discharge. The verbalization of the dream and also the dream itself are a substitute for discharge. (p. 282, freely translated here)

In the German language literature, the question concerning the communicative function of dream telling was taken up by Morgenthaler (1986) under the term *Traumdiagnostik* (dream diagnostics) and by Deserno (1992) as *funktionaler Zusammenhang von Traum und Übertragung* (the functional connection between dream and transference), and further developed by Ermann (1998), who saw dream analysis as relationship analysis.

The transcript excerpts in the following will serve to illustrate what is meant by the communicative function connected with the sharing of dreams.

Do these dreams show me to be very odd? (session 7)

The first passage presented here is from Amalie X's seventh session and thus quite at the beginning of her analytic treatment.

After telling some stories about teaching school, Amalie shared a dream:

Passage 1[2]

1 P: oh yes but I am concerned about something else entirely (2) and it's (6) hm (15) ...
2 A: yeah ...
3 P: yeahhaaaa (laughs) I'm embarrassed, as it were ...
4 A: hmm ...
5 P: well, yeah, I had a dream last night and ...
6 A: yeah ...
7 P: and I would actually like to know whether it, hm (7), makes me totally weird compared to others (3).

This announcement of having had a dream is obviously connected with shame (I'm embarrassed, line 3). And the dream is announced together with a very specific concern (line 7). This concern forms the contextual frame for the telling of the dream.

Her actual telling of the dream then takes place in her third try. The dream was the following (here translated from the German):

> And I dreamed there was a woman; she looked like a Madonna by Raphael, and she came in the door; it was probably some kind of wedding night. Well, that's what it seemed to me, and uh, her dress was very low-cut and more transparent than anything else, and she lay down and then came, I'm not sure what, na yeah in any case, a relatively young man came in, and uh, he tried to deflower the woman, and it didn't work, uh, and I think he said so, too. And then a second man came, oh yeah the first man he also, uh, practically like a child, he allowed himself to be breastfed, and the second man, he, yeah, he managed to do it, yeah, as far as I remember.

In the dialogue on this dream, Amalie expressed her astonishment that her dreams could have such concrete and undisguised sexual content, and she asked herself whether this was normal, as dreams usually appeared in a more encoded form. In the further course of the conversation, it became apparent that Amalie was not very interested in the specific content of her dream or the question as to what it might mean for her. Instead, she told the dream mainly in connection with her question at the start: she wanted to know whether this kind of dream showed her to be odd or weird as compared to other people, and further, whether she was different from others in the whole area of sexuality.

Sharing a dream opens up communicative possibilities

Amalie used dream telling in session 7, and in numerous other sessions, such that through referring to the dream, she could express something that could otherwise not have been communicated in this way or at all. The sharing of the dream serves first and foremost to prepare the way, as an introductory preparation to be better able or able at all to speak about delicate, difficult, or shameful things. The sharing of the dream is meant to create a kind of atmosphere for this. The mode of dream telling is eminently suitable for this purpose. Dreaming happens at night and nowhere else other than inside oneself. And yet it does not feel as if one had produced it all by oneself: The German expression *mir hat geträumt* (it came to me in a dream) in the passive voice illustrates this point. There is no subject, no I, that sees itself as the author of the night-time scene. Instead, the dreamer experiences the dream as something that happens to him or her, that comes from the outside. And yet, of course, the dreamer himself or herself is the director and producer of this short and often surreal film that plays at night on the inner dream screen. The dreamer is never merely an uninvolved spectator—even though it often feels just and only that way.

This subjective feeling that the dream is one's own but also alien creates a great deal of freedom for the dreamer to position herself. She herself can determine the extent to which she can and wants to appropriate this mental product or can and wants to leave it in distanced foreignness. In the case examined, Amalie used the dream in a very specific way. To paraphrase, she was saying, "What these two men and the Madonna have to do with me I really don't know. But what interests me is, is it actually normal to dream about sexual things in such an open way? And while we are on the topic, am I normal in my sexuality, or am I very odd?"

How do you say goodbye to your analyst? (session 517)

A second passage, which is taken from the final session (session 517), shows Amalie's specific handling of her dreams very clearly.

How do you do this in the very last therapy session? How do you say goodbye to your analyst after more than five years and more than 500 sessions?

Passage 2

1   P: Oh (hh.) (3) (hh.) (hh.) oh dear; (hh.) (14) how do the politicians put it

2   so nicely when it's their birthday, (1) just a normal workday. (hh.) (hh.) (2)

3   just a normal workday (53) hm (hh.) (hh.) (exhales very deeply) (2) I'll

4   tell you a dream;

5   A: Hm

6   P: Hm; (4) heard there are patients that just don't show up for their final sessions I

7   was close to doing that; (2) or (1) not saying anything more (.) you can do that, too (2)

8   you can do all of that sure (7) I dreamed that (1) Doctor *171

9   walked somewhere, (.) NO (.) that's not right at all; *59 (3) among colleagues and (2) I don't know

10   I laughed about him or people laughed about him (.) because of the way he did this or that;

11 A: Went, you mean walked away

12 P: No he ran.

13 A: (–) hm Yeah.

14 P: But I think it was Mrs. *95 and it was about (.) ending analysis and and (hh.) uh

15   somehow they were (.) making fun of him how he did it ah yeah it was HIM!

This excerpt is from near the beginning of this session, after the analyst had given Amalie a questionnaire to take with her to fill out for evaluation purposes. What is noticeable is that Amalie's opening (line 1) is spoken in a pronouncedly hesitant way and accompanied by moans and groans. It gives the impression that it is not easy for her to speak. What she says in line 2 makes it clear that she would like this occasion, the final session of her analysis, to be handled as normally as possible. She knows full well, of course, that this is not a normal session, but she would like to treat it as though it were. But she also knows that the analyst expects her to view this as a special session. What to do? Ah, she had a dream last night … and conveniently, it was about ending analysis (line 14).

Passage 3 is part of the dream dialogue about the first dream, where the scene changes to a cemetery, and where elderly ladies and shoehorns play a central role. After line 6 Amalie then tells a second dream.

Passage 3

1 P: I can only say again that your wife =
2 A: h = hm
3 P: Got into the shoe very well. (0.5) and I could only do it with the aid of a shoe horn. (1) (moans)
4 A: It was also a question of how much help you got here and (1.5) uhm
5 P: You know I still wanted to tell you quick what I [dreamed] last night
6 A: [h = hm]

At this point Amalie tells her second dream of the last session:

> Among many other things. When it, it, I have a kind of intercom, a kind of door opener, with a telephone, and it rang and somebody said, "I just want to find out from you what interpretation is, or how you interpret." And then I said, "Are you an academic?" and then the voice said yes and then I pushed the button, and then it was not a woman who came up the stairs as I had expected, from her voice, but a whole family, a whole lot of people, men, women, most of them older, and they said we are all anthroposophists and downstairs below me, that was at home in my apartment in the dream, a door opened quickly and *239 handed out a book and said "Here's everything you want to know about interpretation." And then as they stood at my door they said "So we are anthroposophists." And then there was a big piano in my apartment and it was suddenly a complete mess: it was horrible! There was a dress lying on the glass table, and underpants on the couch. And it was terrible and in the dream I was thinking but I tidied up when *197 came, and, it was, then, I didn't think it was so terribly tragic then and I just stuffed everything under the couch cushion. And I tried to tidy up a little. And then we talked about,

hermeneutics, or, somebody suddenly went to the piano and I don't know what else. In any case it didn't look like guests in my apartment. And that was astonishing. Yesterday evening I talked to a woman acquaintance on the telephone and she told me she had been invited somewhere and there it was astonishing there. The place stank and stank of cats and everything was strewn around, pants, a man's athletic pants on the table and, it was terrible she said. A dirty apartment. That conversation was yesterday evening and … That's it, looked in my apartment like it never looks. And recently at the X-ray I met a very interesting man who was an anthroposophist, from *955.

Just after this dream report, the conversation continues with the following passage:

Passage 4

1 P: But I believe you wanted to say something else (2) how much help I got do you want to know that

2   in grams and decimal points? I can't give you [an answer].

3 A: [hm] No and not that I wanted to know that and it was (.) your thought. and it was (.) a thought

4   about the (.) shoehorn (.) and on help.

5 P: Yes (hh.) (5)

In passage 3, line 4 the analyst, starting out from the first dream, addresses something that has been in the air since the last session: what did the analysand actually receive here in therapy; what does she take with her when the final session is over? Perhaps the analyst would like to hear his patient say with gratitude that the treatment had helped her a lot, the therapist had done a good job, and that parting was difficult for her. And how does Amalie react to this remark? She does not utter one syllable in response to that request (passage 3, line 5) and instead tells the analyst another dream. In passage 3, line 5 (I still wanted to tell you quick) it becomes clear that she has no intention of devoting full and detailed attention to what happened in the dream or to invite the analyst to join her in examining the last dream carefully. The function here is very similar to the function of her telling of the first dream. Here again the focus in on handling a communicative task, a task that Amalie solves by sharing a dream. It is interesting that with this the topic is not over and done with. Passage 4, line 1 refers directly back to the conversation prior to her telling the dream (passage 3, line 4). Amalie's comment unmasks the suspected expectations of her analyst. The analyst states neutrally in line 4 (passage 3): It was also a question of how much help you got here. In Amalie's rephrasing she stresses that it is the analyst who much desires to know this (passage 4, line 1). Using an extremely sarcastic metaphor, she lets him know what she thinks of this request. She depicts the analyst as a bookkeeper who seeks to measure the treatment success in precise quantities—in numbers, grams, and decimal points. By portraying the whole undertaking as absurd, she has done with the topic surely and finally.

Results

In session 517 Amalie does not tell the two dreams so that she can talk about an important concern, which had been the case in session 7. Instead, here she shares dreams so that she does *not* have to talk about something: she thus can initially avoid the topic of saying goodbye to the analyst and avoid an evaluative look back at her therapy. But it is interesting that telling the dream does not mean that these topics are done. The beginning sequence of the first dream deals explicitly with the current conversation context—namely, how do you end analysis. In the second instance of dream telling, after recounting the dream, Amalie immediately and explicitly takes up the question that the therapist had asked before the dream, although her comment does not match the preferred expectation. In both instances the conversation gets back to the original topic via the detour of a dream.

It was found that Amalie used this very particular pattern often. The undisguised sexual dream in session 7, which is taken as a given and about which one cannot do anything, serves as a welcome opportunity to be able to speak at all about the shameful topic of sexuality, which is connected with a lot of insecurity (session 7). And when it is time to say goodbye to the therapist and there is the question about how this is to be best handled, and when the analyst even wants to know what he has given the patient, it is extremely advantageous to have one or two dreams that you can tell, so as to get through the delicate and difficult farewell ceremony more easily (session 517).

What is happening here, actually? What does this very specific use of dreams mean?

Dream telling as a triangulating mode of communication

Introducing a dream into the conversation establishes a triadic form of communication out of a dyadic one. This is equivalent to a form of regulation of relations between analyst and analysand. This function is found so consistently in Amalie's therapy, from the start of treatment to the end, that it can be assessed as very important. I call it the triangulating function of sharing dreams. Stated very simply and independently of dream telling, the meaning of triangulation is as follows: in a triangle, the relationship between two points is regulated by reference to the third point (Grieser, 2003).

In many cases Amalie introduces a dream narrative to modulate and regulate her direct relationship to the analyst via the triangulating factor of the dream. This is not only distancing herself from the here and now, but it is also often a successful achievement of a compromise, in that the dream continues to take up the topic of the analytical relationship but does so in the dream mode and thus in the mode that is more distanced and entails less responsibility. A look at several passages reveals a clear interactive pattern that shows how the temporary distancing of herself from the here and now of the analytic relationship via the detour of the dream accomplishes a new approach towards being able to talk about delicate, shameful, or unpleasant things.[3]

Dream telling in the service of wish fulfilment

Whereas this triangulating function plays a constant central role in Amalie's analysis from the start to the end of treatment, another interesting phenomenon in handling dreams in the sessions develops, starting at approximately the middle of her analysis. More and more, Amalie tells not only her own dreams but also other people's dreams, such as her boyfriend's or her mother's. But not only that—she also interprets these dreams in the presence of her analyst. She thus performs dream interpretations of other people's dreams. And she apparently expects that the analyst will take a position on her interpretations.

In the second half of her analytic treatment, Amalie involves her analyst more and more in using the dream sessions as a kind of further education course in dream interpretation. This is shown on the basis of three guiding principles in working with dreams:

1. Amalie's aim is not interpretation of the contents of her dreams in a cooperative dialogue; instead, she is interested in the act of interpreting dreams itself.
2. Her goal is to learn and master the art of dream interpretation, an art to which she ascribes a phallic quality.
3. The way to her goal is via participation in the analyst's art of interpretation, which she perceives as phallic (for a detailed derivation of this function, see Mathys, 2010).

This development, described only briefly here, reaches its logical conclusion in the last analytic session, session 517. The manifest dream story and its starting point are about no less than the high point of Amalie's interpretation abilities: people come to her to learn, from her, what interpretation is and how it is done.

The positioning of this dream narrative in the last session of her therapy is decisive. Immediately before Amalie tells the dream, the analyst posed the question as to what help she had received from her analysis. This is followed by Amalie telling her dream about "interpretation for anthroposophists". Based on this sequence, the analyst's question about what help she had received in the analysis can now be answered conclusively from Amalie's point of view: in the analysis she learned what interpretation is. Amalie positions herself as a self-appointed, successful interpreter (of dreams), who does not need anything more and who distances herself from any form of gratitude for what she has received. In her dream, people who want something from her make a pilgrimage to her door, and she gives them something—namely, instructions on interpretation. With this literally dreamlike triumph, she need not fear to part from her analyst, and at the end of the session—that is, at the end of her therapy—she can say to him, "I have to go now."[4]

Conclusion: the telling of dreams has a multitude of communicative functions

To the practising dream analyst, I propose a differentiated attitude of reception. The analyst must find out what a patient's dream telling is all about. A kind of triage is necessary.

If on the part of the analysand there is a recognisable desire for interpretation that finds expression in a wish to learn something about the content of a dream together with the analyst, then work on the content of the dream stands in the foreground. This is the classical work of dream analysis, for which a wide range of different approaches exist.

But it is possible, as in most of the cases of dream telling by Amalie X, that a dream is being "deployed" by the analysand mainly for its communicative potential. The analyst's task is then to find out what function the sharing of the dream has. Communicative-functional dream analysis thus examines this question: what is the analysand telling me, when he or she shares with me precisely this dream at precisely this point in time?

The communicative functions can be various:

- The dream can be told primarily for purposes of containment, that is, as a way to move indigestible material to the outside. According to Deserno (2007), we can assume that in psychoanalysis the container-contained model is used the most frequently, and used "mono-conceptually", meaning without any connection to other approaches (see, for example, Weiss, 2002).
- A dream can be very illustrative of the presence of a transference tendency (Deserno, 1992; Ermann, 1998).
- Dreams can be shared with the analyst in the service of resistance, of course (Freud, 1900; Moser, 2003).
- It is a very interesting phenomenon, if for the dream dialogue between analysand and analyst particular patterns of interaction can be discovered, as was the case in the example presented here. Through this and with the aid of the psychoanalytical concept of enactment, it was shown that dreams can be told in the service of wish fulfilment. In the present case, the wish for phallic features was phrased in the form of competency in dream interpretation.
- Finally, sharing a dream can constitute an attempt at triangulation, an opportunity so to speak to use the dream to say something in a roundabout way (Mertens, 2005/2006).

For Amalie X, this latter function is central and might be expressed as follows: "I refer to a third instance so as to be able to speak about a topic at all that I cannot bring up in the direct, dyadic constellation. I can only put forward the topic by referring to something that I myself produced but that now, at the moment of telling it, seems foreign to me (which is most welcome) and where I can for now leave open the issue of whether I see this as my own personal issue or view it with distance as alien to me."

In this regard, the telling of dreams serves as a playful form of communication with a great degree of freedom for analysands to present topics that they cannot otherwise bring up in the same way or at all—and is thus also a possible way to expand the dyadic form of the analytic relationship to a triad and to regulate it.

Notes

1. The psychoanalytic treatment of "Amalie X" was tape-recorded in its entirety as a German specimen case by Kächele et al. (2006). In the total of more than 500 sessions, Amalie X told ninety-five dreams, distributed over seventy-two sessions. Sometimes she told more than one dream in a therapy session. The basis of this study is our transcription of the tape recordings of these "dream sessions". At the start of her therapy, the patient Amalie X was a thirty-five-year-old, single teacher. Her reason for initiating therapy was considerable vulnerability to depression accompanied by low self-esteem. Starting in puberty Amalie X had a somatic illness, the main symptom of which was idiopathic hirsutism, or unwanted, male-pattern, excessive hair growth all over the body. Due to her inhibitions, which her idiopathic hirsutism only reinforced, Amalie X had not yet had any sexual contacts at the time of the initial interview.

2. For detailed transcription rules, see Appendix. The method used here was conversation analysis, which is a qualitative, ethno-methodological procedure for analysis of interaction. The principle of conversation analysis is to carve out how the participants in the conversation implicitly interpret each other, in that they respond to the other person's last utterance or "turn" in the conversation (Deppermann, 2001; Peräkylä, 2004; Streeck, 2004).

3. In the symposium at the Sandler Conference in Frankfurt, a member of the audience objected that the dream as a triangulating element was not comprehensible, because it was clearly something produced by the patient and not any third party thing. This comment starts out from a metapsychological understanding of the dream and not from the experience of the patient and the way that she uses the dream in the sessions. Although analysands know intellectually that no one other than themselves produces their dreams, this personal mental product, the dream, feels alien enough for them to see it and treat it as something coming from outside. The fact that strange and outlandish dreams do

have something to do with the dreamer, and what that is exactly, is after all the very process that must be accomplished and worked out in psychoanalytic dream sessions but that is not given per se and assumed from the start.

4. Here the focus is not on what the latent content of the dream is. What is crucial is how Amalie uses it. Here she of course starts out from the manifest form of the dream.

APPENDIX: Transcription Symbols
(Simplified from Drew & Heritage, 1992)

Symbol	Meaning
P	The patient (speaker designation)
A	The analyst (speaker designation)
[	Starting point of overlapping speech
]	Endpoint of overlapping speech
(2.4)	Silence measured in seconds
(.)	Pause of less than 0.2 s
( )	Inaudible word
.hhh	Inhalation
hhh.	Exhalation
.	Falling intonation at the end of an utterance
?	Raising intonation at the end of an utterance
,	Flat intonation at the end of an utterance
((word))	Transcriber's comments
*171, *59, *95	Code of a person's name

References

Bartels, M. (1979). Ist der Traum eine Wunscherfüllung? *Psyche, 33*: 97–131.

Bergmann, M. S. (1966). The intrapsychic and communicative aspects of the dream: Their role in psychoanalysis and psychotherapy. *International Journal of Psychoanalysis, 47*: 356–363.

Boothe, B. (2006). Wie erzählt man einen Traum, diesen herrlichen Mist, wie porträtiert man seinen Analytiker? In: M. Wiegand, F. von Spreti & H. Förstl (Eds.), *Schlaf und Traum. Neurobiologie, Psychologie, Therapie* (pp. 159–169). Stuttgart, Germany: Schattauer.

Deppermann, A. (2001). *Gespräche analysieren.* Opladen, Germany: Leske & Budrich.

Deserno, H. (1992). Zum funktionalen Zusammenhang von Traum und Übertragung. *Psyche Zeitschrift für Psychoanalyse und ihre Anwendungen, 46*: 959–978.

Deserno, H. (2007): Traumdeutung in der gegenwärtigen psychoanalytischen Therapie. *Psyche Zeitschrift für Psychoanalyse und ihre Anwendungen, 61*: 913–942.

Drew, P. & Heritage, J. (1992). Analyzing talk at work: An introduction. In: P. Drew & J. Heritage (Eds.), *Talk at Work* (pp. 3–65). Cambridge, UK: Cambridge University Press.

Ermann, M. (1998). Träume erzählen und die Übertragung. *Forum der Psychoanalyse, 14*: 95–110.

Ferenczi, S. (1913). *To Whom Does One Relate One's Dreams? Further Contributions to the Theory and Technique of Psycho-analysis.* London: Hogarth.

Freud, S. (1900). Die Traumdeutung. *Gesammelte Werke: Vol. 2/3.* Frankfurt, Germany: Fischer.

Freud, S. (1916/1917). Vorlesungen zur Einführung in die Psychoanalyse. *Gesammelte Werke: Vol. 11* (pp. 79–234). Frankfurt, Germany: Fischer.

Grieser, J. (2003). Von der Triade zum triangulären Raum. *Forum der Psychoanalyse, 19*: 1–17.

Kächele, H., Albani, C., Buchheim, A., Grünzig, H.-J., Hölzer, M., Hohage, R., Jimenez, J. P., Leuzinger-Bohleber, M., Mergenthaler, E., Neudert-Dreyer, L., Pokorny, D. & Thomä, H. (2006). Psychoanalytische Einzelfallforschung: Ein deutscher Musterfall Amalie X. *Psyche, 60*: 387–425.

Kanzer, M. (1955). The communicative function of the dream. *International Journal of Psychoanalysis, 36*: 260–266.

Klauber, J. (1969). Über die Bedeutung des Berichtens von Träumen in der Psychoanalyse. *Psyche, 46*: 280–294.

Mathys, H. (2010). *Wozu werden Träume erzählt? Interaktive und kommunikative Funktionen von Traummitteilungen in der psychoanalytischen Therapie.* Giessen, Germany: Psychosozial.

Mertens, W. (2005/2006). Anmerkungen zu Fritz Morgenthalers Buch *Der Traum. Journal für Psychoanalyse, 45/46*: 31–51.

Morgenthaler, F. (1986). *Der Traum: Fragmente zur Theorie und Technik der Traumdeutung.* Frankfurt, Germany: Campus.

Moser, U. (2003). Traumtheorien und Traumkultur in der psychoanalytischen Praxis (Teil 1). *Psyche, 57*: 639–657.

Peräkylä, A. (2004). Making links in psychoanalytic interpretations: A conversation analytical perspective. *Psychotherapy Research, 14*(3): 289–307.

Streeck, U. (2004). *Auf den ersten Blick. Psychotherapeutische Beziehungen unter dem Mikroskop.* Stuttgart, Germany: Klett-Cotta.

Weiss, H. (2002). Reporting a dream accompanying an enactment in the transference situation. *International Journal of Psychoanalysis, 83*: 633–645.

CHAPTER THIRTEEN

ADHD—illness or symptomatic
indicator for trauma? A case study
from the therapy comparison study
on hyperactive children at the Sigmund
Freud Institute, Frankfurt

Katrin Luise Laezer, Birgit Gaertner, and Emil Branik

In the last fifteen years there is an increasing number of clinical
and theoretical contributions regarding the so-called attention
deficit hyperactivity disorder (ADHD) in psychoanalytical literature. For a long time the rapid growth in the number of children
diagnosed with ADHD had been denied. The scientific and everyday-
scientific discourse used to be quite limited. Etiological considerations
had been restricted to genetic and neurochemical factors (see, e.g.,
Hopf, 2000, p. 279). Even in the domains of child psychoanalysis and
psychotherapy a psychodynamic treatment of ADH children was
seen as contraindicated, and child psychiatrists exclusively conducted
therapies.

Meanwhile, not only in the public dialogue, but also in the scientific
community, critical and warning statements concerning the increasing
and often uncritically applied diagnosis "ADHD" and the frequent
pharmacological interventions have come up. In the last ten years
many psychoanalysts have modified their conceptual view of ADHD,
trying to understand children with this diagnosis as patients with neurotic impairments and thus treating them psychotherapeutically. They
could no longer deny that the ADH diagnosis is at best a descriptive

one, which subsumes and conceals various and in parts severe psychological disorders. Thus, in the last few years numerous individual clinical studies and theoretical conceptualisations concerning the ADH syndrome were published (see, for example, in Germany: Borowski et al., 2010; Bovensiepen, Hopf & Molitor, 2004; Dammasch, 2009; Heinemann & Hopf, 2006; Leuzinger-Bohleber, Brandl & Hüther, 2006; Leuzinger-Bohleber et al., 2011; Neraal & Wildermuth, 2008; Staufenberg, 2011; Warrlich & Reinke, 2007). The development of symptoms which are characterised by attention deficit hyperactivity disorder vary significantly: "… we observe many different levels of psychic structure in so-called ADHD-children" (Leuzinger-Bohleber, Brandl & Hüther, 2006, p. 27).

A psychodynamic understanding of the ADH syndrome may thus contribute to the discovery of the idiosyncratic psychic histories of these children (Leuzinger-Bohleber, 2010). The following case study illustrates the significance of *one* of various etiological factors (however, a very important one): the pathological effect of early, cumulative (loss-) traumatisations, which eventually leads to a behaviour finally diagnosed as ADHD, often after years of "mute" and hence undiscovered symptom development. When presenting the biographical development of this boy (we call him "Anton"), it is particularly important for us to draw attention to the successive accumulation of traumatic stress and to carefully describe the systematics behind the escalating dialogue between child and environment. We believe that Anton is by no means a single case in the still increasing group of children diagnosed with the so-called ADH syndrome. By now, the Frankfurt Effectiveness Study has offered differentiated insights into the biographical development of fifty children diagnosed as suffering from ADHD and oppositional defiant disorder (ODD). A shockingly high number of these children had been exposed to high psychological and psychosocial distress. A significant number of them had suffered from *trauma* in a strict sense—i.e., unforeseen, extremely dangerous events, both external and internal, which exposed the ego of the child to unbearable anxiety and pain.

Before presenting the case of Anton, we would like to outline briefly the current state of research addressing the relationship between ADHD and trauma as well as the research context of the Frankfurt Effectiveness Study.

ADHD and trauma

Recently, the *Journal of Infant, Child and Adolescent Psychotherapy* published a special issue on "Attention Deficit Hyperactivity Disorder: Integration of Cognitive, Neuropsychological and Psychodynamic Theoretical Perspectives in Psychotherapy".

Within it, Kate Szymanski, Linda Sapanski, and Francine Conway summarise that "a growing body of research has developed to examine the relationship between exposure to traumatic events in childhood and attention deficit hyperactivity disorder (ADHD) (Cuffe, McCullough & Pumariega, 1994; Daud & Rydelius, 2009; Famularo, Fenton, Kinscherff & Augustyn, 1996; Ford, Rascusin, Daviss, Fleisher & Thomas, 2000; Husain, Allwood & Bell, 2008; Lipschitz, Morgan & Southwick, 2002; McLeer et al., 1998)" (2011, p. 51).

The literature review by Szymanski and colleagues (2011) explored the questions whether or not trauma is a risk factor for ADHD and whether or not ADHD could be seen as masking symptoms of trauma. In a well-known follow-up study on severely deprived Romanian orphans adopted before they age of forty-three months, Stevens et al. (2008) found that these children not only developed ADHD-associated symptoms of inattention and hyperactivity—but that these symptoms were linked to dismissed attachment and conduct problems (Szymanski, Sapanski & Conway, 2011, p. 53). Szymanski and colleagues also refer to the study by Famularo, Fenton, Kinscherff & Augustyn (1996), showing that nearly one-third of severely maltreated children met criteria for an ADHD diagnosis. Another study by Ford et al. (2000) demonstrated the relationship between chronic trauma and disruptive disorders. In this research, children diagnosed with ADHD and oppositional defiant disorder (ODD) were at higher risk for past exposure to traumatisation (Szymanski, Sapanski & Conway, 2011, p. 53).

Szymanski and colleagues identified trauma as a risk factor for ADHD claiming that the traumatic exposure substantially impacts a child's ability to regulate his/her affect. Children who experienced trauma "are prone to be easily overwhelmed, overreact to minor stresses, have difficulties with self-soothing, react excessively in response to neutral stimuli, and have trouble modulating their anger" (Szymanski, Sapanski & Conway, 2011, p. 53). All these symptoms are linked to the DSM-IV-TR criteria of post-traumatic stress disorder (PTSD). Therefore, they argue, it is possible that a clinician might misinterpret symptoms (such as problems with affect regulation, behaviour regulation, stress tolerance, mood lability, aggression, depression, and anxiety) "for symptoms of ADHD without even acknowledging a possibility of trauma history" (Szymanski, Sapanski & Conway, 2011, p. 54).

The study by Conway, Oster, and Szymanski (2011) reviewed charts of eighty-seven hospitalised children, using the hospitalised child and adolescent trauma and psychopathology (HCATP) questionnaire which had been developed by the research team. The researchers propose that experiences of chronic adverse situations during childhood, also referred to as complex trauma, cannot be denied in ADHD symptomatology because it is strongly correlated with behaviour that is common among children who have deficits in mentalisation (Conway, Oster & Szymanski, p. 61). The data analysis showed that children diagnosed with ADHD compared to non-ADHD children experienced higher correlations between insecure attachment and environmental complex trauma events in early life including adoption, foster care placement, maltreatment, ACS involvement, and death of their mother, father, or caregivers (Conway, Oster & Szymanski, p. 65). Moreover, the majority of ADHD children lived in chronically stressful environments where they witnessed violence in their homes or parental substance abuse (Conway, Oster & Szymanski, p. 65). Therefore, this study offers empirical evidence "that environmental stressors and disturbances in attachment relations are more likely to be found among ADHD children compared to their non-ADHD counterparts" (Conway, Oster & Szymanski, 2011, p. 67).

The researchers of the Frankfurt Prevention Study by Leuzinger-Bohleber et al. (2011) were able to differentiate between subgroups of children who had been diagnosed with ADHD, based on numerous and extensive single case observations as well as statistical data from the original sample of the 500 children of an intervention group, applying a psychoanalytic perspective on each child's idiosyncratic psychic and psychosocial situation. One subgroup out of seven was defined as "ADHD and trauma" (Leuzinger-Bohleber et al., 2011, p. 40).

In our Frankfurt Effectiveness Study we also found several children who suffered from traumatic experiences in early life and developed ADHD symptoms (see also Leuzinger-Bohleber, 2010). Therefore, we will briefly introduce this ongoing study.

The Frankfurt ADHD and ODD Effectiveness Study (2006, ongoing)[1]

Between 2003 and 2006 the Sigmund Freud Institute, in cooperation with the Institute for Psychoanalytic Treatment of Children and Adolescents, conducted the Frankfurt Prevention Study (FPS). The FPS could show that a two-year psychoanalytic (non-psychopharmacological) prevention and intervention programme in kindergarten resulted in a statistically significant decrease in ADHD symptoms, such as aggressive, anxious, and impulsive behaviour (Leuzinger-Bohleber et al., 2010, 2011).

Recognising the FPS-indicated benefits of psychoanalytic treatment for ADHD children, and the opportunity to deepen the established research collaboration with child analysts in Frankfurt, the Frankfurt ADHD and ODD Effectiveness Study was initiated in 2006. The study investigates the differential benefits of psychoanalytic and behavioural/medical treatment and treatment as usual (TAU) for ADHD and ODD children. Using a naturalistic controlled design and combining quantitative and qualitative approaches, we address the question, whether subgroups among ADHD and ODD children might be affected differentially by psychoanalytic treatment or behavioural/medical intervention or treatment as usual.

Method

Participants

Children, aged six to eleven, met ICD-10 criteria (International Classification of Diseases, WHO, 2010) for ADHD (F90.1 Hyperkinetic disorder associated with conduct disorder; F90.0 Disturbance of activity and attention) or for ODD (F91.3 Oppositional defiant disorder) as determined by parent interviews and teacher reports, using the diagnostic system for mental disorders in children and adolescents (DISYPS-KJ) (Döpfner & Lehmkuhl, 2003).

Allocation to treatment

The children meeting the ICD-10 criteria for ADHD or ODD were allocated, according to their first contact, to the intervention group (psychoanalytic treatment) or to one of the control groups

(b. behavioural/medical treatment, c. treatment as usual (TAU), d. untreated control group), i.e., the child was assigned to the psychoanalytic treatment group if parents had first consulted a psychoanalyst or the psychoanalytic outpatient clinic.

Treatment groups

a. *Psychoanalytic treatment.* In accordance with the manual for psychoanalytic treatment (Staufenberg, 2011), treatment was conducted by a psychoanalyst in private practice. Usually, children in psychoanalytic treatment saw the therapist twice a week, for two years on average. Parents saw the therapist once in two weeks.
b. *Behavioural/medical treatment.* Children within the behavioural/ medical treatment group attended either a six-week attention and concentration training programme (Marburger Konzentrationstraining: Krowatschek, Albrecht & Krowatschek, 1990), meeting once a week for two hours, accompanied by a parent training programme, or they attended a two-week anti-aggression training programme that took place in the hospital, daily from 8am to 7pm (anti-aggression training: Grasmann & Stadler, 2008). At the beginning, children in the behavioural/medical treatment group were examined and diagnosed by a psychiatrist and medicated accordingly, if needed.
c. *Treatment as usual (TAU).* This treatment refers to a low-frequency child psychiatric treatment that includes parent counselling and optional medication, ergotherapy, social training, and parents' management training.
d. *Untreated control group.* The untreated control group was selected from the untreated control group of the Frankfurt Prevention Study.

Procedure

Participants within the psychoanalytic treatment group were screened after completing the assessment sessions with the analyst. The children and parents were then invited to the Sigmund Freud Institute for further assessment. Consequently, each child who had met the criteria for ADHD or ODD was recruited for psychoanalytic treatment. The same procedure was applied to recruitment for behavioural/medical treatment and for standard treatment. In each family, parents and child were invited to the Sigmund Freud Institute for assessment at three measurement time points: pre-measurement, post-measurement, and follow-up measurement one year after finishing treatment. Furthermore, parents, children, and teachers were asked to complete questionnaires half-yearly.

Measures

- *Diagnostic system for mental disorders in children and adolescents* (Doepfner & Lehmkuhl, 2003). The DISYPS-KP consists of different types of data: a parental questionnaire (that can be used as a structured parent interview), a teacher questionnaire, and a self-reporting questionnaire (for children aged eleven to eighteen). The clinical assessment is performed by clinicians and psychological professionals using the DISYPS-KP checklists for ADHD and ODD which are related to the stipulated symptoms in DSM-IV and ICD-10.
- *Conners teacher rating scale* (Conners, 2001). The CTRS-S includes four subscales: hyperactivity, attention deficit, conduct problem, and ADHD index.
- *Conners parent rating scale* (Conners, 2001). The CPRS-S includes the same four subscales: hyperactivity, attention deficit, conduct problem, ADHD index.
- *Child behaviour checklist* and the *teacher report form*, respectively (Achenbach, 1991, Arbeitsgruppe Deutsche Child Behavior Checklist, 1998) for assessment of the children's comorbidities.
- *Culture fair test* (CFT-20R: Weiss 2008). In seeking to apply a culture-fair intelligence test, we use this IQ test for our study children often coming from a family with a migration background.
- The child's behaviour during examination was reported by the observation questionnaire *"behaviour during examination"* (VWU: Doepfner, Schurmann & Froelich, 1998).
- Using the *"d2 test of attention"* (Brickenkamp & Zillmer, 1998), we obtained a consistent and valid measure of visual scanning accuracy and speed.
- *"Schweinchen-Schwarzfuss Test"* is a projective, psychoanalytically proven instrument for children. This narrative story stem test, including seventeen cards with black and white drawings, features a little

pig with a black foot as the main character (Corman, 2006). The test was tape recorded and transcribed, permitting the researchers to consider the inner psychic states and fantasies of the child.

- The *inventory for the assessment of the quality of life in children and adolescents* (ILK: Mattejat & Remschmidt, 2006) was completed by children as well as by parents and therapists. The ILK addresses seven different areas of life such as school, family, and friendship, and provides the opportunity to compare the different perspectives.
- Primary data included a questionnaire of behaviour that provides information about the first years of life, personal disease history, traumatic experiences, and family history (Englert, Jungmann, Lam, Wienand & Poustka, 1998).

In the frame of this large empirical outcome study we document and analyse psychoanalytical treatments of "ADHD children" by qualitative psychoanalytic research methods. The case material is documented carefully. Its condensation and interpretations of transference/countertransference reactions, enactments in the therapeutic setting, etc. are discussed in a group adhering to the so-called method of expert validation (see Leuzinger-Bohleber, chapter 5 in this volume). The following case study is the product of such a careful and quite time-consuming expert validation in the clinical research group. The case study may illustrate our attempt to combine clinical and extraclinical psychoanalytical research in this project as well as in other ongoing intervention and prevention studies at the Sigmund Freud Institute (see www.sigmund-freud-institut.de).

Case study: Anton

When Anton is born in a small town in one of the poorest countries of eastern Europe, his parents' relationship is already broken; his father, a young soldier in the national army, left the twenty-year-old mother during her fifth month of pregnancy. She suffered extremely from the abandonment; she and the father had lived four years together prior to this in her parents' house. It was too late to abort, and from this time on, the pregnancy was overshadowed by ambivalence, grief, shame, and desperation. After a long and complicated birth there was a certain postpartum relief for mother and child; Anton was breastfed for five months, and the mother reported that her care for the child posed no problems. However, she suffered under the social norm of being an unwed, single mother, and also for being an abandoned woman. Even her parents, in whose home she continued to live with her baby, denied her any assistance and did not support her or her child.

In the following four years, mother and child developed an inseparable and couple-like relationship—Anton took control over his mother, and she was not able to act as an adult. From the age of two Anton was in child care, and his mother went on and continued her studies. The boy, however, still slept with her in the same room, and in many respects he continued to have the upper hand. For example, he insisted she accompany him on every toilet visit (this compulsive behaviour towards the intimacy with his mother concerning the toilet rituals continued until he was nine years old). The research group came to the conclusion that mother and son, having for the first four years nearly an exclusive dyadic relationship, and living in antagonistic and hostile surroundings, retreated as if being on an island, just the two of them—however, paying the price of loss of generation boundaries, and the missing triangular relationship. There was no contact with the father, although he played an idealised and dangerous phallic symbol in Anton's fantasy (as an armed soldier going to war).

The young mother could not overcome the narcissistic damage, and came to the realisation that there was no prospect of work in her home country. When Anton was four years old, she, as a twenty-four-year-old, left him with her parents, and moved to Germany, surviving without any knowledge of the language. She found work as a maid, cashier, and also as a sales associate. Anton was left behind as if a mute. During the psychoanalytic sessions, the traumatic loss wove itself like a red thread through his therapy, expressing itself by means of autistic and panic situations. Left behind, Anton turned to his grandmother and became very close to her. He not only slept in her room, but in her bed. The grandfather was moved out of his own bedroom for the next four years. The boy continued to hold this spot next to his grandmother, also during the sporadic visits from his mother. Later, the child therapist would formulate this in her report as follows: for the patient, it seemed too risky to be able to rely on the mother; she represented herself as too insecure. Next to the grandmother, his relationship to other children, and also his relationship to the animals in the village (horses and dogs) played an important role and were a significant consolation factor for the boy.

After entering school, his psychological situation worsened. The seven-year-old boy was teased because he could not prove that he had a father or mother. His narcissistic situation, being abandoned by both parents, progressively developed into desolation, and for the first time, the boy became a problem child. He was unable to concentrate and had poor comprehension. Deeply disturbed by the development of her child, and driven by strong guilt feelings, the mother decided spontaneously to bring Anton to Germany and place him in year two. The abrupt move reactivated the traumatic feelings of loss, uprooting, and alienation. Not only did Anton lose his grandmother, but also his trusted homeland, the common language, and his animals. He felt alienated, isolated, and in a new way completely left out. His reaction to his new life situation was disturbed, and he developed massive, psychological symptoms, especially auto-erotic, stereotyped movements, such as swinging and cradling. Additionally he suffered from homesickness and phobias, especially fears of being alone, and of the darkness. In her first consultation the mother reported that he was often sad and depressed, and was treated for many psychosomatic symptoms (vomiting, diarrhoea, stomach aches). In school he was noticeably restless, lacked interest, and exhibited an inability to concentrate. He was regularly a disturbance to his classmates, talking out of turn, and generally disregarding rules. These behaviours meet the diagnostic criteria of a so-called "hyper kinetic disturbance of social behaviour" (ICD-10). The empathetic teacher not only noticed the boy's drive, but also commented in the teacher's questionnaire: "Anton seems restless, sometimes wound up, and also sad."

At home, a vicious circle occurred between mother and son, caused by the omission of necessary boundaries on the one hand, and guilt feelings of the seemingly crippled mother on the other. She complained about his need to rule: "When Anton doesn't get his way, he shuts himself out." However, the power struggle could overshadow the frustrated child's resistance with some effort against his regressive yearnings. While falling asleep, nine-year-old Anton sucked his thumb, and continued to demand the common trips with his mother to the toilet, appearing altogether fixated on the pre-Oedipal level as in the previous symbiotic oneness with her. His stubborn fascination with war games must be understood as a complex determination. On the one hand it points to the boy's enormous anger against the factual omnipotent mother, who is accessible to him—an anger that he also realises as a dangerous impulse towards the only accessible figure he has to split off and fight for at the same time. But, on the other hand, Anton is internally, almost in a compulsive way, occupied with his fantasised father; he continually refers to him as a war hero, with phallic and dangerous qualities. Later on, in therapy, he admits to his wish to see him again, but at the same time, he is afraid of him: "… even if we were to meet, and what would happen, if my father did not recognise me, and accidentally shot me?" (taken from the therapist's report). The mother regularly shaves the boy's head, and thus unconsciously creates a military-like figure in her son, as a substitute for the child's lost father.

Despite the obvious psychological distress of the eight-year-old boy escalating over the years, and the fact that already his mere presence in school fulfilled the profile of the hyperkinetic disorder, the "outraged messages of the hyperactive child" (cf. Neraal & Wildermuth, 2005) remained unanswered. For many of the children examined in our study, only the *formulation* (by school, parents, nursery, or paediatrician) of an ADHD suspicion provides reason for utilising help and initiating interventions (of different kinds).

In the presented case of this boy, his mother needed almost one year until she was able to respond to the obvious distress of her child. Only after the mother meets a nineteen years older man in Germany, subsequently marrying him quickly, is she able to break away from her being crippled; only now, her own guilt feelings and her worries about Anton can advance into a common initiative. She takes the advice of a paediatrician and seeks out psychotherapeutic help.

Psychoanalytic treatment

In the initial session, there was evidence of tension between mother and son. The therapist reports: "The boy appears as if not to belong to this mother …." When the child is alone in a session with the therapist she reports that the boy succumbs into an autistic-like stare, covering up a panic fear that the mother might not return. When the therapist succeeds in giving the boy an opportunity to speak about his fear of separation, he warms up, and begins reluctantly to describe his home country, the grandmother, and the animals living there. At the end of the first session, when the mother wants to make another appointment with the therapist, the boy tried deliberately to throw a glance at her (the therapist's) diary. In a very egocentric manner he gives the impression that her diary should also be available to him—and with this intrusive scene, he gives us a view into his inner world, where objects blend without boundaries.

Anton belongs to those children in our study who are quite successful in recognising and working through their conflicts in a therapeutic setting. Without going into a detailed reconstruction of the treatment process, one very important central developmental line needs to be discussed here as it became of great importance in the therapeutic process later on: *separation and triangulation*.

Two years after the beginning of therapy, the symptoms of hyperkinetic disturbances in social behaviour have virtually disappeared. Even with the new family situation (including an additional child) causing extreme conflicts of feelings in the now ten-year-old boy (hate, rivalry, envy, separation anxiety), there is yet a sense of relief, as a chance for triangulation exists—necessarily in the stepfather figure—and the possibility of separating from the mother.

Previously, during numerous therapy sessions it became clear how much he not only missed his biological father but also feared and heroically glorified him. Moreover, the full extent of the *unconscious identification of the boy with the wishes of his mother* could be understood and worked through, and Anton was able to revoke some parts of his initial symptoms: the loud symptoms in school, which led to the diagnosis of the hyperkinetic syndrome in the first place, as well as the obsessive war games with which he unknowingly targeted the father and were needed to keep his biological origin alive, and the symptoms expressing his protest against forgetting his roots.

Anton could henceforth let his hair grow (against the mother's protest) and thus overcame his unconscious identification with the lost father. When the burden of fear and depression successively subsided, and the developmental cessation of the prior years dissolved, the boy could make positive strides in school and sports for the first time, and his ego functions began to unfold.

Now, finally, Anton could successfully defend himself against the smooth shave of his head still preferred by his mother, and he let his hair grow, by which he redressed both externally his military appearance, and internally the unconscious identification with the lost father. In particular he freed himself with the changed physiognomy from the maternally delegated grief function and emphasised his desire for his own self.

As a result, the heavy burden of uncertainty, anxiety, and depression successively reduced and the earlier developmental stagnation of the boy dissolved, simultaneously expanding his social radius by which he gained self-confidence for the first time.

This overall undoubtedly positive development would not have been possible without the accompanying psychotherapeutic work with the mother (and also with the stepfather Anthony). In the efficacy study we have found the experience that the holding function developed by the contact between *the family of these children and the therapist* is of crucial importance for the prognosis of the treatment of the child. In the twice-weekly meetings Anton's mother was able to understand and be aware of her deep feelings of guilt regarding her son. Gradually it became possible for her to open up to the therapist and to understand the relationship between her own suffered damages and the traumatic interference in the development of her child. Only on these premises could a psychological space develop in the mother-son relationship, in which the fixation on the symbiosis could be overcome and the separation of objects could be accepted without a paralysing anxiety arousal. Towards the end of the psychotherapy of her son and in connection with starting a new family, the mother saw her loss-anxiety and her unresolved past returning, which gave rise to her decision to start a psychotherapy of her own. In the follow-up interview—one year after Anton's treatment was completed—she was convinced that her son had benefited greatly from psychotherapy. He became calmer, could now express his feelings and felt much more confident regarding his relationships with friends. More importantly however, she could now acknowledge that it had been a challenge for herself and her husband and she, the mother, had learned to understand herself much better and to accept her own guilt. This improved her relationship with her child significantly.

Conclusion

With this case study we wanted to illustrate how a cumulative traumatisation in childhood can lead to emotional withdrawal, to "emotionally-driven emergency responses" (Kugele, 1998, p. 60 [translated for this edition]) as well as serious disturbances of the affective communication between child and the environment—all of which can be misunderstood as a genetically or neurobiologically caused attention deficit as in the ADHD diagnosis. Psychoanalytic authors have often referred to this relationship of "early pathological conflicts, such as an unresolved object-loss ..." and the development of a hyperkinetic syndrome, and described how due to "reason of denial of separation a disturbance of the capability to symbolize and therefore also a paralysis of the fantasy-experience can be developed. If so, the world is not equipped sufficient enough any more with symbolic meaning and therefore an impairment of attention can evolve" (Hopf, 2000, p. 279 [translated for this edition]).

However, the tension between empirical knowledge about ADHD versus knowledge gained from clinical experience remains (Conway, Oster & Szymanski, 2011; Eresund, 2007). We agree with Salomonsson (2011) that psychoanalysis "may contribute in two ways to ADHD treatments. It might complement standard treatments by helping the child to grow emotionally, and it might increase our understanding of the internal world of these children" (p. 89). According to the previously mentioned literature review and the empirical findings, traumatic biographical factors, and their impacts on the internal world and emotional vulnerability of those children—as well as societal and cultural factors—should be taken as seriously as the findings of neurobiology and brain research when talking about ADHD (Leuzinger-Bohleber et al., 2011, p. 43).

The Frankfurt ADHD and ODD Effectiveness Study might not only offer an adequate way to address this specific psychodynamic aetiology of attention deficit hyperactivity disorder—it could also show which developmental possibilities and benefits the psychoanalytic treatment in comparison to other treatments can establish for the severely burdened children and their parents.

Note

1. We are very grateful for the fruitful cooperation with the Institute for Psychoanalytic Child and Adolescent Psychotherapy, Frankfurt/Main and all child psychoanalysts in private practice; the Child and Adolescent Psychiatry Department of the Johann-Wolfgang Goethe University, Frankfurt/Main, the Child and Adolescent Psychiatry, Asklepios Clinic, Hamburg/Harburg, and the University of Applied Science, Frankfurt/Main.

References

Achenbach, T. M. (1991). *Integrative Guide to the 1991 CBCL/4–18, YSR, and TRF Profiles.* Burlington, VT: University of Vermont, Department of Psychology.

Arbeitsgruppe Deutsche Child Behavior Checklist (1998). *Elternfragebogen über das Verhalten von Kindern und Jugendlichen; deutsche Bearbeitung der Child Behavior Checklist (CBCL/4–18). Einführung und Anleitung zur Handauswertung. 2. Auflage mit deutschen Normen, bearbeitet von M. Döpfner, J. Plück, S. Bölte, K. Lenz, P. Melchers & K. Heim.* Cologne, Germany: Arbeitsgruppe Kinder-, Jugend- und Familiendiagnostik.

Borowski, D., Bovensiepen, G., Dammasch, F., Hopf, H., Stauffenberg, H. & Streeck-Fischer, A. (2010). Leitlinie zur Aufmerksamkeits- und Hyperaktivitätsstörungen. *Analytische Kinder- und Jugendlichenpsychotherapie, 146:* 238–253.

Bovensiepen, G., Hopf, H. & Molitor, G. (Eds.) (2004). *Unruhige und unaufmerksame Kinder. Psychoanalyse des hyperkinetischen Syndroms.* Frankfurt, Germany: Brandes & Apsel.

Brickenkamp, R. & Zillmer, E. (1998). *The d2 test of attention.* Seattle, WA: Hogrefe & Huber.

Conners, C. K. (2001). *Conners' Rating Scales—Revised. Technical Manual. Instruments for Use with Children and Adolescents.* New York: Multi-Health Systems.

Conway, F., Oster, M. & Szymanski, K. (2011). ADHD and complex trauma: A descriptive study of hospitalized children in an urban psychiatric hospital. *Journal of Infant, Child, and Adolescent Psychotherapy, 10:* 50–72.

Corman, L. (2006). *Der Schwarzfuß-Test. Grundlagen, Durchführung, Deutung und Auswertung.* Basle, Switzerland: Ernst Reinhardt.

Cuffe, S. P., McCullough, E. L. & Pumariega, A. J. (1994). Comorbidity of attention deficit hyperactivity disorder and post-traumatic stress disorder. *Journal of Child and Family Studies, 3:* 327–336.

Dammasch, F. (2009). Der umklammerte Junge, die frühe Fremdheitserfahrung und der abwesende Vater. *Kinderanalyse, 17:* 313–334.

Daud, A. & Rydelius, P.-A. (2009). Comorbidity/overlapping between ADHD and PTSD in relation to IQ among children to traumatized/non-traumatized parents. *Journal of Attention Disorder, 13:* 188–198.

Doepfner, M. & Lehmkuhl, G. (2003). *Diagnostik-System für psychische Störungen im Kindes- und Jugendalter nach ICD-10 und DSM-IV (DISYPS-KJ).* Berne, Switzerland: Hans Huber, Hogrefe.

Doepfner, M., Schurmann, S. & Froelich, J. (1998). *Therapieprogramm für Kinder mit hyperkinetischem und oppositionellem Problemverhalten THOP: Materialien für die klinische Praxis.* Weinheim, Germany: Beltz.

Englert, E., Jungmann, J., Lam, L., Wienand, F. & Poustka, F. (1998). *Basisdokumentation Kinder- und Jugendpsychiatrie (BADO)*. Kommission Qualitätssicherung DGKJP/BAG/BKJPP.

Eresund, P. (2007). Psychodynamic psychotherapy for children with disruptive disorders. *Journal of Child Psychotherapy, 33*: 161–180.

Famularo, R., Fenton, T., Kinscherff, R. & Augustyn, M. (1996). Psychiatric comorbidity in childhood post traumatic stress disorder. *Child Abuse & Neglect, 20*: 953–961.

Ford, J. D., Rascusin, C. G. E., Daviss, J. R., Fleisher, A. & Thomas, J. (2000). Child maltreatment, other trauma exposure, and posttraumatic symptomatology among children with oppositonal defiant and attention deficit hyperactivity disorders. *Child Maltreatment, 5*: 205–217.

Grasmann, D. & Stadler, C. (2008). *Verhaltenstherapeutisches Intensivtraining zur Reduktion von Aggression. Multimodales Programm für Kinder, Jugendliche und Eltern*. Vienna: Springer.

Heinemann, E. & Hopf, H. (2006). *AD(H)S—Symptome, Psychodynamik, Fallbeispiele—psychoanalytische Theorie und Therapie*. Stuttgart, Germany: Kohlhammer.

Hopf, H. (2000). Zur Psychoanalyse des hyperkinetischen Syndroms. *Analytische Kinder- und Jugendlichen Psychotherapie, 107*(3): 279–307.

Husain, S. A., Allwood, M. A. & Bell, D. J. (2008). The relationship between PTSD symptoms and attention problems in children exposed to the Bosnian War. *Journal of Emotional and Behavioral Disorders, 16*: 52–62.

Krowatschek, D., Albrecht, S. & Krowatschek, G. (2004). *Marburger Konzentrationstraining (MTK) für Schulkinder*. Dortmund, Germany: Modernes Lernen.

Kugele, D. (1998). Affektive Verarbeitungsmöglichkeiten traumatisierter Kinder. *Analytische Kinder- und Jugendlichen Psychotherapie, 29*(1): 57–69.

Leuzinger-Bohleber, M. (2010). Early affect regulations and its disturbances: Approaching ADHD in a psychoanalysis with a child and an adult. In: M. Leuzinger-Bohleber, J. Canestri & M. Target (Eds.), *Early Development and Its Disturbances: Clinical, Conceptual and Empirical Research on ADHD and Other Psychopathologies and Its Epistemological Reflections* (pp. 185–206). London: Karnac.

Leuzinger-Bohleber, M., Brandl, Y. & Hüther, G. (Eds.) (2006). *ADHS—Frühprävention statt Medikalisierung: Theorie, Forschung, Kontroversen*. Göttingen, Germany: Vandenhoeck & Ruprecht.

Leuzinger-Bohleber, M., Laezer, K. L., Pfenning-Meerkoetter, N., Fischmann, T., Wolff, A. & Green, J. (2011). Psychoanalytic treatment of ADHD children in the frame of two extraclinical studies: the Frankfurt preventions study and the EVA study. *Journal of Infant, Child, and Adolescent Psychotherapy, 10*: 32–50.

Lipschitz, D. S., Morgan, C. A. & Southwick, S. M. (2002). Neurobiological disturbances in youth with childhood trauma and in youth with conduct disorder. *Journal of Aggression, Maltreatment & Trauma, 6*: 149–174.

Mattejat, F. & Remschmidt, H. (2006). *Inventar zur Erfassung der Lebensqualität bei Kindern und Jugendlichen (ILK). Ratingbogen für Kinder, Jugendliche und Eltern.* Berne, Switzerland: Hans Huber, Hogrefe.

McLeer, S. V., Dixon, J. F., Henry, D., Ruggiero, K., Escovitz, K., Niedda, T. & Scholle, R. (1998). Psychopathology in non-clinically referred sexually abused children. *Journal of the American Acadamy of Child & Adolescent Psychiatry, 37*: 1326–1333.

Neraal, T. & Wildermuth, M. (Eds.) (2008). *ADHS—Symptome verstehen—Beziehungen verändern.* Giessen, Germany: Psychosozial.

Salomonsson, B. (2011). Psychoanalytic conceptualizations of the internal object in an ADHD child. *Journal of Infant, Child, and Adolescent Psychotherapy, 10*: 87–102.

Staufenberg, A. (2011). *Zur Psychoanalyse der ADHS. Manual und Katamnese.* Frankfurt, Germany: Brandes & Apsel.

Stevens, S. E., Sonuga-Barke, E. J., Kreppner, J. M., Beckett, C., Castle, J., Colvert, E., Groothues, C., Hawkins, A. & Rutter, M. (2008). Inattention/overactivity following early severe institutional deprivation: Presentation and associations in early adolescence. *Journal of Abnormal Child Psychology: Official publication of the International Society for Research in Child and Adolescent Psychopathology, 36*: 358–398.

Szymanski, K., Sapanski, L. & Conway, F. (2011). Trauma and ADHD—association or diagnostic confusion? A clinical perspective. *Journal of Infant, Child, and Adolescent Psychotherapy, 10*: 51–59.

Warrlich, C. & Reinke, E. (Eds.) (2007). *Auf der Suche. Psychoanalytische Betrachtungen zum AD(H)S.* Giessen, Germany: Psychosozial.

Weiss R. (2006). *Grundintelligenztest Skala 2 (CFT 20-R).* Göttingen, Germany: Hogrefe.

CHAPTER FOURTEEN

No intermediate space for dreaming? Findings of the EVA study with children at risk

Nicole Pfenning-Meerkoetter, Katrin Luise Laezer, Brigitte Schiller, Lorena Katharina Hartmann, and Marianne Leuzinger-Bohleber[1]

Introduction

OECD states in a recent report: "… only in a few countries in Europe have children with a migration background such a bad level of education as in Germany …" (Klingholz, 2010, p. 129, translation: the authors). Every fourth child with a migration background leaves German schools without a formal qualification. Many of them will follow the steps of their parents and end up in a life without work on the fringe of society. The differences between these children and those who are born in a privileged family have never been as large as in recent years in Germany. Early neglect, violence, and an increase of psychosomatic and psychic illnesses such as depressions and drug abuse are some of the well-known consequences.

Seventy per cent of violent adolescents have been physically abused as children. Twenty to thirty per cent of these children will turn into violent adults (see, e.g., Egle, Hoffmann & Joraschky, 2000).

Therefore, early prevention for "children at risk" is seen as one of the most important societal tasks nowadays. Findings from psychoanalysis, developmental psychology, and the neurosciences agree how promising and rewarding such early supports and interventions have proved to be. Since the innovative findings of René Spitz in the 1940s, many psychoanalytical researchers have been engaged in clinical, empirical, and interdisciplinary developmental studies investigating the short-term and long-term effects of early emotional neglect, trauma, and violence (see, e.g., Emde, 2011; Fonagy & Luyten, 2009; Rutherford & Mayes, 2011). De Bellis and Thomas (2003) summarised many studies which reveal that early experiences of violence and emotional neglect lead to the development of post-traumatic stress disorder (PTSD) in children and adolescents. They estimate that in the USA around three million children are suffering from such early traumatisations.

In particular, the findings of attachment research concerning the so-called disorganised children (type D, see below) are alarming. According to many long-term studies these children have a poor prognosis. It is very likely that these children will show more destructive aggression, severe psychic problems, and low school achievements already in elementary school (Green, Stanley, Smith & Goldwyn, 2000; Lyons-Ruth, Alpern & Repacholi, 1993). Most of these children have experienced violence and other traumatisations by their primary caregiver. Fonagy (2007) considers this as "attachment trauma" (see also Fonagy, 2010; Lyons-Ruth, Bronfman & Atwood, 1999).

Although more research is necessary on this topic the experts already agree that these children need early help and support. Such support is, of course, essential for the children and their families, but also saves society a great amount of future expense as the Nobel Prize winner James J. Heckman (2008) was able to show. He investigated the data from the famous Perry School Study from an economical perspective. This study—perhaps the most well-known of all High/Scope research efforts—examined the lives of 123 African Americans born in poverty and at high risk of failing in school. From 1962–1967, three- and four-year-old subjects were randomly divided into a group which received a high-quality nursery school programme based on High/Scope's participatory learning approach, and a control group which did not receive the nursery school programme. In the last follow-up study ninety-seven per cent of the participants still living were interviewed at the age of forty. Additional data were gathered from the subjects' school, social services, and arrest records.

The findings of the study show that forty-year-old adults who attended the nursery school programme received higher incomes, were more likely to keep a job, had committed fewer crimes, and were more likely to have graduated from high school than adults who did not attend the nursery school programme (see, e.g., Schweinhart, Barnett & Belfield, 2005). Heckman could show that every dollar invested in early prevention saves more than eight dollars for society in later years.

Due to its rich knowledge concerning early development and trauma psychoanalysis is able to contribute a great deal to the field of early prevention. The Sigmund Freud Institute (SFI), in close cooperation with the Institute for Psychoanalytic Child and Adolescent Psychotherapy (IAKJP), has been engaged in several early prevention programmes since 2003: the Frankfurter Prevention Study, "Starthilfe", "EVA", and "First Steps". In all these projects we are aiming to combine the specific psychoanalytical, interdisciplinary, and intergenerational research skills of the SFI, in cooperation with the IAKJP and the specific skills of experienced child and adolescent psychoanalysts. We consider this combination as innovative and productive, as we would like to summarise in this short chapter.

The EVA research project[2]

In the Frankfurt Prevention Study (FPS), the psychoanalytically oriented prevention programme was conducted and evaluated in a representative sample of all 140 public kindergartens in the city of Frankfurt. This included kindergartens situated in urban areas with a high concentration of social problems as well as wealthier urban districts. Although in these "privileged facilities" we also encountered children who were in urgent need of psychotherapeutic help and support, this number was as expected much higher in kindergartens situated in urban areas with high rates of unemployment, migration, and a large number of families dependent on public support. Morever, it became apparent that parents from those "privileged facilities" who were advised to seek psychotherapeutic help for their children preferred to organise such help in private, on their own—often because of fear of social humiliation. However, for families in kindergartens located in urban districts with a high concentration of social problems it was inconceivable to go to private practice to see a psychotherapist. That is why in the EVA study we decided to concentrate on these kindergartens.

For the selection of a representative sample we drew upon a basic representative survey carried out in the context of the Frankfurt Prevention Study, checked for the current accuracy of the socio-economic data, and combined those findings with recent social indicators (see Laezer, 2011). In that context it seems interesting that the kindergartens, which were chosen based on the cluster-randomised controlled design, were all located in districts of the former industrial workers, and are nowadays mainly inhabited by migrant families (a high percentage of them Muslim), and affected by high unemployment rates.

Modified prevention proposal

All our prevention projects are based on psychoanalytical concepts of early development and early prevention, and aim at improving the quality of the professional relationship between educators and "high risk children", hoping—in the light of research on resilience—to offer these children alternative "good enough object relations".

The psychoanalytical prevention programme "Early Steps" consists of various elements:

- A two-weekly supervision of the kindergarten team by experienced child psychotherapists
- Weekly counselling by experienced child psychotherapists in the institutions, individual advice for educators, parents
- Psychotherapy in the facilities of the kindergarten for those children who display severe clinical symptoms
- Work with parents
- In the second year, administration of the Faustlos violence prevention curriculum (Cierpka & Schick, 2006)
- Individual mentoring of children in their transition from kindergarten to primary school.

Fortnightly supervision by experienced analytic child psychotherapists

In all prevention projects the team supervision proved to be extremely helpful. At the beginning of the Frankfurt Prevention Study, many team members as well as kindergarten leaders were sceptical about the additional time and effort connected to the fortnightly case supervision, given the already packed daily routine. When the Frankfurt Prevention Study ended, all teams, without exception, asked for a continuation of the supervision. In the evaluation interviews they described the benefits of the supervision as follows:

- Enhancement of the professional understanding of the children, their psychic and psychosocial development, the unconscious dimensions of their thinking, feeling, and acting, of traumatisations and their transgenerative transmission, as well as of the social status of the children within their peer group and multicultural conflicts, etc.
- Insight into countertransference reactions to certain children in their specific situation as a precondition for professional acting, improvement of the perception of one's own emotional reactions including feelings of guilt and shame, but also of aggressive impulses towards the child
- Insight into the tremendous feelings of powerlessness given the suffering of many children as well as into one's own inability to make any changes to the domestic or societal conditions as a prerequisite for a more adequate reaction (e.g., instead of expulsion of certain children from the group, resignation, withdrawal, or psychosomatic reactions)
- Increase of the team cohesion; reciprocal support instead of acting out of destructive rivalry, envy, or resentment
- Necessity of the analysis of the interaction of societal, institutional, and individual biographical factors, also with the aim of working against feelings of resignation given certain political structures.

The supervisors, who also regularly exchanged their experiences, repeatedly expressed their appreciation for the tremendous integrative accomplishments of the teams in these kindergartens and the unrecognised approval of their hard work by the public and in the media. They also expressed their concerns about the high number of sick notes and the daily overload (due to the extended working hours, the low wages, and limited number of team members, etc.). They also emphasised the significance of conceptual work and highlighted the expertise of the kindergarten leaders, etc.

A short example for illustration:

One of the educator's reports about a four-year-old boy, Eli, from a West African country, who is scarcely bearable for the group due to his aggressive-destructive behaviour.

He is like a small, savage animal. When he started visiting the kindergarten one year ago he couldn't speak one German word, he wasn't toilet trained, he used his hands to eat, and didn't seem to know the simplest social rules. In the meantime he seems to speak German quite well. However, as soon as there is the smallest conflict, he totally pushes over the edge, loses control, hits, bites, and repeatedly injures other children badly. Actually, one of us is constantly busy with him; you must not lose sight of him. I think we cannot keep him in our institution ... Also, now, his little brother is going to visit our kindergarten. This child seems to cry all night, so that the mother fears a dismissal.

I am furious about the mother ... she is more interested in her make-up and her clothes than her children. On Eli's first day she already left him here for five and a half hours without any time for familiarisation and seemed to be happy that she got rid of him ....

What seems strange to me, is that Eli seems to like to go to kindergarten—despite his ongoing conflicts. If the mother wants to punish him, she lets him stay at home. (educator)

After the educators had the opportunity to intensively express their anger concerning Eli's mother and their wish to remove the family from the institution, the atmosphere slowly changes: The question comes up, why Eli's mother appears to be so cold and "arrogant".

Now, it comes to my mind, that Mrs X once told me in passing that her husband died on the day when her second son was born ....
Could it be, that the mother isn't arrogant at all, but lives in some kind of a state of shock and is emotionally solidified? (supervisor)

More and more information comes through, which confirms this assumption: the family comes from an African country which is affected by a long-standing civil war. "I wonder if the parents had to flee? What did they experience ...?"

At the end of the supervision we conclude that it would be very important to learn more about the family background. The child therapist of the kindergarten will try to get into conversation with the mother.

At the next supervision, the head of the kindergarten reports that the child therapist told her that Mrs X lost her husband in a plane crash. The message about the tragedy caused a premature delivery. Mrs X lives socially totally isolated in a two-room apartment and is dependent on welfare. Probably, she is still in a dissociative state, which is interpreted by the educators as "cold", "inapproachable", and "arrogant". What seems impressive is the fact that the small brother always cries at night: "Mama, Mama, where are you ...?", although the mother is not absent. "He seems to sense that his mother is psychically absent, though physically she is present," the supervisor notes. She explains the team some short-term and long-term consequences of traumatisations (state of shock, dissociation, cracking of the parental holding function and empathy, etc.). Thanks to this information it becomes clear why Eli flourishes in kindergarten: in the kindergarten he experiences conflicting, yet emotionally resonant object relations with the educators.

"In contrast to his traumatised mother you let yourself get emotionally touched by him—he doesn't deflect off you." (supervisor) Due to the supervision a deeper understanding of Eli and his psychic situation and his situation within the family emerges. None of the educators wants to exclude Eli from the institution any more—all wish to support him, his brother, and their mother—as far as this is possible.

The mother of Eli is able to take some crisis intervention sessions by the child therapist, which leads to a visible relief: "The face of the mother did change—it is not that numb any more: she seems to somehow return to life." "The small boy doesn't cry any more at night, and Eli's aggressive breakthroughs seem to diminish."

Weekly offers by experienced child analysts in the kindergarten: counselling of educators as well as parents and realisation of child therapies in the facility

This example may illustrate why it is necessary that experienced analytic child therapists as well as supervisors work in these institutions as therapists and consultants. A profound clinical expertise seems to be indispensable to us, in order to perceive the dark shadows of the psychic and psychosocial situations of many of these children and their families and not to deny them—with the aim of "holding" and "containing" them in their misery, as far as this is possible.

In the above mentioned facility there are children from fifty-eight different nations. However, the few German children included in the study are often affected by traumatogenic family constellations, too.

Therefore an exemplary case:

Two nursery school educators request a consultation together with the two heads of a kindergarten. They have observed a remarkable change in the five-year-old Acra over the last few weeks: she seems lacking in concentration, is "fluttering" and is often:

> oddly wound up, hysterical, and then strangely collapsing ... Now we spotted her playing weird games with a boy—she was making movements under a blanket which seemed to be sexual movements ... furthermore she is recently drawing paintings with strange erotic content. Is there possibly a sexual assault in progress? We did not want to report this in the overall supervision, since we do not want to arouse false suspicions. (educator B)

Regarding the family situation it turned out that the mother had sent away Acra's biological father, who suffered from severe physical disability after an accident, half a year ago. She is now living together with her new partner,

> and flourishes evidently—she pays attention to her looks and seems to be in love .... Being on the tram, I happened to see her embracing her partner tightly and kissing him ... Acra and her little brother were standing next to them but the couple barely noticed them. (educator B)

We discuss the assumption that Acra's erotic behaviour could be a perhaps understandable identification with the mother, who is beginning to brighten up after many years bearing the heavy burden of her disabled husband. However, Oedipal fantasies and feelings of guilt might also play an important role (see "crashes", seemingly depressed absence of the child, etc.).

A second assumption concerns the suspicion that there might exist an actual sexual assault. The mother's new partner picks Acra up from nursery school every day and does not seem to keep much distance from her. Acra shows, in the perception of the educators, a mixture of fear and excitement in these situations. They assume that Acra will be alone at home with the man for a few hours before her mother returns home.

Together we discuss the possibilities by which way these two assumptions can be verified (conversation between the educators and the mother, if possible further (mutual) conversations with the child psychotherapist, who is present in the kindergarten weekly, contact with the paediatrician of the family, with whom the institution is in close contact, systematic observation of the behaviour of Acra, and further mutual advisory services before undertaking any further steps).

The child psychotherapists do not only offer counselling and advice as shown in the example above, but they also provide psychotherapy for some children in the institution, which includes intense conversations with the parents. Within the first two years it could be possible to reach sixteen children therapeutically.

These therapies are usually very difficult, but also very impressive and often lead to astonishing results. Since the therapies are not yet completed, the child therapists will report about their experiences at a later time (see elaborated therapy report from the Frankfurt Prevention Study in Leuzinger-Bohleber, Fischmann & Vogel, 2008).[3]

Research design and first results

In this framework we will not describe the design of the study in detail, but we would like to mention that thanks to the participation of the IDeA centre (Centre for Individual Development and Adaptive Education of Children at Risk, www.idea-frankfurt.eu), we are able to apply more elaborate, extraclinical research options than in the Frankfurt Prevention Study. Therefore, we are supplementing the initial multi-perspective study design both with further methods of self and external assessment of children, educators, and parents, and with a newly developed instrument for measuring the attachment behaviour, the MCAST.

"Manchester Child Attachment Story Task" (MCAST) (Green, Stanley, Smith & Goldwyn, 2000)

Various studies have given proof that a secure attachment type is a protective factor in child development (see overview in

Leuzinger-Bohleber, 2010). It can be roughly summarised as: secure attached children are more creative already in nursery school, develop a more adequate social behaviour, and are less involved in aggressive-destructive conflicts than insecure attached children. Therefore, one of the main goals of the EVA project is to support especially high risk children with the disorganised attachment type by applying the psychanalytical prevention programme—in the best case to develop and transform the attachment type towards a secure attachment.

In the MCAST, using a standardised doll-play completion task, which was developed by the research group around Jonathan Green, the examiner plays various attachment relevant stress situations, which are videotaped. Afterwards, the video material is analysed with respect to thirty-three attachment specific characteristics.

In doing so, it is examined how children react within the play when facing a dangerous situation in which the attachment system is activated. From attachment research it is well known that a child only actively explores its environment (i.e., being able to learn) when it feels save. As soon as it perceives a threat, the exploratory behaviour stops

Figure 1. Attachment diagnostics using the Manchester Child Attachment Story Task.

and the attachment system is activated by seeking protection from the primary caregiver. The MCAST method examines systematically which attachment style the nursery school children have developed. Therefore the children are confronted, after an initial scene, with four attachment relevant situations of distress (nightmare, hurt knee, tummy ache, child loses mother in shopping centre). By dealing with the distress situation four attachment types can be diagnosed:

- In the dangerous situation, a securely attached child immediately seeks the protection of its primary caregiver. For instance, when it wakes up due to a nightmare, it calls for its mother who provides comfort (attachment classification: type B)
- A child with an insecure-avoidant attachment pattern has learned that it has to comfort itself in a dangerous situation: it will probably put a plaster on its wound on its own when it has hurt its knee (type A)
- An insecure-ambivalent attached child is neither able to comfort itself in a dangerous situation, nor does it have an inner security to receive help from its primary caregiver. Instead it is often plagued by aggression and despair when it is confronted with distress and shows an ambivalent reaction pattern (alternately seeking proximity and distance: type C)
- A disorganised attached child has not developed a coherent attachment pattern due to its own history of severe traumatisation or by growing up with traumatised caregivers: it reacts confused or shows uncontrolled reactions when confronted with a dangerous situation (type D).

First results from the MCAST

The analysis of the initial measurements before the intervention started have now been completed. We were able to examine 286 children. Of these, 238 could be included in the analysis.

The first results of the initial measurement could already show that the EVA study includes a high percentage of high risk children (attachment type C and D and in a less severe degree type A, in total 65 per cent). In our sample, there are remarkably few children with a secure attachment type (35 per cent) and many with a disorganised attachment pattern (23 per cent) which is often characteristic of severely traumatised children. These children urgently need professional help as early as possible.

Table 1. The table compares the distribution of attachment types from previous studies, which were conducted with children without any special risks, to the EVA project. This is characterised by a low proportion of children with a secure attachment (type B) (see van Ijzendoorn and Sagi-Schwartz, 2008, pp. 898–899).

Country	Number of examined children	Insecure-avoidant attachment type (type A)	Secure attachment type (type B)	Insecure-ambivalent attachment type (type C)	Insecure-disorganised attachment type (type D)
West Europe (various samples, van Ijzendoorn & Kroonenberg, 1988)	510	28%	66%	6%	Has not been examined yet
USA (21 samples, van Ijzendoorn et al., 1992)	1584	21%	67%	12%	Has not been examined yet
Israel Cities (Sagi et al., 2002)	758	3%	72%	21%	3%
EVA study, Frankfurt	238	33%	35%	9%	23%

Two brief examples

Mohammed (four years old) plays in the story "A child suffers from severe tummy ache":

> Mohammed-doll calls for his mummy. She comes immediately and asks: "Oh, where does it hurt?" "Here, my tummy—it really hurts a lot." "I will make you some hot tea and a hot-water bottle, then you will feel better very soon ...." "Go to bed—you will stay at home today. I will read a story for you, then you will forget your

tummy ache soon ...." All story themes of Mohammed show a similar structure: he therefore belongs to the group of the securely attached children.

Ali's (three years old) stories, in contrast, indicate a different, a disorganised attachment pattern:

> When the Ali-doll loses his mother in the shopping centre and—in the game—eventually finds her, he is beaten by her in the first place. Subsequently he beats her—and continues to lose control. He disarranges the whole dolls' house and buries the mother-doll impulsively under the furniture, "so she is finally dead ...." He is not able to free himself from his aggressive destructive mood: a quarter of an hour later he is busy killing the mother-doll in the play.

As mentioned above, Fonagy (2007) explains that due to careful empirical studies, the prognosis for three-year-old children like Ali, who experience an aggressive outbreak in separation situations, is poor: many of the young delinquent offenders who Fonagy examined had shown such an early childhood behaviour and a disorganised attachment pattern.

When Ali's mother, in the conversation with the educators, was confronted with Ali's behaviour and the fact that his aggressive outbreaks did not only appear in the doll-play but also in nursery school, she reported similar situations from home and accepted a health insurance financed child and family therapy in the kindergarten. The migrant mother had just had a divorce from her second alcoholic and abusive husband and lived in a desolate psychic and psychosocial situation. The professional support by an experienced, Turkish speaking child therapist from the Institute for Psychoanalytic Child- and Adolescent Psychotherapy, proved to be of great help for her and her son.

Time will tell whether we will succeed in demonstrating empirically that with "Early Steps" we are able to help children like Ali to transform their problematic attachment type (C/D) into a secure attachment type and therefore enhance their prospects for a creative psychological and psychosocial development.

However, on the basis of clinical-psychoanalytic experiences there is no doubt that children like Ali, i.e., 23% of the disorganised attached children in our sample, do urgently need psychotherapeutical help, as the following examplary case will illustrate.

A case study of Mesud, six, years eight months

To this day I have been treating my little patient for 125 hours and have had thirty meetings with his parents. This family would not have been able to come to a practice on a regular basis. The therapy is held in a small room at the kindergarten, to which I bring my own toys. Of course you can hear the other children now and then, but the room is located one storey above the other rooms. Therefore the two of us are surrounded by the kindergarten and separated at the same time. The kindergarten is located within a social hot spot and surrounded by a large fence.

When I meet Mesud for the first time he is four years and eight months old.

He is a small, delicate boy, who seems absent-minded at times, without contact, and then again demonstrating curiosity for his counterpart and the room. On his head there is a bald spot, where he suffers from circular hair loss. His eyes are large and brown and his expression seems absent and lost at times. His poverty and the extent of his exposure shows in his worn, sometimes even unkempt clothing and (especially impressing to me) his impractical, open, and apparently too small house shoes, which could cause him to suffer a dangerous fall when jumping up and down the stairs. At one point I witness him tugging at his mother's skirt whining "Sausage, sausage", seemingly pressing tears from his eyes. The mother looks at me seeking help and yet showing resignation. She is totally detached. She does not know what to do with him. There is no "splendour in the eye of the mother" (a famous formulation by Heinz Kohut).

When we start therapy Mesud is five years and one month old.

In our first session he paints and depicts an utter chaos with an array of building blocks, on which he comments in sentences partially lacking any kind of grammatical structure or a flow of words, which seem incoherent to me. This is about death and dying, fire and destruction. Everyone dies, even objects. There is no salvation, no help. A bridge over a rapid river breaks down. In the face of all of this the little guy shows no fear. There is a stream of words pouring out of him, while he makes no eye contact. In a way I vanish into the stream alongside other pieces of his inner world.

The mother gives an account of a boy who is cheeky towards the paediatrician, will not listen at all, is afraid of nothing, and just runs off. Apparently he does as he pleases and also bites other children. This is the first sign of the discrepancy in the mother's perception and mine, which is similar to the kindergarden teacher's.

Mesud has two older siblings (a sister of 6,1 years, a brother of 5,1 years). He was 3,4 years old, when another sister was born.

The mother herself can almost be depicted as an overstrained older sister. She seems to be restrained by concretistic–associative thinking patterns, a state which often complicates our communication. She speaks of phobic fears and at the same time offers admissions of guilt for not being a fit mother. The father comes across as depressed. The mother feels guilty towards the little patient and tries to fulfil small materialistic requests, in an irritated manner. When interacting with the mother the patient behaves analogical to a two year old with language defects. It is said that the father let him get away with everything, but showed no more interest in him upon the younger sister's birth. The older sister motivates the little patient to arts and crafts work, at the same time criticising, scolding, and beating him. Recently he had showed me a very painful-looking flesh wound. The sister had dragged him over the carpet, giving him a carpet burn, where raw flesh could be seen. It seems as if not a single member of the family takes any interest in him. The father has been chronically ill for the past decade. He comes from the Middle East, as does the mother. The mother was born in Germany and went to a German school. She has seven siblings. The youngest sister is studying at a university. She herself has never had a good relationship with her mother. In general her family diminishes and criticises her. She also speaks about depressions occurring during her pregnancy with the little patient's younger sister.

The family is in a state without chances, poor, unknowing, and depressed.

I also do not understand anything during our sessions; I am confused and try to seek out the sense in recurring visions of water, fire, a bridge, a street, and plummeting vehicles. A collapse. I bring a round wooden arch, which could function as a bridge, and stable building blocks. I speak of fire, which is so frightening and yet exciting, of the possibilities of help and repair for anything that is broken, and how awful it must feel when one is caught up within all of this. His sense of self seemed determined by the danger of being washed away, incinerated, or crashed. He managed to express this by ways of painting or with single words.

During the following sessions he develops an object fixated oral aggression. In his fantasy the entire kindergarten and I are being followed and devoured by dangerous animals. I behave badly, I am imprisoned, punished, and killed. In these cases he is highly aroused, which is depicted in fire-water images, as if he possesses no threshold, everything is rushing into him absolutely undifferentiated. I have the impression that I am witnessing what Winnicott describes as "aroused love", which also involves "an imaginary attack on the mother, at the same time though the aggressive component leads to a recognition of the Non-Ego-World and the early constitution of a sort of ego" (Winnicott, see Stork, 1994, p. 216).

Simultaneously an archaic superego becomes visible, hinted at by the dangerous animal and myself, which has the wish to preserve the good (me and the kindergarten) by devouring us and enriching itself with this cannibalistic deed, prosecuted by the superego. While painting, the concept of a "bad, stupid" boy surfaces. He is shot and run over by a train. I begin pondering over the boy out loud. What is it that makes him bad and stupid? Fire, water, he says and scrawls over the painting in black. I ask if there is any help for the boy? The following I have to put together myself, for his words are incoherent. The mother hates the boy and beats him. He states this without any emotion, but looks like a little bird that has fallen from the nest. I point out that the boy must be very sad. He agrees. I try to hoist the feeling, which I see as predominant, into his consciousness, by connecting it to language, so the word "sad" obtains a tangible sense. We are at a stage of development where words could be occupied libidinously.

I am relieved to see that from now on there are differentiated people to be found in his paintings. Within a fragile object relation there is a self with and against others. A children's book full of people and scenery (similar to the *Where is Waldo?* books), which we read at the begining of the session, becomes a storyline along which he can attribute certain activities to certain people, and becomes a conversation starter for another topic.

He develops a kind of joy, when recognising me and "our" book.

Then I lose him again and I have to stay very close by his side, inward and outward. He continually walks up to the window and gazes outside. He can see the house he lives in and where his mother and sister are. I get up (which I usually only do in perilous situations) and stand beside him. We both gaze out of the window. First we call out the colours of the cars, ensuring we are each seeing what the other is seeing. He smears saliva onto the window. He says its burning—fire, fire. (During a conversation with the parents I am informed that there actually was a fire in their house.) Alternating ,we draw each other's attention to the rain, the snow, the birds, etc.

Very often his desire to be understood by others strikes me as weak. But he speaks in understandable sentences and reiterates and understands the sentences we read together. Sometimes he seems deflated, without any connection to the world, and I think of psychosis and autism, also because his language skills have developed, but he is also showing signs of an adhesive identification.

Sometimes it is as if I were moving a child emotionally, on a basis which it has never before experienced in such intensity. This causes him to seek out shelter, while at the same time greeting it with joy. Therefore there are occasions on which he retreats to a day bed, so that I can only see his back, putting me into non-existence. I see this retreat as avoidance of contact with reality, as a place where fantasy and omnipotence persist unaudited (according to John Steiner (1993)). Only seldom does he leave this place to face me, once to speak to me of his fear of the dark man, whom he had seen on a book cover. He does not really speak, but brings forth a few sentences, which do make sense though. Sometimes he seems so lonely and unattainable that it leads me to reconsider psychosis immanent phases. His retreat is also a defence mechanism in order to bind dangerous and destructive behaviour. At the same time it sets a boundary. Then for the first time we were able to link his fear of the dark man, who wants to hurt him, to the urge to destroy the computer in the room.

Our sessions have gained structure, because he now understands they have a beginning and an end. He dashes up the stairs into the therapy room when I ask him to. He now sorts his ambivalent feelings towards me, his sense of separation, by using my own words "our time is up", getting up and leaving, but coming back when I inform him that it is not so. Sometimes he will lie by the open door, his feet towards the stairs and his head in the room. There is a density between us; I feel bad for coming so close, as if were making a promise to him, a relationship which I will not be able to maintain because I will have to leave him. He changes passivity to activity: he wants to leave me. He mumbles, of it being too much and he would rather go back to the group. A book, which he has chosen from the bookrack in our room, becomes an object of junction, by its main theme, which is oral satisfaction, which he can obtain self-sufficiently. The boy in the book is obese and forbidden to consume fast food. Mesud on the other hand can eat everything. His aggressive and libidinous desires have found a self-induced way of expression. He is able to experience himself and at the same time, realises his sensitivity towards separation (by "tying" me to the chair) and his fear of being overpowered. Yet he is capable of using me as a "container".

The sessions before and after the summer vacation (2010) show the trials of mastering his separation-aggressions and the defence mechanisms towards separation fear and pain. I am lathered in lotion, bombed with stinkbombs, and poked by a syringe. He lies on the floor and wants to leave. He stands at the top of the stairs for quite a while. This gives me the chance to note that he must find me to be really mean and bad, because I am going on holiday, which makes me the master of time. I also tell him that he cannot get up and remain at the staircase, because he is not 100% sure that I will return. He mumbles something along the lines of "asshole" and leaves. During the summer vacation he had developed a tic: he would stick out his tongue and contort his face. The family had travelled to their home country. There he was perceived as an "idiot". He understood nothing and was not understood by anyone.

When he sticks his tongue out at me, I try to translate the situation into the following: he wants to say something mean to someone he actually likes and he has difficulties finding the right word in his mind and mouth. After this long break, he is extremely occupied with "crossing me out" or minuses, while attributing pluses to himself. He paints a picture of me, covering the entire page and then crosses me out. Playfully, I object and state how mean it is to be crossed out. But I am satisfied that he has found this clarity and wants to be a "plus" for himself. At the same time he discovers the game of drawing me and crossing me out. He triumphantly dances about the room chanting "Crossed out! Crossed out!" The following sessions start with a game of hide-and-seek. I have to find him, but I also have to hide under a blanket, which he then pulls away. The moment of happily looking into each other's eyes, the joy of retrieving is most important (according to Winnicott maybe even the moment of creating). At the same time there are moments, outside therapy, where he looks through me and does not seem to recognise me. A lack of time prevents the exact description of thinking and symbolising processes which have developed here, because Mesud could use me as a development object of the likes of Ann Hurry.

In terms of instinct development it is clear that Mesud no longer dabbles in a regressive oral undertow; instead he is securely moving along an anal instinct level: everything evolves around running away, staying, holding on, letting go, and integrating good and bad feelings towards me—I have to run after him. He degrades me as a minus, while he is a plus; he is also showing phallic tendencies in wanting to be victorious.

Mesud does not wet himself any longer or bite other children; he listens to adults. When playing he capable of building stable bridges and streets and most importantly he no longer runs away.

Mesud is 6, 8 years old now, but is far from the development level of a school child. An application to an integration-school[4] has been issued, which gives him the chance to join an I-class at a regular school. When the case worker of the local school board came to visit the family, Mesud asked his mother if this was Miss Schiller's husband. An Oedipal relation might be conceivable.

Summary

Many of the children of our ongoing prevention studies, such as Mesud, are growing up in an environment which does not offer them any *intermediate space for dreaming and playing*. What has psychoanalysis to offer these children?

This question was within the focus of this short chapter.

We know that the wish to support disadvantaged children has a long and renowned tradition in psychoanalysis; many famous psychoanalytic personalities have been engaged in "applied psychoanalysis" or "psychoanalytic pedagogics", such as August Aichhorn, Bruno Bettelheim, Anna Freud, Fritz Redlich, Chezzi Cohen, and Alois Leber in Frankfurt. We did not focus historical perspectives here but tried to illustrate our attempt to combine clinical and extraclinical psychoanalytical research in this field. Identifying with a "basic research attitude" (Leuzinger-Bohleber, 2007), we tried to make use of the large body of clinical and empirical psychoanalytical knowledge on trauma, early emotional neglect and maltreatment of "children at risk", and their parents and teachers in institutions in problematic areas of the city of Frankfurt. In contrast to other conceptualisations, e.g., in the field of psychoanalytic pedagogics, we are trying to realise what we call *"outreaching psychoanalysis"*, a psychoanalysis which leaves the psychoanalytic ivory tower of the private offices and tries to offer an intensive understanding of unconscious processes in individual children and their parents—"in the field itself", in close cooperation with the teachers. A differentiated understanding of complex, mostly unconscious processes of a certain child which manifest themselves in emotional and social behaviour in the kindergartens, with other children or the teachers, and which sometimes evoke intensive affective reactions and fantasies in the teachers, countertransference feelings, projections, and projective identifications, as well as impulses to get rid of the child, of fragmentation and rigid separation, often proves to be extremely helpful for the team. In our view it is one of the presuppositions for the professionalism of the teachers working with these "children at risk", including the capability to hold and to contain these often severely traumatised children (see case examples above).

Taking into account the findings of contemporary research on resiliency, we are hoping to contribute to the professional capabilities of the teachers to offer alternative, safe object relations to the children at risk, particularly to the 23% disorganised children, in spite of the daily distress and the extreme frustrations which the teachers have to withstand in their daily work. Alternative secure object relations have proved to be extremely important for some of these children in order to develop resilient behaviour (see, e.g., Hauser, Allen & Golden, 2006). Therefore the attempt to understand the psychic world of these traumatised children is focused upon in the regular team supervisions. The understanding of the unconscous functioning of these children at risk often proves very helpful for the teachers and creates a new, more relaxed and more integrative atmosphere in the kindergartens.

A second dimension of the "outreaching psychoanalysis" is created by the weekly presence of a experienced child psychoanalyst in the kindergartens. They offer their professional skills and experiences to the teachers (e.g., in their observations of a certain child or a group of children), the parents, and some of the children in the setting of individual child therapies in the kindergartens. These children and their parents would never find their way to the private practices of the child psychoanalysts. As far as we know this conceptualisation is relatively new. We are trying to establish a *professional dialogue* which takes into account the different professional skills of the teachers as well as the child psychoanalysts: the teachers remain teachers, the psychoanalysts remain psychoanalysts! The professional identities are not confused or mixed up: it has proved to be very important that the teachers recognise and feel the deep respect and acceptance of their own professional skills and competencies. This is a presupposition for a productive exchange and creative joint problem-solving in the service of each individual child and its family. Often the cultural background as well as the specific situation of immigrant families are not well known to the therapists. They need the knowledge of the educators—and sometimes of the social workers of other institutions of the city—for adequate interdisciplinary analyses of the problems as well as the unconscious dimensions in the behaviour of a certain child. This is one reason why we are talking about a "basic attitude of research": therapists as well as supervisors have to discover—to "research"—the foreign world of the children at risk—as well as their ubiquitous unconscious developmental conflicts and fantasies. All the therapists and the supervisors have regular meetings in which they are exchanging their observations and insights.

In the framework of the EVA project we have the unique chance to combine clinical and extraclinical psychoanalytical research. We were not able to discuss methodological questions here (see www.sigmund-freud-institut.de). We have reported only some of the preliminary findings, e.g., that 23% of all the children investigated showed a disorganised attachment pattern—for us a sign that our project really has reached the kindergartens with many "children at risk" who urgently need our psychoanalytical prevention programme.

As the case study of Mesud may have illustrated, at least for some children the child analysts engaged in our study may help these children, to open some intermediate spaces for dreaming, and for playing—for their own psychic development.

Notes

1. The EVA Study takes place at the Centre for Research on Individual Development and Adaptive Education of Children at Risk (IDeA), which is supported by the Landesoffensive zur Entwicklung wissenschaftlich-ökonomischer Exzellenz (LOEWE) of the State of Hessen, a large initiative for supporting excellent research in the State of Hessen, Germany. The centre was supported from 2009 to 2011 and, after re-evaluation by an international team of evaluators in March 2011, the support will continue until 2014 (see: www.idea-frankfurt.eu). Thirty-five professors and around sixty scientists from educational sciences, neurosciences, psychology, and

psychoanalysis are investigating children-at-risk from interdisciplinary perspectives.

2. We would like to thank the research team of the EVA project at the Sigmund Freud Institute for their careful and intensive work: P. Ackermann, S. Becker, T. Fischmann, M. Hauser, L. Hartmann, K. L. Läzer, V. Magmet, M. Müller-Kirchof, V. Neubert, N. Mazaheri Omrani, H. Pauly, N. Pfenning-Meerkötter, M. Schreiber, Y. Soltani, M. Teising, I. Weber, M. Weisenburger, (principal investigator: M. Leuzinger-Bohleber).

We would like to thank the child therapists and supervisors from the Institute for Analytic Child and Adolescent Psychotherapy: A. Wolff, F. Dammasch, D. von Freyberg-Döpp, M. Hermann, N. Lotz, I. Nikulka, M. Palfrader, J. Raue, H. Seuffert, B. Schiller, K. Wagner, C. Waldung.

We would like to thank the translators: L. Hartmann and R. Tovar. The following summary is based on a recent German publication: Leuzinger-Bohleber, M., Fischmann, T., Läzer, K. L., Pfennng-Meerkötter, N., Wolff, A. & Green, J. (2011): Frühprävention psychosozialer Störungen bei Kindern mit belasteten Kindheiten. *Psyche—Z Psychoanal*, 56: 989–1023.

3. In all previous prevention projects it became clear, particularly for the so-called "high risk children" (especially the disorganised type) how important the transition from nursery school to elementary school is. Therefore, for these children and their families in the second phase of the EVA project an individual mentoring is provided to support them in their transition to school. The inspiration for this approach is the "Kassel student aid project" (see Garlichs, 1996).

4. This is special school type in the German school system for children with particular pedagogical challenges, connecting the children to the regular school system and employment network in their region.

References

Cierpka, M. & Schick, A. (2006). Das Fördern von emotionalen Kompetenzen mit FAUSTLOS bei Kindern. In: M. Leuzinger-Bohleber, Y. Brandl & G. Hüther (Eds.), *ADHS—Frühprävention statt Medikalisierung. Theorie, Forschung, Kontroversen* (pp. 286–301). Göttingen, Germany: Vandenhoeck & Ruprecht.

De Bellis, M. & Thomas, L. A. (2003). Biologic findings of post-traumatic stress disorder and child maltreatment. *Current Psychiatry Reports*, 5: 108–177.

Egle, U. T., Hoffmann, S. O. & Joraschky, P. (Eds.) (2000). *Sexueller Mißbrauch, Mißhandlung, Vernachlässigung. Erkennung und Therapie psychischer und psychosomatischer Folgen früher Traumatisierungen*. Stuttgart, Germany: Schattauer.

Emde, R. N. (2011). Regeneration und Neuanfänge. Perspektiven einer entwicklungsbezogenen Ausrichtung der Psychoanalyse. *Psyche—Z Psychoanal, 65*: 778–807.

Fonagy, P. (2007). Violent attachment. Unpublished paper given at the conference, "In Gewalt verstrickt—psychoanalytische, pädagogische und philosophische Erkundungen", Kassel University, Germany, 9–10 February.

Fonagy, P. (2010). Veränderungen der klinischen Praxis: Wissenschaftlich oder pragmatisch begründet? In: K. Münch et al. (Eds.), *Die Psychoanalyse im Pluralismus der Wissenschaften* (pp. 33–81). Giessen, Germany: Psychosozial.

Fonagy, P. & Luyten, P. (2009). A developmental, mentalization based approach to the understanding and treatment of borderline personality disorder. *Development and Psychopathology, 21*: 1355–1381.

Garlichs, A. (1996). An der Seite der Kinder. Das Kasseler Schülerhilfe-Projekt. In: D. Hänsel & L. Huber (Eds.), *Lehrerbildung neu denken und gestalten* (pp. 153–164). Weinheim, Germany: Beltz.

Green, J., Stanley, C., Smith, V. & Goldwyn, R. (2000). A new method of evaluating attachment representations in young school-age children: The Manchester Child Attachment Story Task. *Attachment and Human Development, 2*: 48–70.

Hauser, S. T., Allen, J.-P. & Golden, E. (2006). *Out of the Woods: Tales of Resilient Teens*. London: Harvard University Press.

Heckman, J. J. (2008). Early childhood education and care: The case for investing in disadvantaged young children. *CESifo DICE Report, 6*(2): 3–8.

Klingholz, R. (2010). Ausländer her. *Der Spiegel, Nr. 35*, 30 August, pp. 129–131.

Laezer, K. L. (2011). *Erfahrungen mit der Aufmerksamkeit—Ergebnisse zweier empirischer, psychoanalytischer Studien zum sogenannten "ADHS"*. Unpublished paper given at the 58th VAKJP "Psychoanalyse der Aufmerksamkeit. Über Reize, ihre Verarbeitung und deren Entwicklung", Munich, Germany, 30 April.

Leuzinger-Bohleber, M. (2007). Forschende Grundhaltung als abgewehrter "common ground" von psychoanalytischen Praktikern und Forschern? *Psyche—Z Psychoanal, 61*: 966–994.

Leuzinger-Bohleber, M. (2010). Early affect regulation and its disturbances: Approaching ADHD in a psychoanalysis with a child and an adult. In: M. Leuzinger-Bohleber, J. Canestri & M. Target (Eds.), *Early Development and Its Disturbances: Clinical, Conceptual and Empirical Research* on *ADHD and Other Psychopathologies and Its Epistemological Reflections* (pp. 185–206). London: Karnac.

Leuzinger-Bohleber, M., Fischmann, T. & Vogel, J. (2008). Frühprävention, Resilienz und "neue Armut"—Beobachtungen und Ergebnisse aus der Frankfurter Präventionsstudie. In: D. Sack & U. Thöle (Eds.), *Soziale Demokratie, die Stadt und das randständige Ich* (pp. 149–177). Kassel, Germany: Kassel University Press.

Leuzinger-Bohleber, M., Fischmann, T., Läzer, K. L., Pfenning-Meerkötter, N., Wolff, A. & Green, J. (2011). Frühprävention psychosozialer Störungen bei Kindern mit belasteten Kindheiten. *Psyche—Z Psychoanal*, 65: 989–1023.

Lyons-Ruth, K., Alpern, L. & Repacholi, B. (1993). Disorganized infant attachment classification and maternal psychosocial problems as predictors of hostile-aggressive behavior in the nursery school classroom. *Child Development*, 64: 572–585.

Lyons-Ruth, K., Bronfman, E. & Atwood, G. (1999). A relational diathesis model of hostile-helpless states of mind. In: J. Solomon & C. Goerge (Eds.), *Attachment Disorganization* (pp. 33–70). New York: Guilford.

Rutherford, H. J. V. & Mayes, L. C. (2011). Primäres mütterliches Präokkupiertsein: Die Erforschung des Gehirns werdender und junger Mütter mithilfe bildgebender Verfahren. *Psyche—Z Psychoanal*, 65: 973–988.

Sagi, A., Koren-Karie, N., Gini, M., Ziv, Y. & Joels, T. (2002). Shedding further light on the effects of various types and quality of early child care on infant mother attachment relationship: The Haifa study of early child care. *Child Development*, 73: 1166–1186.

Schweinhart, L. J., Barnett, W. S. & Belfield, C. R. (2005). *Lifetime Effects: The High/Scope Perry Nursery school Study through Age 40*. Ypsilanti, MI: High/Scope Press.

Steiner, J. (1993). *Psychic Retreats: Pathological Organizations in Psychotic, Neurotic and Borderline Patients*. London: Routledge.

Stork, J. (1994). Zur Entstehung der Psychosen im Kindesalter. *Kinderanalyse*, 2: 208–248.

van Ijzendoorn, M. H. & Kronoenberg, P. M. (1988). Cross-cultural patterns of attachment: A meta-analysis of the Strange Situation. *Child Development*, 59: 147–156.

van Ijzendoorn, M. H. & Sagi-Schwartz, A. (2008). Cross-cultural patterns of attachment: Universal and contextual dimensions. In: J. Cassidy & P. R. Shaver (Eds.), *Handbook of Attachment* (pp. 880–906). New York: Guilford.

van Ijzendoorn, M. H., Sagi, A. & Lambermon, M. W. E. (1992). The multiple caretaker paradox: Data from Holland and Israel. *New Directions for Child Development*, 57: 5–24.

PART V

DREAMS IN MODERN LITERATURE

CHAPTER FIFTEEN

Orders of the imaginary—Freud's *The Interpretation of Dreams* and the literature of classical modernity

Peter-André Alt

Preliminary methodological and systematic considerations

Since Descartes, the dream has remained confined to the tenebrous zones of the incomprehensible, of the meaningless. The European Enlightenment all but imposed a ban on interpretation by declaring the dream to be the epitome of the absence of meaning. It fell to Freud's theory of dreams to release the dream from the stranglehold prompted by this designation. Psychoanalysis constitutes the first scientific system since the oneirocritic of classical antiquity purporting to construe the dream according to the idea of a strict inherent structure. With the notion of the unconscious there appeared a new framework of meaning, which attributed to the dream a distinct status of an alphabet of signs with meaningful denotation. Freud went on to evaluate his own scientific achievement in this connection when, borrowing one of Friedrich Hebbel's phrases, he declared in 1914 that with his theory of dreams he had the overpowering impression of having "disturbed the sleep of the world" (Freud, 1914d, p. 21).

Freud opened up four new fields in the theory of dreams capable of developing productive forces in the practice of interpretation. 1. Dream content is a product of a secondary thought process in so far as it arises in the distortion of unconscious dream thinking; it thus stands in contrast to a primary thought process, which occurs beyond the reach of consciousness. 2. The source of the dream is located in the unconscious; the topology of this unconscious supplies the human being's psychic apparatus with a structure which, in turn, constitutes the dream-work. 3. The function of the dream resembles language the signs of which, analogous to human speech, are linked (post-Freudian psychoanalysis as elaborated by Jacques Lacan was the first to discover such common features). Condensation, displacement, consideration of representability, and secondary revision, each functioning according to a unique linguistic pattern, constitute the elements of dream-work which begins in the unconscious and concludes in the preconscious. 4. The dream possesses a latent dream thought that deviates from its manifest content, and which arises in the production of the wish; by way of an act of censorship, this thought is then transformed into the pictures of the manifest dream content and fed into the dream narrative.

The construction of human psychic individuality acquires its specific profile through these four fields. When considering the epistemological architecture of Freud's theory, each of the single fields may, in turn, be attributed four central concepts: thought, space, language, and time. In their particular forms, each of these constitutes the epistemological universals of Freudian dream theory from which it may be inferred that consciousness possesses a structural anchor in the unconscious through which it then obtains its specific economy in the back and forth interaction with these energetic forces (according to Paul Ricœur, 1974). 1. In the dream, *thought* is a process that does not follow exclusively regulatory functions, but rather continues to be subject to the influences of primary processes occurring in the unconscious. 2. The *space* of the dream represents a labyrinth, an order difficult to comprehend and with perplexing structures; it is clearly evident though that Freud provides a modern version of early modern topology of the brain with its allocation of storage spaces, as drawn from Aristotle and Galen, for the human being's psychological functions. 3. The *language* of the dream is a system of connections which, while following the rhetoric of corresponding rules, no longer recognises a conscious productive speaker. 4. In the dream, by contrast, the significance of *time* is subordinate to the processes of wish-fulfilment in which the past (as residue of memory) and future (as object of wish-production), in accordance with the famous conclusion of *The Interpretation of Dreams*, virtually amalgamate organically.

Thus, the psychic individuality of human beings does not constitute an objective phenomenon, but rather appears in respective imaginary forms of unconscious representation, like in dreams, which, in turn, result from the processing of a primary economy of drives incapable of consciousness (libido) (Ricoeur, 1974, p. 156ff.). The expressive force which this model of interpretation claims is, for the most part, underestimated because it is considered as a discovery, where it is in fact a new creation of the intellect. Consequently, by means of an appealing, though nonetheless mistaken simile, Michel Foucault (1971) claimed that in so far as it had hoped to also penetrate into those spheres behind psychic life by means of the advancing knowledge of consciousness, research in psychology prior to Freud had stood with its back to the unconscious; however, psychoanalysis undertook a frontal approach to those hitherto ignored zones of the psyche so as to recognise and understand them in their immediacy (Foucault, 1971, p. 448). This comparison overlooked the creative intellectual act, which Freud achieved by making the unconscious the central theoretical field of psychology. Here, the scenario of an independent construction of a second sphere of thought would be more accurate: in contrast to what Foucault's assumption would have us believe, Freud did not perfect his insights by way of a change of perspective, but rather via an architectonic achievement that facilitated the construction of the unconscious. The object of knowledge which generated the theory did not exist previously in a different form; the apparent discoverer crossing the ocean of knowledge is in reality an architect in possession of the expertise of technical design. Theoretically, psychoanalysis had taken the decisive step towards the modern conception of the individual which, though programmed independently, is nevertheless subject to heterogeneous psychic influences. It thereby concludes, as its self-characterisation attests, that series of stages of grand disillusionment in Western modernity beginning with Copernicus through to Kant, Darwin, and Freud (cf. also Luhmann, 2000, p. 351, note 66).

It was precisely owing to Freud's theory that the dream was to become legible for the first time since antiquity, namely, interpretable—something which, in turn, made it possible for psychoanalysis to exert such a pervasive influence on modern literature. The genuinely hermeneutic objectives of *The Interpretation of Dreams* made it one of the key texts for poetic fiction. However, it belongs to one of literature's own laws that it not only critically adopted Freud's model, but also productively rewrote it. Literary knowledge is always constituted of the results of those acts of reworking, transformation, and decomposition that generate impure combinations of biographical experience and theory. It is this finding which is to be examined in the following by way of three authors each of whose texts expresses their own unique relationship to Freud's theory of dreams: Hugo von Hofmannsthal, Arthur Schnitzler, and Franz Kafka.

The theatre of dreams: Hugo von Hofmannsthal

As Carl Jacob Burckhardt would say of him in November 1923, for von Hofmannsthal "psychology" was a means to "penetrate myth (Burckhardt, 1954, p. 356f.). The tragedy *Oedipus and the Sphinx* (as inspired by one of Josephin Péladan's dramas (1903)), was originally planned as a second part of a trilogy. The premier of the drama, which was directed by Max Reinhardt at the Deutsches Theater in Berlin on 2 February 1906, is a typical example of such a procedure. The piece begins with a dream narrative, in a quasi anamnestic discussion, where Oedipus recounts to his servant Phoenix how he had requested the oracle at Delphi to investigate the growing suspicion in Phocis claiming that he is not the son of Polybus. Apollo provides the answer to the question as to his own identity by way of a dream. In the dream Oedipus encounters two levels of knowledge. Initially, he traverses the chain of generations of which he is an unwitting part: " ... my inner self underwent continual renewal. Others would always be around me, and their sublime forms would merge with one another in flames (von Hofmannsthal, 1979, p. 395) Oedipus dreams the dream of life which is governed by the principle of generation propagating generation. One cannot help but note the influence of Schopenhauer's philosophy, with its trans-individual metaphysics of the will, on the young von Hofmannsthal, which has been well researched. In a later study of 1850 called *Transcendente Spekulation über die anscheinende Absichtlichkeit im Schicksale des Einzelnen*, Schopenhauer emphasises, "that, in some sense, the subject of the grand dream of life amounts to one thing only, namely, the will to live. ... It is a grand dream of the kind all Being dreams, though such that all its persons also dream it. Hence, all things are intertwined and in consonance" (Schopenhauer, 1977, p. 242). Evidently, in von Hofmannsthal's drama Oedipus's dream of life likewise draws inspiration from Schopenhauer's theory of the will.

On the second level in Oedipus's narrative, the dream of life is followed by the incest dream, which the hero experiences as an intoxicated Dionysian heightening of his existence. He slays an unknown man and unites "with a woman, in whose arms I felt godly". Crime and the erotic are intimately linked with one another: the slain man, over whose face a towel has been draped, lay prostrate beside the bed of desire. During the course of metamorphosis, the beloved is transformed into Oedipus's mother who, in turn, becomes the god Apollo who proclaims to the horrified hero that the dream will find fulfilment in reality: "… the desire to slay/you have atoned for by your father, by your mother/atoned for the desire of embrace, thus is it dreamt,/and thus it will come to pass" (von Hofmannsthal, 1979, p. 396f.). Paul Ricœur noted that from the perspective of psychoanalysis, Sophocles's *Oedipus* tragedy represents nothing other than a "dream" (Ricoeur, 1974, p. 529). von Hofmannsthal's adaptation of the myth follows through this finding to its full literary conclusion. Here, the dream is an oracle which the god no longer announces, but discloses in the role of the interpreter. What the dream narrates in pictures is fulfilled during the course of events as pre-established law, as entelechy. Naturally, what is revealed is not a higher divine truth, but far more a metaphysical principle of life the consequence of which is the obliteration of individuality. The figure of Oedipus characterises the nucleus of the doctrine of the will going back to Schopenhauer and that announces itself in the dream when he asks: "Why/did I not shatter into fragments, as that woman/ in Delphi my bed did approach? Wherefore/still this cursed dream of these last days?" (von Hofmannsthal, 1979, p. 473). The drama seeks to descend into the "furthest most depths of the apocryphal cavernous kingdom of the ego" (according to one of von Hofmannsthal's formulations in a letter to Hermann Bahr dating from August 1904), to "find the no-longer-me, or the world" (von Hofmannsthal, 1937, p. 473; cf. also Worbs, 1983, p. 298).

It was from Freud, whose *The Interpretation of Dreams* he had studied closely in 1903, that von Hofmannsthal adopted the motivation for the events from desire; the source of what Oedipus dreams originates in his erotic desire, as indicated by the "lust" which pulsates through his veins. Entering the chain of generation, by contrast, characterises the realm of the will which, for Schopenhauer, is directly connected with drives: the sublation of individuation (the "not-shattering"), the merging with the father's blood, the "life dream" ("like whipped water, my life is in turmoil within me") (von Hofmannsthal, 1979, p. 396). The enraptured celebration of being to which Oedipus abandons himself upon arriving in Thebes is, in turn, reminiscent of Nietzsche's philosophy of

the unconditional presence and plenitude of life. In the dream it is characterised by way of the leitmotif of divine intoxication linking the erotic
drive to a primary aesthetic category, which refers to Nietzsche's writing on tragedy and his concept of the Dionysian. What may be affirmed
in this connection is that in terms of its genealogy, Nietzsche traces the
dramatic treatment back to the phenomenology of the "dream" and
the "vision". In the dream, the intoxicated choir beholds its "Lord and
Master Dionysus" (Nietzsche, 1999, p. 62f.). When von Hofmannsthal
has Oedipus's dream culminate in a heightened Dionysian reality in
the conclusion—hence, beyond good and evil—in doing so he activates
that aesthetic programme of musical tragedy conceived by Nietzsche as
an original form of classical genre history.

Oedipus's dream is construed by a threefold perspective comprising Schopenhauer's metaphysics of the will, Nietzsche's concept of
life, and Freud's theory of desire. He arrived at the oracle initially
by way of this triadic meaning, which intimates the progression to
von Hofmannsthal's Stygian tragedy. Oedipus consummates the destiny of his drives under the dictate of an elementary incestuous desire,
as directed by the will and in Dionysian, orgiastic celebration of life. In
this way, von Hofmannsthal connects three distinctive theoretical fields
of reference in an emphatically idiosyncratic manner. His representation of dreams is not the product of an uncritical adoption of psychoanalysis as was attempted several years later by Leonhard Frank and
Franz Werfel; von Hofmannsthal's representation rather transgresses
the confines of a homogenous system and opens out into a characteristic ambiguity. This procedure is facilitated by the technology of the
drama, which sustains the threefold foundation of the dream model
through its aesthetic arrangement: here, desire, will, and celebration
constitute the poetic structural figures that enable von Hofmannsthal
to stage his version of the Oedipus myth. In the dream, they appear
as tightly grouped together, whereas, as the tragedy progresses, they
unfold according to the law of an (artistically produced) dramatic
entelechy. *Desire*: by a turn of tragic irony, the same desire that aids
Oedipus's escape from the foster-mother now forces him into the arms
of his true mother. The model of the plot complies with the principle
of parapraxis, which, in this context, is transferred from its integral
psychic venue, the unconscious, to the field of dramatic composition.
In his essay of 1904, which von Hofmannsthal found highly interesting, Hermann Bahr compared the poetic effects of the tragedy with the

processes of psychoanalytic therapy: both prescribe "a dreadful course of treatment recollecting everything evil". In this sense, within the aesthetic space of the tragedy, Oedipus undergoes a course of treatment according to the dictates of the vicissitudes of drives that were imposed on him. *Will*: Oedipus's approach to Thebes—something which releases the drama from the constraints imposed by psychoanalytic didactic demonstration—amounts to his self-interpolation into the chain of his lineage—that magical force leading to abolishment of his individual commitment to the world dominated by will. Proclaimed by the people as saviour and future ruler, the hero does not embody the principle of individuality, but a general law of the will: "In my veins//I hold the world ..." (von Hofmannsthal, 1979, p. 466). Finally, the *celebration*: the tragedy disembogues into the orgiastic celebration of the royal coronation and the virtually ecstatic union with Iocaste. According to the stage directions, Oedipus now reveals himself "in a state of tremendous agitation", "drunken", and "exultant" (von Hofmannsthal, 1979, p. 480f.). Here, the underlying Acheronian tenor of the drama is interrupted by a pathos of life's celebration, for the opera-like tendencies of which Max Reinhardt's staging, directed for the masses at the Schuhmann Circus Berlin, provided the appropriate setting.

In von Hofmannsthal's work, the three central theoretical figures of dream interpretation constitute the model of dramatic composition. It is no mere coincidence that, unlike Sophocles's protagonist, Oedipus appears subject to the dictates of a dream. The stage directions emphasise repeatedly that he either "appears as if sleepwalking", or else emerging "as if from a heavy dream" or acts "as if in a conscious dream state". Similarly, the murder of Laius follows "as if in a dream state" (von Hofmannsthal, 1979, pp. 383, 390, 389, 409). The dream comprises the order according to whose laws for life the hero acts. When encountering Oedipus for the first time, Iocasta also perceives the realisation of a "dream"; the Sphinx calls out to him, "Hail to thee, Oedipus! Hail to him who dreams deep dreams" (von Hofmannsthal, 1979, pp. 463, 476). By contrast, in an ironic gesture emerging as the plot unfolds, Creon explains: "... a King does not dream, a King's dream/ originates from within him before becoming manifest in deed ..." (von Hofmannsthal, 1979, p. 421). Naturally, in the dramaturgic model of the tragedy, it is precisely the triadic substantiation of the dream idea that prohibits discerning only the reflection of psychoanalytic patterns of explanation. von Hofmannsthal had arranged the three meanings of the dream such that they reciprocally delimit and alienate themselves. Bolstered by Schopenhauer's philosophy, an experimental field of the will emerges from Freud's major archaeology of the ego; by way of a Nietzschean perspective this dark metaphysics then evolves into an aesthetic instance of Dionysian transfiguration; Aristotelian catharsis, namely, the idea of tragic purification assumes an orgiastic dimension in the theatrical ritual of the musical celebration of life. Literature renders the Oedipus material, now disenchanted by Freud's work, a plurivalent status and hence, in so doing, a modern aesthetic signature. It sublimates, as it were, the scientific pacification of myth once again returning it to a zone of ambivalence.

The dreams of the Doppelgänger: Arthur Schnitzler

Among the outstanding pre First World War German-speaking authors, it was unquestionably Arthur Schnitzler who possessed the most profound grasp of psychoanalysis. He had read Freud's *The Interpretation of Dreams* as early as March 1900, shortly after its publication, in other words, long before the work had begun to make any public impact. Schnitzler would review all the first editions of Freud's major works up until the 1920s. Between 1904 and 1925, he would keep a collection of notes under the title "On Psychoanalysis", which was meant to serve as the foundation for a treatise on the—in his view, suspect—category of "psychic" normality, which had occupied a key position in Freud's studies on hysteria. Schnitzler's earlier literary texts frequently contain sequences in which a psychoanalytic interpretation of dreams were defined *avant la lettre* (in this connection one thinks above all of the drama *Der Schleier der Beatrice* (1899)). But what of those works evidently already familiar with Freud's teachings? Among the later works, it is the *Traumnovelle* (1926) which is of particular significance: in Stanley Kubrick's filmic adaptation it was above all the title *Eyes Wide Shut* which was most remarkable. The text featured for the first time in the Berlin journal *Die Dame* in several instalments between 1925 and 1926, going into a second edition, along with other later stories, in the volume entitled *Traum und Schicksal* in 1931, the year of Schnitzler's death.

The dissolution of the everyday, the sublation of automated perceptual processes, erotic fantasies, and experiments with deceit form the thematic structure of this story of a marriage, which finally led to a reinforcement of the status quo reuniting the partners who had drifted apart. Once again, the work narrates the desire for heightened experience in life, again it is the dream that discloses this; in this case, evidently, with the double meaning which was to remain constitutive of Schnitzler's novella. Fridolin, whose nocturnal adventure assumes the appearance of a dream, and who visits an erotically permissive masked ball incognito without invitation, falls in love with an unknown person before just managing to escape the fatal rage of the enigmatic host at the end by way of disclosing his identity. By contrast, the dream of his wife, Albertine, which comments on this experience (temporally synchronous), and in which Fridolin is disloyal, appears real; whereas, for his part, he sacrifices himself and dies in an ethos of unconditionality for her. A chiastic rhetorical pattern characterises the relationship between dream and reality. When, after some considerable hesitation, Fridolin confesses to Albertine the matter of his adventure at the masked ball, he does so as if it "were a dream". The converse tendency is indicated at the end of the novella: "And no dream ... is wholly dream" (Schnitzler, 1961, p. 502f.). This obfuscation of dream and reality leads to a remarkable doubling effect. Fridolin performs both in his erotic fantasy and at the same time in Albertine's dream; by contrast, and as can be clearly discernable towards the end, Albertine not only lies dreaming on her bed, but shares the same identity with the striking bearer of the mask whom Fridolin had encountered at the ball. The double of each of the respective persons must in the end be cast off and perish so that the spouses may once again discover one another. Hence, the self-sacrificial Fridolin in the dream meets with his demise, as does the beautiful *inconnue* of the night. The doubling of the person, which itself comprises an element of the dream logic permeating the events in the novel, must be revoked so that morality may triumph and so that the picture of an empirically stable reality may emerge from the bewildering reflections of the dream. However, the effect of the shock of simultaneity persists; the externally harmonious finale is incapable of offsetting this effect as the reader has meanwhile lost trust in the objectivity of a system of reality located beyond the imagination.

Schnitzler's text not only narrates the revelation of erotic wishes between people in nocturnal dreams and waking fantasies; it also provides a modern version of the *Doppelgänger* motif observed in Romanticism, which Freud, in a form not entirely lacking in irony, likewise pursued when congratulating Schnitzler on his 60th birthday on 14 May 1922 in a letter which later became famous ("I have avoided you out of a kind of fear of a Doppelgänger") (Freud, 1955, p. 97). As is well known, the theme sparked interest in psychoanalysis at an early stage; one recalls Otto Rank's essay on the subject of the *Doppelgänger* in the third year of *Imago* (1914), and Freud's treatise on "The Uncanny" (1919h), which drew above all on the work of E. T. A. Hoffmann. While Schnitzler's novella plays with the duplication of its characters, by no means does it serve the purpose of generating surprising illusory effects (such as are to be found in the fantasy literature of Romanticism), but is sombre proof that the significance of the thin red line separating dream and reality appears less distinct. Fridolin and Albertine move through the text in duplicate form, entangled in the network of dreams, engulfed by a world of fantasy from which they must finally escape in order to retain their own identity. Schnitzler's play with the diffusion of the imaginary and the real necessarily explodes the boundaries of the psychoanalytic concept of the dream. It is not the dreamer's wishful thinking, but far more the destabilisation of his reality which the novella's *Doppelgänger* motif conveys. In the final analysis, its diagnosis corresponds to the consequences of the Freudian theory of dreams: the contemporary modern individual has lost the illusion of an objective reality to those virtual structures to which his mind gives birth.

Writing as if in a dream: Franz Kafka

The productive literary impact of Freud's interpretation of dreams reveals itself where one extends its model of a language-like approach to the preconscious to the narrative structures themselves. That the processes of narration and of dreaming may conform to similar principles is shown in the work of Franz Kafka in an exemplary manner (cf. concerning the following considerations; also Alt, 2001). It is above all the techniques Kafka employs in his approach to space and time that are often subordinated to those patterns of dream narration as observed by Freud (cf. Engel, 1999, p. 248ff.; Foulkes, 1965; Stern, 1984). The structure of his prose conforms to displacements, superimpositions, and sudden leaps, apparently located somewhere beyond the logic of everyday rationality. Among some of the most disconcerting reading experiences in this connection are such processes of shifting disturbance and irritation, most of which, as already noted by Adorno, remain for the most part entirely without comment (Adorno, 1955, pp. 254ff). However, it is precisely this dispensing with explanations, the incorporation of the irrational into an immanent narrative procedure yet to be transgressed, which is what links Kafka's stories to the architecture of dreams; Freud's theory of linguistic forms of representation of the latent content in the manifest content of the preconscious is repeated here in the very structure of the epic itself.

Kafka identifies the approach to such constructions by way of examining autobiographical dream material, of which he makes copious notes in diaries and letters. In the processes, two groups emerge: the nocturnal dreams, which he explicitly distinguishes as such, and the day dreams, which are, for the most part, dictated without any further explanation or literary embellishment (cf. the structure of Kafka, 1992). Kafka's official employment at the Prague *Arbeiter-Unfall-Versicherungs-Anstalt* (Employee Accident Insurance Institute) would go to two o'clock in the afternoon; having enjoyed a meal he was in the habit of reclining on a sofa and occasionally in bed for considerable lengths of time, as a rule sleeping properly only having taken his obligatory stroll, which he would take before sitting down to write late into the evening (Kafka, 1999, p. 204). A "life of manoeuvrings" is how he would refer to this daily routine at the end of August 1920 in a letter to Milena Jesenská (Kafka, 1999, p. 229). It was in such a comatose state spent during the afternoons in bed or lolling on the sofa that Kafka would ponder images and beginnings of narratives, at times also complete stories. Such transitional stages would mediate the "semi-somnolent fantasies", as Kafka would describe them in a diary entry dated 26 February 1922 (Kafka, 1994d, p. 223; cf. also Kafka, 1994b, p. 42; 1994c, p. 182; 1994d, p. 216; 1967, pp. 264, 501; Guntermann, 1991, p. 76). As can be seen, these fictive worlds at the threshold of sleep and waking consciousness which these comatose states would invoke possess their own poetic dimension. Being aware of this Kafka consequently jotted down his dreams in his notebook. For readers, such notes possess a unique ambiguity since they are barely distinguishable from literary sensibility and fragments.

> Setting a protocol for his own dreams, Kafka practises the act of literary imagination. The biographical dream material opens up a further terrain for him, in which he can probe the possibilities of picture production and the construction of stories in the preliminary stages of free literary invention. Making note of dreams initially means working out structural patterns without necessitating a leap into unprotected poetic fantasy. As narrative model, the dream provides the decisive impulse; by way of its interconnections, layering, and superimpositions he presents narrative techniques, which Kafka himself seeks to imitate perfectly in order to arrive at a satisfactory

form of writing. In a diary entry dated 17 December 1911, he suspects that his desire to write a biography of his self originates in an intimation that its development "would be as easy to do as noting down his own dreams ..." (Kafka, 1994b, p. 232).The linguistic reproduction of the dream content in the journal permits casual access to literary production. It allows for the intricate process of writing on a difficult experimental field to be tested in immediate confrontation with the linguistic structure of the unconscious. At the same time, it offers the opportunity for strategically overcoming those massive authorial inhibitions and blocks, which Kafka would suffer in periodic cycles. It is precisely this apparent revisionary character of the protocols that deceives the writer by concealing the creative achievement of the act of writing. Since the dream constitutes an open store of fantasy generation free of any strategic calculation, it is capable of significantly influencing and inspiring the literary construction of an author such as Kafka who worked without drafts and structural schemes (cf. Engel, 1999, esp. p. 241ff.).

Without doubt, the encounter with the linguistic structure of the unconscious constitutes Kafka's major force as author. The fact that he initially dreams numerous of his stories, and later, by acts of the imagination builds them into an augmented fictive context, may be shown by way of some examples. This finding is especially relevant in the case of the novels, the epic worlds of which are organised according to the laws of dreams as selectively inspired by authentic dream material. Finally, though no less importantly, this should be estimated in its role in the narrative construction itself, which, in Kafka's case, follows those "structures of associations" understood by Novalis to be one of the common features of dream and poetry (Novalis, 1978, p. 241ff.).

The connection between dream and narrative is particularly evident in the novel *The Trial* (1914). As the story goes, the protagonist of the work, Josef K., is arrested one morning while still in bed. The transition from sleep to waking consciousness appears as characterised by a kind of precarious tension which, as noted in Kafka's diary entries, can be evoked by unconscious fantasies. In the first chapter of the manuscript version of the novel, K. tells the guards carrying out the arrest: "At least while asleep and dreaming one seems to be in an essentially different state than when awake", since it threatens to reveal the feigned character of such a difference in the hidden connection between dream and reality (Kafka, 1997, p. 37). Later Kafka struck out these, all too revealing, sentences without replacing them. Hence, Josef K.'s story might be construed as a dream fantasy on the threshold to waking reality, as a narrative picture puzzle of a sense of guilt discovering a linguistic pattern to represent itself prior to waking consciousness.

Similarly, the opening part of the novel *The Castle* (1922) would lead one to suppose that the following story bears the character of a dream. K., who arrives in the village late one evening, falls into a deep sleep at the inn: "It was warm, the farmers were quiet, his tired eyes surveying them a little before he then fell asleep." K.'s dream begins the moment the narrator explains that the hero is woken by a representative of the castle administration. Interestingly enough, it appears that K. completes the interrogation to which he is subject in a state of trance. At this stage, the novel clearly discloses the extent of doubt about the presence of his consciousness: "'And must one have permission to stay over night?'" asked K., as if seeking to convince himself that, perhaps, he had not been dreaming the previous message" (Kafka, 1994a, pp. 9f.). When, later in the novel the hero penetrates ever further into the labyrinth of the village world, this happens according to the dictate of the dream from which he appears no longer to awake.

The hypothesis that Kafka's novels narrate the dreams of their heroes is more than a mere footnote among the sheer endless series of commentaries his works have prompted. It has rather set the conditions which any reading of his texts must follow. It is precisely because these conform to the narrative structure of dreams that all conventional interpretative art must fail. In this case, an approach based on the contradiction-free interpretability of a literary work would be doomed to failure. What constitutes the originality of Kafka's prose is not the fact that it exhibits contradictory structures of meaning (an attribute it has in common with works by numerous other authors of modernity from Rilke and Musil through to Joyce); its essential characteristic is shown far more in the propensity to flout the laws of rational argumentation, rhetorical coherence, and formal arrangement in epic material. It inherits such a composition from the dream, the narrative pattern of which, as Kurt Tucholsky emphasised in an early review dating from 1920, Kafka's novels and narratives quite evidently imitate (Born, 1979, p. 95f.). The reason why Josef K. can be at once guilty and not guilty, impostor and victim, becomes understandable only against the background of the logic of dreams as staged here. Kafka's writings adopt the techniques of displacements, superimpositions, and transpositions from the rhetoric and narrative economy of the dream—the art of distorting objective space and time coordinates and the licence for the reconfiguration or transformation of figures, buildings, and localities. Whoever misjudges the formal premises of this poetics of dreams and the rules constituting the basis of their turbulences, fails as a reader of Kafka: clasping to the guidebook of reason, he instead rambles along through a world of crazed meanings.

Summary

In his *Minima Moralia* (1951), written in 1944, Theodor W. Adorno writes: "Between 'it dreamed me' [es träumte mir] and 'I dreamed' [ich träumte] lie ages of the world. But which is truer? So little do spirits send dreams, so little is it the ego which dreams" (Adorno, 1951, p. 252).

The subject, as the dictum suggests, is not master of his dreams. This disagreeable message of psychoanalysis appears to replace an older with a new power structure. Just as in the prophetic dream of classical antiquity the ego resembles an empty leaf inscribed by a divine writ, so the ego of the Freudian theory of dreams dwells in an inhospitable location in which unwieldy drives are operative. It is at this point that the literature of modernity sets in with a critical and productive impulse. In that it transfers the dream as medium of an imaginary world into its fictive reality, it provides it with the kind of ambiguity that remains incomprehensible to a closed scientific system. The way in which the literature of modernity narrates its dream-stories indicates that however intense the shadow of psychoanalytic knowledge may be, it still retains a unique capacity for portrayal and interpretation beyond theoretical thought. The dreams of literature are aesthetic events possessing autonomous rank and unique ambivalence the significance of which defies access by a homogenous explanatory approach.

The human drive to contrive linguistic images is as old as its world of culture. As Nietzsche remarked about this drive and its relationships to the dream in his lectures on rhetoric in Basle, in 1873: "It perpetually bemuses the rubrics and cells of the concepts by arranging new transfers, metaphors, metonyms; it perpetually shows the desire to form anew the given world of alert human beings as colourfully and irregularly unconnected and without consequence, and so appealing as it is in the world of dreams" (Nietzsche, 1993, p. 381). The drive to metaphor and the dream obey the same laws. As a medium of the drive to metaphor, literature consequently disposes over the freedom to once again transfer modern psychoanalytic knowledge about the dream into imaginary structures and to direct it through a theatre of pictorial associations. Robert Musil characterised this freedom in *The Man without Qualities* (1930–1942) with a plausible formula: the "sense of possibility", which eludes the power of the factual encompasses "not only the dreams of neurasthenic people, but also the not yet awakened intentions of God" (Musil, 1978, p. 16). This sense of possibility is aesthetically determined. As a way of simulating reality, it thrives on the scope which the arsenal of imagination opens up to it. Modern literature also draws on such a scope when exploring the vast terrain of dreams. The cartographic material which it uses for this derives from the store of knowledge of psychoanalysis. However, the journey itself leads into uncharted territory—beyond Freud.

References

Adorno, T. W. (1951). *Minima Moralia. Reflexionen aus dem beschädigten Leben.* Frankfurt, Germany: Suhrkamp, 1981. [*Minima moralia: Reflections from Damaged Life.* London: Verso, 2005.]

Adorno, T. W. (1955). *Prismen. Kulturkritik und Gesellschaft* (3rd ed.). Frankfurt, Germany: Suhrkamp, 1987. [*Prisms.* London: Spearman, 1967.]

Alt, P.-A. (2001). Erzählungen des Unbewußten. Zur Poetik des Traums in Franz Kafkas Romanen. [Narratives from the Unconscious. About the Poetic of the dreams in Franz Kafka's Novels.] In: F. R. Marx & A. Meier (Eds.), *Der europäische Roman. Festschrift für Jürgen C. Jacobs* (pp. 153–174). Weimar, Germany: VDG.

Born, J. (Ed.) (1979). *Franz Kafka. Kritik und Rezeption zu seinen Lebzeiten 1912–1924.* [Franz Kafka: Critique and Receiption in his life time 1912–1924.] Frankfurt, Germany: Fischer.

Burckhardt, C. J. (1954). Begegnungen mit Hugo von Hofmannsthal. [Encounters with Hugo von Hofmannsthal.] *Die Neue Rundschau,* 65: 341–357.

Engel, M. (1999). Literarische Träume und traumhaftes Schreiben bei Franz Kafka. Ein Beitrag zur Oneiropoetik der Moderne. [Literary Dreams and Franz Kafka's Dreamlike Writing. A Contribution to the Oneiropoetic in Modern Times.] In: B. Dieterle (Ed.), *Träumungen. Traumerzählungen in Film und Literatur* (pp. 233–262). St. Augustin, Germany: Gardez!-Verlag.

Fick, M. (1993). Ödipus und die Sphinx. Hofmannsthals metaphysische Deutung des Mythos. [Oedipus and the Sphinx. Hofmannsthal's Metaphysical Interpretation of the Myth.] *Jahrbuch der deutschen Schillergesellschaft*, 32: 259–290.

Foucault, M. (1971). *Die Ordnung der Dinge. Eine Archäologie der Humanwissenschaften*, U. Köppen (Trans.). Frankfurt, Germany: Suhrkamp, 1974. [*The Order of Things: An Archaeology of the Human Sciences*. London: Routledge, 1996.]

Foulkes, A. P. (1965). Dream Pictures in Kafka's Writings. *Germanic Review*, 40: 17–30.

Freud, S. (1900a). The Interpretations of Dreams. *S. E.*, *5*. London: Hogarth Press.

Freud, S. (1914d). On the History of the Psychoanalytic Movement. *S. E.*, *14*: 7–66. London: Hogarth.

Freud, S. (1955). Briefe an Arthur Schnitzler. [Letters to Arthur Schnitzler.] *Die Neue Rundschau*, *66*: 95–106.

Guntermann, G. (1991). *Vom Fremdwerden der Dinge beim Schreiben. Kafkas Tagebücher als literarische Physiognomie des Autors*. [*From Becoming Strange of the Things During Writing. Kafka's Diaries as Literary Physiognomy of the Author*.] Tübingen, Germany: Niemeyer.

Kafka, F. (1967). *Briefe an Felice [Bauer] und andere Korrespondenz aus der Verlobungszeit*. [*Letters to Felice [Bauer] and Other Correspondences in the Time of Engagement*.] E. Heller & J. Born (Eds.). Frankfurt, Germany: Fischer.

Kafka, F. (1982). *Briefe an Milena [Jesenská]*. [*Letters to Milena [Jesenská]*.] Erweiterte und neu geordnete Ausgabe. J. Born & M. Müller (Eds.). Frankfurt, Germany: Fischer.

Kafka, F. (1992). *Träume*. [*Dreamings*.] G. Giudice & M. Müller (Eds.). Frankfurt, Germany: Fischer.

Kafka, F. (1994a). *Das Schloß. Roman. In der Fassung der Handschrift*. H.-G. Koch (Ed.). Frankfurt, Germany: Fischer. [*The Castle*. New York: Knopf, 1954.]

Kafka, F. (1994b). *Tagebücher 1909–1912*. [*Diaries 1909–1912*.] II.-G. Koch (Ed.). Frankfurt, Germany: Fischer.

Kafka, F. (1994c). *Tagebücher 1912–1914*. [*Diaries 1912–1914*.] H.-G. Koch (Ed.). Frankfurt, Germany: Fischer.

Kafka, F. (1994a). *Tagebücher 1914–1923*. [*Diaries 1914–1923*.] H.-G. Koch (Ed.). Frankfurt, Germany: Fischer.

Kafka, F. (1997). *Der Process. Historisch-kritische Ausgabe sämtlicher Handschriften, Drucke und Typoskripte*. R. Reuß & P. Staengle (Eds.). Frankfurt, Germany: Stroemfeld. [*The Trial*. New York: Knopf, 1975.]

Kafka, F. (1999). *Briefe 1900–1912.* [*Letters 1900–1912.*] H.-G. Koch (Ed.). Frankfurt, Germany: Fischer.

Luhmann, N. (2000). *Die Politik der Gesellschaft.* [*The Politics of Society.*] A. Kieserling (Ed.). Frankfurt, Germany: Suhrkamp.

Musil, R. (1978). *Gesammelte Werke* (*Volume 1: Der Mann ohne Eigenschaften*). A. Frisé (Ed.). Reinbek, Germany: Rowohlt. [*The Man Without Qualities.* London: Picador, 1997.]

Nietzsche, F. (1993). *Kritische Gesamtausgabe* (*Volume 2.3: Vorlesungsaufzeichnungen SoSe 1870–SoSe 1871*). [*Critical Edition of the Complete Works.*] G. Colli & M. Montinari (Eds.). Berlin: de Gruyter.

Nietzsche, F. (1999). *Studienausgabe* (*Volume 1: Die Geburt der Tragödie, Unzeitgemäße Betrachtungen I–IV, Nachgelassene Schriften 1870–1873*). [Study Edition (Birth of the Tragedy et al.).] G. Colli & M. Montinari (Eds.). Berlin: de Gruyter.

Novalis, (1978). *Werke, Tageb.cher und Briefe* (*Volume 2: Das philosophisch-theoretische Werk*). [*Works, Diaries and Letters.*] H.-J. Mähl & R. Samuel (Eds.). Munich, Germany: Hanser.

Péladan, J. (1903). *Œdipe et le Sphinx.* Paris: Mercure de France.

Ricœur, P. (1974). *Die Interpretation. Ein Versuch .ber Freud.* E. Moldenhauer (Trans.). Frankfurt, Germany: Suhrkamp. [*Freud and Philosophy: An Essay on Interpretation.* New Haven/London: Yale University Press, 1970.]

Rank, O. (1914). *The Double.* London: Karnac Books, 1989.

Schnitzler, A. (1961). *Gesammelte Werke* (*Volume 1-2: Die erzählenden Schriften*). [*Collected Works.*] Frankfurt, Germany: Fischer.

Schopenhauer, A. (1977). *Zürcher Ausgabe. Werke in zehn Bänden* (*Volume 7*). [Zurich Edition.] A. Hübscher (Ed.). Zurich, Switzerland: Diogenes.

Stern, M. (1984). Der Traum in der Dichtung des Expressionismus bei Strindberg, Trakl und Kafka. [The Dream in the Fiction of Expressionism by Strindberg, Trakl and Kafka).] In: T. Wagner-Simon & G. Benedetti (Eds.), *Träum und Träumen* (pp. 113–132). Göttingen, Germany: Vandenhoeck & Ruprecht.

von Hofmannsthal, H. (1937). *Briefe 1900–1909.* [*Letters 1900–1909.*] Vienna: Bermann-Fischer.

von Hofmannsthal, H. (1979). *Gesammelte Werke* (*Volume 2: Dramen II*) [*Collected Works (Volume 2: Drama).*], B. Schoeller (Ed.). Frankfurt, Germany: Fischer.

Worbs, M. (1983). *Nervenkunst. Literatur und Psychoanalyse im Wien der Jahrhundertwende.* [*Art of Nervous. Literature and Psychoanalysis in Vienna at the Turn of the Century.*] Frankfurt, Germany: Europäische Verlags-Anstalt.

INDEX

Printed in Great Britain
by Amazon

35480662R00192